THE
Professional
WINE
Reference

WRITTEN BY

Frank E. Johnson

THIS SPECIAL EDITION
DESIGNED AND PREPARED BY
GRAPHIC IMAGE, INC.

Library of Congress Catalog Card Number 78-67823

Printed and Bound in the United States of America

Introduction

Beverage Media's Professional Wine Reference is written and edited for the thousands of men and women in the industry who sell wine.

It responds to a need expressed to us repeatedly by members of the wine trade for a practical, handy manual to which they can turn quickly to find precise answers to questions about wines that arise on almost every business day. It is a guide to wine buying decisions, a stimulant to new selling ideas.

The Wine Reference compiles hard, carefully researched facts about the wines of the world. It is concise, pithy, thorough in its coverage. It organizes a vast wealth of information, alphabetically arranged by subject, in an easy-to-use format. Here is an invaluable working tool for the industry, and equally an authority for the wine consumer.

A special Appendix is devoted to wine service and care. Tables list the wines that go best with different foods and show popular wine-cheese affinities. There are guides for storing wine, the best wine serving temperatures, decanting wines, holding a wine tasting.

While the Wine Reference is designed primarily as a handbook of wine facts, it serves, too, as a "refresher" about wines and the wine regions. Whether your knowledge of wine is scant or massive, its 830 alphabetically arranged wine entries will make fascinating reading.

The Author

Frank E. Johnson is a contributing wine editor to Beverage Media and the Associated Beverage Publications, an organization of leading beverage trade journals in the United States, and since 1974 he has been the East Coast editor of Wine World Magazine in California. A student of wine and the wine industry, he has travelled extensively throughout the world's wine regions and is a recognized wine authority. His articles on wines and wine trends and special vintage reports have attracted wide attention in the trade. Among his works is a recent translation from the French of a *History of Wine* prepared for the Union des Grands Crus de Bordeaux.

The Publishers

Beverage Media, Ltd., brings over 40 years of wine and spirits trade publishing experience to the creation of the Professional Wine Reference.

In addition to publishing Beverage Media, a New York publication with an international reputation, the company represents 32 local Associated Beverage Publications which service the nation's package stores, restaurants, wholesalers, vintners and wine importers. Each month, these publications carry thousands of pages of information about wine pricing and brands, vintages, merchandising and sales trends and basic product knowledge.

Beverage Media also publishes Good Hosting, a two million circulation entertainment catalog which features extensive guides for the selection and service of wines.

From this wealth of day-to-day working experience, this practical reference has been compiled by and for wine professionals.

Table of Contents

Maps of World Wine Regions

Appendix

How to Use the Wine Reference

To gain maximum benefit from the use of Beverage Media's Professional Wine Reference, it is advantageous for the reader to become familiar with the way it is designed.

Subjects are alphabetically arranged with each of the 830 entries identified by heavy print. Immediately following the subject title, a pronunciation guide appears in italics. In instances where no pronunciation guide appears, the word is pronounced as it would be spoken in English.

In many of the entries, a word will appear in full capitals, e.g., BURGUNDY. These words indicate a separate cross reference entry on the subject which appears in appropriate alphabetical sequence.

Acknowledgements

We would like to acknowledge various trade organizations and their officials who provided material that greatly assisted the research of important facts regarding their country's wines: The Australian Trade Commission, Austrian National Tourist Office, Bordeaux Wine Information Bureau of New York, Bulgarian Embassy Commercial Couselor, California Wine Institute, Chianti Classico Wine Consortium, Finger Lakes Winegrowers' Association, Food & Wines From France and the Comité National des Vins de France, German Wine Information Bureau and the Stabilisierungsfonds für Wein in Mainz, Hungarian Embassy Commercial Attache's Office, Italian Trade Commission of New York, Portuguese Government Trade Office, Romanian Government Trade Office, South Africa Information Service, Commercial Office of the Spanish Embassy, and the Switzerland Cheese Association of New York. In addition, invaluable help was obtained from many generous importers, suppliers and distributors, too numerous to list individually.

A

Abboccato *(Ah-bo-ka′-tow)*: Italian for "semi-dry."

Abruzzi *(Ah-broot′-zee)*: Mountainous region in east-central Italy, bordering the Adriatic Sea; also called Abruzzo. Red wine of the region, made from the Montepulciano grape, is called Montepulciano di Abruzzo; the white is made from Trebbiano. Both are entitled to D.O.C.

Acescense *(Ah-see′-sans)*: The disagreeable scent of acetic acid or vinegar in spoiled wine; also called volatile acidity.

Acidity: In relation to wine there are two basic kinds of acidity, fixed and volatile. Fixed acidity refers to the natural fruit acids normally present in wine; the most important are citric, lactic, malic and tartaric. Volatile acidity, however, is not a desirable component of sound wine. It is an alternate term for acetic acid or ACESCENSE, which is formed when air and Acetobacter microbes enter wine during or after fermentation. It is called "volatile" because it is given off in the bouquet. There is usually a small amount of acetic acid in all wines, but when detectable in the bouquet it is an indication of spoilage.

Aglianico del Vulture *(Ahl-yan′-ee-co del Vool′-too-ray)*: Fine red wine of the

Basilicata region east of Naples, Italy. Made from Aglianico grapes grown on the slopes of the Monte Vulture, an extinct volcano, it is considered to be one of the region's best wines, and is rated D.O.C.

Ahr *(Are)*: Tributary of the Rhine River south of Bonn, Germany; also a wine region or ANBAUGEBIET. The Ahr is an unusual German wine district in that its light red wines, made from the Spätburgunder (Pinot Noir) grape, are better-known than its whites. The district includes the BEREICH (sub-district) Walporzheim, and the villages of Ahrweiler and Altenahr; production averages about 256,170 cases of red wine, and 201,280 cases of white.

Alameda *(Ahl-a-meed'-ah)*: County located east of San Francisco Bay, California, including the Livermore Valley. With 2,000 acres of vineyards, Alameda is well-suited to the production of fine white wines; Wente Bros., Concannon and Weibel wineries are situated there.

Albana di Romagna *(Ahl-bann'-ah dee Ro-mon'-ya)*: Semi-dry white Italian wine produced in the EMILIA-ROMAGNA district north of Florence. It is entitled to D.O.C.

Aleatico *(Ahl-yah'-tee-co)*: Red Muscat grape variety used for making a fairly sweet wine in central and southern Italy.

Algeria: Presently the seventh largest wine-producing country in the world, Algeria is steadily improving the quality of her table wines, which became famous in 19th century France during the period of colonial occupation. After independence from France in 1962, the Algerian government delimited several of the best wine regions under the laws of *appellation d'origine garantie,* which are similar to the French APPELLATION CON-TRÔLÉE laws. The most important regions are: Coteaux de Mascara, near the city of

Mascara and famous for rich, full-bodied red wines; Medea, near Algiers and noted for good reds and whites; Tlemcen near Oran, another good red and white wine zone; and Dahra, further east near the Mediterranean coast, celebrated for reds. There are now some 520,000 acres of vineyard in Algeria, restricted by law to the traditional producing zones in order to assure the quality of wine exports.

Alicante-Bouschet *(Ahl-uh-con'-tay Boo-shay')*: High-yield red grape variety grown extensively in California and the French Midi. A hybrid developed in the 19th century by L. and H. Bouschet, it is noted for its deeply-colored wine, not its finesse.

Aligoté *(Ah-lee-go-tay')*: Secondary grape variety used for the lesser white wines of Burgundy, which are called ''Bourgogne Aligoté.'' Very pleasant when consumed young, Bourgogne Aligoté is often mixed with Cassis liqueur to make the popular aperitif KIR.

Aloxe-Corton *(Ahl-oss' Cor-tawn')*: Picturesque hillside town in the northern CÔTE DE BEAUNE, Burgundy, named for its excellent red wine CORTON. Wine from the Corton vineyard, and also a very fine white wine from the famous CORTON-CHARLEMAGNE vineyard, is rated Grand Cru (Great Growth). Other renowned vineyards include the CLOS DU ROI, BRESSANDES, and Renardes. The area under vines in the Aloxe-Corton commune is about 600 acres, and the average annual production is approximately 72,300 cases.

Alsace *(Ahl'-sass)*: Important viticultural province in northeastern France, bordering Germany on the Rhine River. Located on the slopes of the Vosges Mountains, the Alsatian vineyard area extends for some 70 miles in a north-south direction from Strasbourg to Mulhouse, along the ''route du vin'' (wine

3

road). Among the most important Alsatian wine towns are Guebwiller, Rouffach, Kayserberg, Riquewihr, and Ribeauvillé.

Being virtually all white, Alsatian wines are similar to those of Germany, yet display a character that makes them uniquely French. The two "noble" grape varieties used in making Alsatian wines are Riesling and Gewürztraminer; both are grown in Germany with good results, but in Alsace the wines are usually drier and more scented. Other good varieties include the Pinot Gris (also called Tokay), Muscat, Pinot Blanc (or Klevner), and Sylvaner.

Alsatian wine labels do not usually bear the name of the town or vineyard from where the grapes were grown, but instead indicate the shipper and also the grape variety used, which by law must be 100% of the indicated variety. Alsatian wines are always shipped in green, fluted bottles that may not be used elsewhere.

Alto Adige (*Al'-tow Ah'-dee-gee*): Mountain river valley in the northern Italian Tyrol near the Austrian border; located around Lake Caldaro (Lago di Caldaro), Alto Adige is an important wine region. It is considered part of TRENTINO; Bolzano and Merano are its two most important towns.

Because Alto Adige is so close to Austria and much of its population is German-speaking, its wines often bear German labels — Lago di Caldaro is also known as *Kalterersee*. Much wine is exported to Germany and Switzerland, but a good deal is sent to the U.S. Red wine produced from the Schiava grape near Lake Caldaro is called CALDARO and is rated D.O.C.; SANTA MADDALENA, grown near Bolzano and also made from the Schiava, is considered the best Alto Adige red wine. Cabernet, Pinot Noir and Merlot are also grown, and are known by their varietal names. Among the Alto Adige white wines, Riesling and Traminer are excellent. The region is also famous for Lagarino, a rosé made from Lagrein grapes.

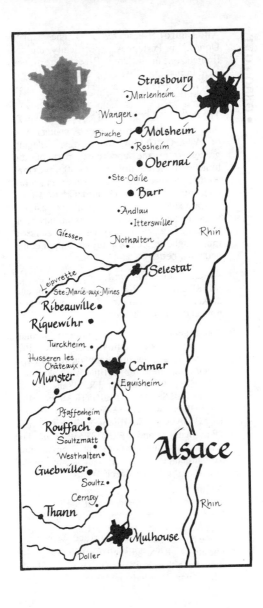

Alto Douro *(Al'-tow Doo'-roe)*: The "Upper Douro," in Portuguese; specifically, the delimited zone on the Douro River where grapes used in making PORT are grown. The Port is first made here on the estate or QUINTA, then brought downstream to Vila Nova de Gaia where it is blended and aged.

Amarone *(Ah-ma-roe'-nay)*: A special type of VALPOLICELLA, for which selected grapes from the uppermost part of the bunches are left to dry on racks after picking, so that the resulting wine is fuller and more concentrated. The term is used with RECIOTO Valpolicellas to indicate that the residual sugar in this normally sweet wine has been fermented, to yield a dry wine. It fetches a much higher price than regular Valpolicella, and ages better.

Amontillado *(Ah-mon-tee-ya'-doe)*: A dry SHERRY of the FINO type, usually fuller and darker in color than most Finos, with a pronounced "nutty" flavor.

Anbaugebiet *(An'-bough-ge-beet)*: German for "region under cultivation." The 1971 German Wine Law authorized eleven specific viticultural areas in Germany as Anbaugebiete: AHR, BADEN, FRANKEN (Franconia), HESSISCHE BERGSTRASSE, MITTELRHEIN, MOSEL-SAAR-RUWER, NAHE, RHEINGAU, RHEINHESSEN, RHEINPFALZ (Palatinate), and WÜRTTEMBERG. The exact legal terminology is "bestimmtes Anbaugebiet" (b.A.) or "designated region." See QUALITÄTSWEIN.

Anjou *(Ahn-zhoo')*: Old French province, now part of the department of the Maine-et-Loire, near Angers on the lower Loire River. Red wines made from the Cabernet Franc grape are called Cabernet d'Anjou; this grape variety is also used for excellent rosés that may be either dry or semi-sweet. Anjou's white wines, produced from the Chenin

Blanc, are superior. To the north, the Coteaux de la Loire includes the district of SAVENNIÈRES, one of the best dry Loire wines made from the Chenin Blanc; to the south, the COTEAUX DU LAYON is known for sweet, luscious white wines, for which the QUARTS DE CHAUME and BONNEZEAUX vineyards are celebrated. SAUMUR is noted for its good whites and also its sparkling wines, made by the Champagne process.

Appellation Contrôlée *(Ah-pell-ah'-syon Kon-troll-ay')*: In French, "controlled place name": the legal authorization for the name of a vineyard or wine region. It is outlined by the Institut National des Appellations d'Origine Contrôlée (I.N.A.O.), the official French government regulatory agency for wines and spirits.

The French wine laws are designed to protect the reputation of a famous wine area and also serve to protect the consumer. The words "appellation contrôlée" on a wine label are apt to be an indication of superior quality, because by law the wine *has* to come from the specified vineyard or wine district. This legislation has been in effect for about 40 years, and it has succeeded in reducing the incidence of wine frauds.

Besides defining the geographical origin of a wine, the laws also specify the approved grape varieties best suited to the area, minimum alcoholic strength of the wine, limits on yield per hectare, pruning methods and other viticultural practices. These provisions work to defend quality by discouraging overproduction.

Appellation d'Origine *(Ah-pell-ah'-syon Dor'-re-zheen)*: In French, "place name of geographic origin"; also, the laws regulating the use of these place names and restricting them to the better wine regions.

A quality hierarchy entitles France's most famous wines to APPELLATION CON-

TRÔLÉE: there are over 200 of these, each one identifying a superior wine in its class. Next come the "Vins Délimités de Qualité Supérieur" (V.D.Q.S.), whose quality does not quite measure up to appellation contrôlée. These wines must conform to certain standards, however, and are usually well-made: they carry a government seal on their labels. At the bottom of the scale are the "vins de pays" (regional wines). Though quality standards for them are not rigorous, they must come from the region indicated on the label, and are relatively inexpensive.

Apulia *(Ah-pool'-ya)***:** Wine district in southern Italy, the "heel" of the Italian "boot." The equivalent of 110 million cases of wine is produced in Apulia each year. Much is used in bulk in the manufacture of VERMOUTH, but there are many fine wines sold under their own names: SAN SEVERO and Castel del Monte, red, white or rosé wines produced near the town of Foggia, are perhaps the most famous and are entitled to D.O.C.

Arbois *(Are'-bwah)***:** Town located in eastern France near the Swiss border, in the JURA Mountains. Arbois is the best-known of several Jura APPELLATION CONTRÔLÉES that all produce similar wines (see CHÂ-TEAU-CHALON). It is famous for *vin jaune,* a white wine made from the Savagnin grape, that undergoes a transformation in cask similar to SHERRY; a process of air-drying the grapes to concentrate them prior to vinification is also used for VIN DE PAILLE. A rosé called Rosé d'Arbois is very popular; both this and a red Arbois is made from the Pinot Noir grape. Average production of all wine types is 185,160 cases.

8

Argentina: Argentina is one of the world's largest wine-producing countries, with more than 750,000 acres under vines; per capita consumption is on the order of ten cases of wine a year. With mass production in giant wineries (BODEGAS), the domestic need for top-quality wine is not great, but many of Argentina's better wines that are exported to the U.S. are excellent value. Red wines are generally more popular than the whites.

75% of Argentina's vineyards lie near the Chilean border, to the west. The climate is very dry, and irrigation is necessary in many vineyards. Principal vineyard areas are in MENDOZA and San Juan provinces, and the Rio Negro territory.

As Americans see them, Argentinean wines are known by their VARIETAL names, of which the most important are Cabernet Sauvignon, Merlot, Malbec (or Malbeck) and Barbera for red wines; Riesling, Chardonnay, Traminer, Pinot Blanc and Sémillon for whites.

Aroma: The fruity, "grapey" scent in a young wine. Aroma should not be confused with BOUQUET, a more complex scent in mature wines, which is achieved through further aging.

Asti: Town in PIEMONTE, Italy, east of Torino (Turin). It is famous for Asti *Spumante*, a very popular sweet sparkling wine made from Muscat grapes; also, good red wines made from Barbera, Grignolino, Nebbiolo and Freisa grapes.

Aszú *(Ahs'-zoo)*: A superior sweet grade of Hungarian TOKAY, made only in the best vintages.

Aube *(Ohb)*: French department in the southern and secondary part of the Champagne region.

Aude *(Ode)*: The second largest wine-producing department in France, after the HÉRAULT. Though chiefly a region of ordinary wines, the Aude has several APPELLATION CONTRÔLÉES, including

FITOU and Blanquette de Limoux, and V.D.Q.S. wines such as CORBIÈRES and part of the MINERVOIS.

Auslese *(Ouse'-lay-zeh)***:** German for "selection." As outlined in the 1971 German Wine Law, a wine labeled Auslese is made from particularly ripe selected grape bunches from which all unripe grapes have been discarded. The legal minimum MUST WEIGHT must be about 90 (varies by area). Auslese wines are usually sweeter and more concentrated than SPÄTLESE, and are more expensive. They are only made in better vintages.

Ausone, Château *(Oh-zone')***:** Famous classified Premier Grand Cru (First Great Growth) of SAINT-ÉMILION, considered one of the very best wines of BORDEAUX; it is celebrated for its body and bouquet. Its name is derived from Ausonius, a Roman poet and consul; about 2,800 cases are made each year.

Australia: The vine is not native to Australia, and so it was only in 1788 that the first vineyards were planted by British settlers at Sydney. Since then, Australia has become a major wine-producing nation; much is consumed on the home market, but the export of wines to the U.S. — and their quality — is increasing. Whereas Australia previously concentrated on making dessert and FORTIFIED WINES, her emphasis now is on quality table wines.

Most of Australia's 60,000 acres of vineyard lie in the south of the continent. The most important wine-producing state is South Australia, which produces two-thirds of the nation's wine; the vineyards surround Adelaide, the state's capital. A notable area for table wine is the Hunter River Valley, north of Sydney in New South Wales; the balance of wine production is largely furnished by Victoria.

In the past, Australia's wines had

GENERIC labels like "claret" or "burgundy," after their European counterparts. Though such practices persist, quality wines are now apt to be designated by their VARIETAL name, such as Cabernet Sauvignon and Hermitage (Shiraz) for red wines. Riesling is the most important white wine variety, but the true Riesling is known as "Rhine Riesling" in Australia, and wine labeled "Riesling" is usually made from Sémillon. In addition, some good sparkling wine is made in Victoria.

Austria: Austria has a heritage of over 1,000 years of viticulture, but today wine is produced only in the eastern half of the country, principally in the environs of Vienna, in Burgenland on the Neusiedler See southeast of Vienna, and in the Wachau district on the Danube River. Much Austrian wine is consumed in taverns as carafe wine, and little of this is exported or even bottled. But what is sent to the U.S. is usually inexpensive and quite good.

There are 122,000 acres of vineyard in Austria. Like Germany, Austria is known more for her fresh white wines than her reds. The principal white grape varieties are Rhine Riesling (the true Riesling of Germany), Italian Riesling, Sylvaner, Gewürztraminer, Grüner-Veltliner (an Austrian specialty), and Furmint — some light, pleasant reds are made from the Spätburgunder (Pinot Noir).

Vienna is most famous for GUMPOLDSKIRCHNER, a fine racy wine, and GRINZING, the popular wine of the Viennese taverns. The town of KREMS in the Wachau is noted for its wines, as is RUST on the Neusiedler See. Some Austrian wines are labeled SPÄTLESE or AUSLESE to designate late picking, though usually these are much less sweet than their German counterparts.

Auxey-Duresses *(Oak'-say Dew-ress')*: Small hillside town in Burgundy's CÔTE DE

11

BEAUNE, to the west of MEURSAULT.
There are 370 acres of vineyard that produce
good, light red wine; the best vineyards are
rated Premier Cru (First Growth) and include:
Les Duresses, Le Val, and Reugné.

Avelsbach *(Ah'-vuhls-bock)*: Wine commune near the RUWER district, Germany;
since 1971 officially part of the district of
TRIER. Its wines are not well-known outside
of Germany, but can be outstanding in good
vintages. The vineyards (EINZELLAGEN) are
Hammerstein, Altenberg, and Herrenberg.

Ayl *(I'll)*: Wine village in the SAAR district,
Germany, with some 178 acres of vineyard.
Ayl often makes some of the Saar's finest
wines; the most famous vineyards
(EINZELLAGEN) are Kupp, Scheidterberg,
and Herrenberger.

B

Baco *(Bah'-co)*: Group of HYBRID vines,
named after Maurice Baco, who perfected
them. Baco vines are grown successfully in
the eastern United States, where they have
good immunity to frost. The best-known is
Baco Noir, or Baco No. 1.

Badacsony *(Bad'-ah-chony)*: Wine area located on the north shore of Lake Balaton,
Hungary; named after Mount Badacsony, an
extinct volcano. Primarily white wines are
produced, such as Riesling, which is called
Badacsonyi Rizling, and two specialties:
Badacsonyi Szürkebarat *(Soor-kee-ba-rat')*,
a medium-dry wine with an earthy bouquet,
and Badacsonyi Keknyelu *(Kek'-nyuh-lew)*,
a light and elegantly dry wine that may be the
best of Hungary's white wines.

Baden: Situated in southwestern Germany along the Rhine River, Baden is that country's third largest wine region. Previously, only tourists who visited Baden's famous Black Forest knew the delights of the wines, but Baden is now taking an active interest in exports and is moving in the direction of high-quality wines. Some 90% of all Baden wine comes from the Z.B.W. wine cooperative in Breisach.

The 1971 German Wine Law delimited Baden into several sub-districts or BEREICHE: *Bodensee,* along Lake Constance, noted for a light red wine called "Seewein"; MARKGRÄFLERLAND, to the south of the city of Freiburg, where the Gutedel (Chasselas) variety predominates; *Kaiserstuhl-Tuniberg,* named for the KAISERSTUHL, a volcanic hill where some of Baden's best wines are made from Ruländer (Pinot Gris); *Breisgau,* famous for a light rosé called WEISSHERBST; *Ortenau,* the home of Affenthaler, a local red wine shipped in an amusing "monkey bottle"; *Bergstrasse-Kraichgau,* around the city of Heidelberg; and *Badisches Frankenland,* further inland near the region of FRANKEN, which ships its wines in the squat BOCKSBEUTEL flask native to Franken. There are over 30,000 acres of vineyard in Baden; one-fourth of the wines are red, made mostly from Spätburgunder (Pinot Noir) — rare in Germany.

Bandol *(Bahn'-dol)***:** Located just to the west of Toulon on the French Mediterranean coast, Bandol is one of the better wines of PROVENCE, and it is rated APPELLATION CONTRÔLÉE. Also a resort area, the region produces red, white and rosé wines — the latter are perhaps the most famous. Principal grape varities used in making red and rosé Bandol wines are Grenache and Mourvèdre; for white, Clairette and Ugni Blanc. The area under vines is 300 acres, and the average annual production is about 45,750 cases.

13

Banyuls *(Bahn-yulz′)*: Sweet French FORTIFIED WINE produced south of Port-Vendres on the Mediterranean coast, near the Spanish border. One of several sweet wines (vins de liqueur) made within the area of Grand Roussillon, Banyuls is considered to be the best. It is grown on very steep, rocky hills extending over 6,920 acres.

Barbaresco *(Bar-ba-ress′-co)*: Excellent and full-bodied red wine from the district of PIEMONTE in northern Italy, generally regarded to be one of Italy's best. Made from the Nebbiolo grape in a delimited region around the town of Alba, like its neighbor BAROLO, it ages well but in comparison to Barolo it is lighter and matures sooner. Average production is approximately 10,850 cases a year.

Barbera *(Bar-bear′-ah)*: Good-quality red wine grape, widely used in northern Italy and also in California, where 20,400 acres have been planted. In PIEMONTE, where it is most successful, the wines entitled to D.O.C. are called Barbera d'Asti, Barbera di Monferrato, and Barbera di Alba.

Bardolino *(Bar-do-leen′-o)*: Attractive light red wine produced on the eastern shore of Lake Garda near Verona, Italy. Made from a blend of Corvina, Rondinella and Molinara grapes, like its neighbor VALPOLICELLA, it is best when consumed quite young — usually before it is three years old. Over a million cases a year are produced.

Barolo *(Ba-roll′-o)*: One of the best red wines of the district of PIEMONTE in northern Italy; possibly the greatest of those that are made from the Nebbiolo grape. The D.O.C. region of Barolo consists of 24,700 acres to the southwest of the town of Alba; over 300,000 cases are produced in a typical vintage.

Barolo is full and tannic when young, but

14

mellows to perfection after several years of aging. It is usually shipped in thick brown glass bottles, and when mature it is apt to throw a heavy sediment.

Barsac *(Bar'-sack)*: Commune in Bordeaux famous for its sweet white wines — the northernmost part of the district of SAUTERNES. Although Barsacs are legally entitled to the name Sauternes, most wines from this equally famous commune will bear the name Barsac.

In comparison to wines from Sauternes, Barsacs tend to be a bit drier. They are fine naturally sweet wines made from Sémillon, Sauvignon Blanc and Muscadelle grapes that have gained in sweetness from the action of the "noble mold" (POURRITURE NOBLE).

The most famous Barsac estates or CHÂTEAUX are Coutet and Climens, classified as First Growths (Premiers Crus) in 1855. The Barsac châteaux rated Second Growth (Deuxième Cru) include Myrat, Doisy-Daëne, Doisy-Vedrines, Broustet, Nairac, Caillou, and Suau. Annual production of all Barsac averages about 183,000 cases per year.

Bâtard-Montrachet *(Bah'-tarr Monrah-shay')*: One of the best white wines of the CÔTE DE BEAUNE, Burgundy. Made from the Chardonnay grape, the wine often rivals even MONTRACHET, which is more famous. The Grand Cru (Great Growth) vineyard is 29 acres large, divided equally between the adjoining communes of PULIGNY- and CHASSAGNE-MONTRACHET; there are some 3,700 cases made each year.

Beaujolais *(Bo'-sho-lay)*: One of the best-known French wines, Beaujolais is celebrated for its fresh, fruity qualities. Most of it is red, made from the Gamay grape, although there is some excellent white Beaujolais (Beaujolais Blanc) that is made from the Chardonnay.

The Beaujolais district contains about

15

42,500 acres of vineyard, situated between MÀCON and Lyon in southern Burgundy. The land is very hilly, and the soil is rich in granite. Ordinary Beaujolais must have at least 9% alcohol; if it reaches 10% it may be called "Beaujolais Supérieur." Better Beaujolais, known as "Beaujolais-Villages," comes from a smaller area to the north, consisting of thirty-five authorized communes whose wines share similar characteristics.

The very best Beaujolais, however, is not called Beaujolais at all, but goes under the name of nine *crus* (growths), which may legally be called Burgundies: BROUILLY, CÔTE DE BROUILLY, CHÉNAS, CHIROUBLES, FLEURIE, JULIÉNAS, MORGON, MOULIN-À-VENT, and ST. AMOUR. These wines are apt to be richer and fuller than ordinary Beaujolais, because the maximum yield per acre is much less (427 gallons, as opposed to 535 gallons). They are also somewhat more expensive.

Beaujolais is a wine to be enjoyed young, usually before it is three years old. It is one of the few red wines that tastes best when chilled. 8½ million cases of Beaujolais are produced annually; wine from the nine *crus* amounts to about 1.7 million cases.

Beaumes-de-Venise *(Bome'-duh Ven-ease')*: District in the CÔTES-DU-RHÔNE region, France, producing both a sweet FORTIFIED WINE made from the Muscat grape, and a dry red. The latter is probably better-known in the United States.

Beaune *(Bone)*: Beaune is the center of the Burgundy wine trade; it gives its name to the CÔTE DE BEAUNE, the southern portion of the CÔTE D'OR. Many of Burgundy's most important shippers have their cellars in Beaune; the town is also famous for a charity hospital, the HOSPICES DE BEAUNE, which derives its income from a number of vineyard holdings. Each November, an auction is held

16

of the wines of the Hospices that generally establishes prices for the Burgundies of that vintage.

There are 1,327 acres of vineyard in Beaune; among these are a number of good vineyards rated Premier Cru (First Growth), located to the west of the town. The most famous of these are Fèves, GRÈVES, and the CLOS DES MOUCHES. Other excellent vineyards include the CLOS DU ROI, BRESSANDES, and MARCONNETS. The average annual production of all Beaune wine is about 99,500 cases.

Beerenauslese *(Bearen-ouse'-lay-zeh)*: German for "berry selection." As specified in the 1971 German Wine Law, a wine labeled Beerenauslese is a special AUSLESE made from individually selected, fully ripened grapes affected by the "noble mold" (EDELFÄULE) and picked berry by berry. The resulting wine is rich and high in residual sugar; the legal minimum MUST WEIGHT must be about 120 (varies by area). Though rare and rather expensive, Beerenauslesen are among the world's very greatest wines.

Bereich *(Buh-ryke')*: German for "area" or "region." As outlined in the 1971 German Wine Law, a Bereich is a sub-region within a larger ANBAUGEBIET (region under cultivation). It may extend over several wine-producing villages and vineyard areas within the Anbaugebiet that produce wines of similar type; however, these wines never carry the name of a single vineyard. See GROSSLAGE, EINZELLAGE.

Bergerac *(Bear'-shair-ack)*: City and viticultural area in the Périgord region, southwestern France, situated some 60 miles to the east of BORDEAUX. While most of Bergerac's wine is ordinary and is apt to be consumed locally, there are two exceptions: PÉCHARMANT, located to the north of the city

17

and known for its red wines, and MONBAZ-ILLAC, famous for its old château, which produces sweet white wines similar to SAUTERNES.

Bernkastel *(Bearn'-cast'l)***:** Famous wine village in the MOSEL district, Germany, with some 500 acres of vineyard. Owing to good soil and exposure, Bernkastel often makes some of the region's best wines, but it is important to know that under the 1971 German Wine Law, Bernkastel is also a BEREICH or sub-region, and that much of the so-called "Bernkasteler Riesling" shipped to the U.S. is merely regional wine and does not actually come from Bernkastel. To be sure of getting the best, one should buy an estate-bottled wine (ERZEUGER-ABFÜLLUNG) made from one of Bernkastel's leading vineyards or EINZELLAGEN: Doktor (the most famous and expensive), Graben, Lay, Bratenhöfchen, Matheisbildchen, Schlossberg and Johannis-brunnchen.

At their best, the wines of Bernkastel are spicy, scented, and well-balanced; they are among the most noble of all wines made from the Riesling grape.

Bianchello del Metauro *(Bee-yan-kell'-o del Muh-tawr'-o)***:** Good-quality white wine produced in the region of MARCHE, Italy, made from Bianchello grapes. Dry and with a golden color, it is rated D.O.C.

Bienvenue-Bâtard-Montrachet *(Be-an-vay-noo' Bah'-tarr Mon-rah-shay')***:** Excellent small vineyard (6 acres) in the commune of PULIGNY-MONTRACHET, in Burgundy's CÔTE DE BEAUNE. Until recently it was part of BÂTARD-MONTRACHET, but now the wines are sold separately. Like its neighbor, it is rated Grand Cru (Great Growth) and is in the same noble class; about 1,430 cases are made each year.

Bingen: Situated at the mouth of Germany's NAHE River where it meets the Rhine,

Bingen is the most western part of the RHEINHESSEN region. Its soft, full-flavored white wines are among the best of the region, owing to favorable exposure and slate soil. Bingen is also the name of a BEREICH (sub-region) extending over many different villages, but the best wines come from some 800 acres around Bingen itself, and are made from the Riesling grape. Leading vineyards (EINZELLAGEN) include Scharlachberg, Kirchberg, Osterberg, Kapellenberg, and Bubenstück.

Blagny *(Blahn'-yee)*: Small hamlet (hameau) in the CÔTE DE BEAUNE, Burgundy, located on the boundary between PULIGNY-MONTRACHET and MEURSAULT. Both red and white wines are made in Blagny; the whites, made from the Chardonnay grape, are better-known. Under French law, wine from the section in Meursault is called "Meursault-Blagny" or just plain "Blagny"; in Puligny-Montrachet, "Puligny-Montrachet, Hameau de Blagny." The former is more common in the U.S.

Blanc de Blancs *(Blawn duh Blawn')*: A white wine produced exclusively from white grapes. Technically it is significant only in the French CHAMPAGNE country in the CÔTE DES BLANCS, where Chardonnay grapes are grown. Most Champagne is made from Pinot Noir, a black grape (see BLANC DE NOIRS), and Champagnes made only from the Chardonnay are delicate, very distinguished and generally more expensive than those made from Pinot Noir.

In recent years "Blanc de Blancs" has been used to label many white wines from other areas without any real justification, since outside the Champagne district almost all white wines are made from white grapes only.

Blanc de Noirs *(Blawn duh Nwar')*: A white

19

wine made from black grapes. The term applies principally to French CHAMPAGNE, most of which is made from the juice of black grapes (Pinot Noir) removed from the skins and fermented separately so that the alcohol produced during fermentation does not extract any color from the skins.

Commercially, most French Champagne is a blend of Blanc de Noirs with some BLANC DE BLANCS to add delicacy, although there are some Champagnes made by small producers that are totally Blanc de Noirs. In the U.S., at least one winery uses "Blanc de Noirs" to identify a sparkling wine made from Pinot Noir according to the traditional French Champagne process.

Blanc Fumé *(Blawn Foo-may')***:** Local name for the Sauvignon Blanc grape grown in the district of Pouilly-sur-Loire in France's LOIRE River valley; the wine that it gives is called POUILLY-FUMÉ or "Pouilly-Blanc Fumé," to be distinguished from the region's more common wines that are made from the Chasselas and are known as Pouilly-sur-Loire.

To avoid a conflict with the French growers by calling their wine Pouilly-Fumé, Californian wineries often use the term Blanc Fumé to identify a VARIETAL wine made from the Sauvignon Blanc that is similar to the French.

Blaye *(Bly)***:** Viticultural district of Bordeaux, situated on the right bank of the GIRONDE estuary opposite the MÉDOC. The better wines of Blaye are red, and are called Premier Côtes de Blaye; they are fruity, supple and generally inexpensive. In addition, a large quantity of lesser-quality white wine is produced, called Côtes de Blaye or "Blayais." Superior wine is made on estates or CHÂTEAUX, the best-known being Châteaux Barbé, Lescadre, Segonzac, and Le Menaudat.

Bocksbeutel *(Bocks'-boy-tul)***:** The rounded,

flask-shaped green bottle used for the white wines of FRANKEN (Franconia), Germany. The name is allegedly derived from the scrotum (Beutel) of a goat (Bock). Similarly-shaped bottles are used in Chile, Australia and Portugal.

Bodega *(Bo-day'-ga)*: Spanish for "wine cellar," although in Spain a "cellar" is usually located above ground. In many Spanish-speaking countries, the term also applies to a large winery.

Bodenheim *(Bo'-den-heim)*: Wine district in the RHEINHESSEN region, Germany, located just to the north of NIERSTEIN, with some 495 acres of vineyard. Both red and white wines are made; the whites are superior, though little-known in the U.S. Most white Bodenheimers are made from the Silvaner grape, but the best wines are Rieslings from individual vineyards or EINZEL-LAGEN, the most famous being Kreuzberg. Kapelle, Hoch, Silberberg, and Burgweg. The Hessian State Domain is a leading producer.

Body: The degree of concentration or substance in a wine, referring to the presence of alcohol and flavors. Rich red wines are generally full-bodied, but this is not always a distinction in certain white wines (such as those of the MOSEL), for they are prized for their light body and any unexpected fullness might be considered a defect.

Bonnes-Mares *(Bawn Marr')*: One of the very greatest red wines of the CÔTE DE NUITS, Burgundy, rated Grand Cru (Great Growth). Full and with a great depth of flavor, a good Bonnes-Mares takes on considerable complexity with age, and is long-lived. The vineyard extends over 37 acres, with 32 acres located in the commune of CHAMBOLLE-MUSIGNY and 5 acres in MOREY-ST. DENIS, to the north, where it borders the CLOS DE TART. About 3,400 cases are made each year.

Bonnezeaux *(Bonn-zo')*: Wine region in the CÔTEAUX DU LAYON district, near the LOIRE River. Bonnezeaux and nearby QUARTS DE CHAUME are considered the best white wine districts of the Côteaux du Layon, and have their own APPELLATION CONTRÔLÉES. Both are made from the Chenin Blanc, and in good vintages the grapes are harvested late, yielding fine, naturally sweet wines. About 250 acres are under vines in Bonnezeaux; there are some 12,000 cases of wine made each year.

Bordeaux *(Bor-doe')*: Important seaport city in southwestern France, situated on the GARONNE River; to the north, the Garonne meets the DORDOGNE River to form the GIRONDE, a tidal estuary and also the name of the department (administrative region) in which Bordeaux is located. The vineyard area entitled to the appellation Bordeaux is immense. One-third of all French wine exported to the United States comes from Bordeaux; from about 346,000 acres under vines, the average wine production is over 30 million cases.

Bordeaux produces a wide variety of red and white wines, though it is perhaps best-known for its reds, known popularly as "clarets." The most famous red wine district of Bordeaux is the MÉDOC, located to the north of the city; the central portion is called the HAUT-MÉDOC, which consists of four principle communes; from north to south, they include: SAINT-ESTÈPHE, PAUILLAC SAINT-JULIEN, and MARGAUX. Fine red wines are also made in GRAVES to the south of the city, and in the adjoining regions of SAINT-ÉMILION and POMEROL 25 miles to the east. The secondary red wine districts include BOURG and BLAYE, located on the right bank of the Gironde opposite the Médoc;

FRONSAC, near Pomerol, and Premières Côtes de Bordeaux south of the city.

The best red Bordeaux wines from great vintages are slow to mature, and need several years of aging in bottle. They are made primarily from the Cabernet Sauvignon grape, a late-ripening variety that gives full, elegant wines, or the closely-related Cabernet Franc. The Merlot, an early-ripening grape prized for the soft, scented wines that it produces, is used principally in Saint-Émilion and Pomerol. Other red varieties include the Malbec and the Petit-Verdot. It is customary for most red Bordeaux to be made from a blend of these varieties, depending on the soil and the region in which they are grown.

Bordeaux is also noted for its white wines; the famous white Graves are very dry, while the regions of SAUTERNES and BARSAC near Graves specialize in sweet wines. The secondary white wine regions include CÉRONS and SAINTE-CROIX-DU-MONT close to Sauternes, and ENTRE-DEUX-MERS, located east of Bordeaux in the area between the Garonne and Dordogne Rivers.

The principal grape varieties used in making white Bordeaux are the Sauvignon Blanc and the Sémillon, which are used to make either the crisp, dry wines of Graves or the rich, sweet wines of Sauternes and Cérons. To make sweet wines, the grapes are harvested late when they are overripe. A third variety, the Muscadelle, is also used in the sweet wine districts.

Almost any wine from Bordeaux is likely to be well-made, but superior wine bears the name of a specific region in Bordeaux from where it comes — the more information given on the label, the better the wine. The best Bordeaux wines are produced on estates called CHÂTEAUX. When the wine is bottled at the estate and not by a shipper in Bordeaux, its label will read: "MIS EN BOUTEILLE AU CHÂTEAU" — château-bottled — which is equivalent to ESTATE-BOTTLED wine in other districts. This system assures the authenticity of fine Bordeaux wines, and also controls quality; most of the great Bordeaux are château-bottled, but there are a few exceptions.

Botrytis Cinerea *(Bo-treet'-iss Sin-uh-ray-'-uh)*: The botanical term for what is known as POURRITURE NOBLE in French and EDELFÄULE in German: "noble mold." It is found in many of the world's wine regions, but only in certain climates and under certain conditions is its action "noble," for rotting of the grapes is a constant fear of wine-growers. In the fall, following a period of warm weather and high humidity, the mold gathers on the skins of the grapes but does not rot them — instead, it causes the skins to shrink and the juice to become concentrated and high in sugar and extracts. It is essential to the manufacture of the best naturally sweet wines, which include the SAUTERNES and BARSACS of Bordeaux, the AUSLESEN of Germany, and the TOKAYS of Hungary.

Botrytis is beneficial only to white grapes, most notably the Riesling, Sémillon, Sauvignon Blanc, and Chenin Blanc. On a limited basis, wines have successfully been made from grapes affected by Botrytis in the United States.

Bouchet *(Boo-shay')*: The local name for the red Cabernet Franc grape in the SAINT-ÉMILION and POMEROL districts of Bordeaux.

Bouquet: The scent of a mature wine, to be distinguished from AROMA, which is given off by young wines. Chemically rather complex, bouquet is a product of bottle age, and most good wines will develop it to a certain degree if allowed to mature. It is created by slow oxidation of the alcohol, fruit acids and other compounds in the wine as it ages — this

Bordeaux

medoc

St-Estèphe · · St-Ciers

Pauillac ·

St-Julien · · **Blaye** · St-Savin

Margaux · Garonne **Bourg**

Blanquefort · **Libourne**

· Pomerol

Vayres · **St-Emilion**

Bordeaux

Pessac · Castillon-la-Bataille

· Cadillac

Cérons · · Loupiac

· Ste-Croix-du-Mont

GRAVES Barsac · **St.Macaire**

Sauternes · **Langon**

Villandraut · Isle

produces new compounds such as esters and aldehydes.

Wines will generally best display their bouquet if swirled in an appropriate glass, so that the volatile compounds may evaporate. Certain mature wines generally possess more bouquet than others, most notably those of MARGAUX (red) or the MOSEL (white).

Bourg *(Boorg)*: Viticultural district of Bordeaux, located on the right bank of the GIRONDE estuary opposite the MÉDOC. Bourg lies just to the south of BLAYE, and the red and white wines of both regions are similar, though the fruity and distinguished red wines of Bourg, made principally from the Cabernet Franc grape, tend to be better-known in the United States.

There are three Bourg APPELLATION CONTRÔLÉES: Bourg, Bourgeais, and Côtes de Bourg; the latter includes a large number of estates or CHÂTEAUX, the most famous being du Bousquet, Caruel, Laurensanne, Mille Secousses, and Rousset.

Bourgeois *(Boor'-zhwah)*: French for "common" or "middle class." Though this term is legally applied to a grade of Bordeaux wine (Cru Bourgeois), most notably in the MÉDOC region, from the quality standpoint it is somewhat misleading. Wine from a Cru Bourgeois CHÂTEAU (or the slightly higher rank, Cru Bourgeois Supérieur) may not be common wine at all — in fact, from a good château in a fine vintage, the wine may occasionally be quite impressive, if not equal in quality to a CLASSIFIED GROWTH château.

Bourgogne *(Boor-gon'-yuh)*: French for BURGUNDY. Bourgogne is also an APPELLATION CONTRÔLÉE, the legal designation for ordinary red or white wine produced within the specified area of Burgundy. Although these wines are not entitled to a COMMUNE appellation and are therefore not as good as other Burgundies from a more specific region, they are generally inexpensive. In poor vintages, or when there is overproduction, many more famous Burgundies may have to be de-classified and given the simpler name "Bourgogne" if they do not meet the standards that apply to them. Wine with the appellation Bourgogne may be given the following designations:

— *Bourgogne.* Red or white wines produced exclusively within the region of Burgundy. The red wines must have a minimum alcoholic strength of 10%; the whites, 10½%.

— *Bourgogne Ordinaire* or *Bourgogne Grand Ordinaire.* Red, white or rosé wines, either de-classified or else not meeting the standards for Bourgogne. The minimum alcoholic strength for red wines must be 9%; for whites, 9½%.

— *Bourgogne Aligoté* (white wines only). Wines from the secondary regions, made principally from the Aligoté grape and not the more distinguished Chardonnay, although some Chardonnay may be used. Minimum alcoholic strength: 9½%.

— *Bourgogne Passe-Tout-Grains* (red wines only). Wines made from Gamay and Pinot Noir grapes vatted together, with at least one-third Pinot Noir. Because in northern Burgundy the Gamay is more productive and produces lesser wines than the Pinot Noir, wines cannot be made entirely from the Gamay with good results, but as inexpensive table wine Passe-Tout-Grains serves a useful purpose. Minimum alcoholic strength: 9½%.

Bourgueil *(Boor-goy′)***:** Town and viticultural district of TOURAINE (a former province, on France's LOIRE River. The district includes two neighboring townships, Bourgueil and St. Nicolas-de-Bourgueil; the latter, being situated on hillier country with a higher concentration of chalk in the soil, is apt to produce better wine.

27

Along with CHINON to the south, Bourgueil generally makes the best red wines of the Loire. Both regions use the Cabernet Franc grape — called Breton locally — which is also used to make a lesser quantity of rosé. Often possessing a fine bouquet of raspberries, Bourgueils may be drunk young but the best improve with some bottle age.

Bouzy *(Boo-zee')*: Village in the French CHAMPAGNE district, located in the northern portion known as the MONTAGNE DE REIMS. In addition to being considered one of the best vineyard areas in the Montagne de Reims for growing red Pinot Noir grapes that are used in making Champagne, Bouzy is also celebrated for its still red wine, called Bouzy Rouge; fine and delicate, it is comparable to a light red Burgundy. Red Bouzys enjoy considerable local fame and are also very popular in Paris; recently some have been shipped to the United States.

Brachetto *(Bra-kett'-o)*: Sparkling red wine from the region of PIEMONTE in northern Italy, named after the grape variety from which it is made. Superior Brachetto is produced near the town of Acqui and is called Brachetto d'Acqui; it is entitled to D.O.C.

Brauneberg *(Brown'-uh-bairg)*: Celebrated wine village of the MOSEL River valley, Germany. There are some 550 acres of vineyard around Brauneberg, four-fifths of them planted in Riesling. The wines are among the Mosel's best; they often rival those of BERNKASTEL, which lies four miles to the east. The leading vineyards (EINZELLAGEN) are: Juffer (the best-known), Juffer-Sonnenuhr, Hasenläufer, Kammer, and Klostergarten.

28

Bressandes *(Bres-sond')*: One of the fine red wines of the commune of ALOXE-CORTON, in Burgundy's CÔTE DE BEAUNE. The Bressandes vineyard extends over 42½ acres and lies near the famous CORTON vineyard; because the two land parcels share similar exposure and soil, the wines are sold either as "Corton Bressandes" or "Corton." They are scented and full-flavored Burgundies, slower to mature than most Côte de Beaune red wines.

There is also a Bressandes vineyard in the commune of BEAUNE to the south, rated Premier Cru (First Growth). It is not so well-known as Corton Bressandes but often produces similar wine.

Brouilly *(Broo-yee′)*: Red wine district in the BEAUJOLAIS region, southern Burgundy, extending over some 2,160 acres. Officially classified as one of the nine *crus* (growths) — those areas that usually produce the best Beaujolais — Brouilly is the southernmost of these, and consists of five associated communes: Odenas, Saint-Lager, Cercié, Quincié, and Charentay. The center of Brouilly is a hill known as the CÔTE DE BROUILLY, a separate district.

Generally quick to mature, Brouillys are among the best-known and most attractive Beaujolais. Their fresh, fruity qualities make them most enjoyable rather soon after they are made.

Brunello di Montalcino *(Broo-nell′-o dee Mon-tahl-chee′-no)*: Excellent red wine from the district of TUSCANY, Italy, made near the town of Montalcino south of the CHIANTI region. Brunello di Montalcino is one of the very finest Italian red wines. It is made from the Brunello grape, a variety similar to the Sangiovese of Chianti. The D.O.C. region of Brunello di Montalcino is 809 acres, and the average annual production of this exceptionally long-lived wine is about 119,300 cases.

29

Brut *(Brute)*: French for "natural" or "unrefined," employed in the CHAMPAGNE district to designate the driest wines. Brut is drier than "Extra Dry," although the latter is often incorrectly assumed to indicate the driest Champagnes.

When a Champagne is ready for market, it normally receives a small amount of sugar solution prior to being shipped: the "liqueur d'expédition." Brut Champagnes receive a minimum amount of sweetening, and are therefore the driest. In the trade, the term Brut is used for both vintage and non-vintage Champagnes, as well as other sparkling wines.

Bual (also **Boal**): A sweet type of MADEIRA, with a fragrant bouquet and a golden color. It is generally served as a dessert wine.

Bulgaria: Although Bulgaria is one of the world's oldest wine-producing areas, many centuries of Moslem rule prohibited wine drinking and frustrated large-scale vineyards until quite recently. After World War II, with a nationalized wine industry and modern wine-making techniques, Bulgaria rose to sixth place among the world's wine exporting nations. Presently there are over 422,000 acres of vineyards, most of them located in the central plains east of Sofia, the capital.

Bulgarian wines are usually named after the grape varieties from which they are made. White wines are produced from Chardonnay, Italian Riesling, Dimiat, and a local variety of Muscat known as Misket. The red wines include Cabernet, Pamid, Gamza, and two uniquely Bulgarian specialties: Mavrud, a dark, flavorful wine, and Melnik, a strong, full-bodied wine made near the town of the same name.

Burgundy (French, **Bourgogne**): Historic old French province, now divided into smaller separate districts or departments, each of them a producer of wine. Specifically, Burgundy refers only to these regions in France; elsewhere, "burgundy" is used loosely as a

GENERIC term to indicate red wine of almost any type. But Burgundy also makes white wines that are among the world's greatest.

The Burgundy vineyards extend over 160 miles south from Auxerre in the department of the Yonne practically down to the city of Lyon. CHABLIS in the Yonne, renowned for its fine white wines, is Burgundy's most northerly wine region. The center of Burgundy is the CÔTE D'OR, to the north and south of the city of BEAUNE, an area that produces some of the region's most famous wines. In the Côte d'Or fine red wines are made in the CÔTE DE NUITS, the northern section, and red and white wines are produced in the southern section — the CÔTE DE BEAUNE.

South of the Côte d'Or is the CHALONNAIS region, named after the city of Chalon-sur-Saône. It consists of four vineyard areas: RULLY, MERCUREY, GIVRY, and MONTAGNY. Further south, the viticultural region of MÂCON, called ''Mâconnais'' in French, yields some excellent white wines; POUILLY-FUISSÉ is perhaps the most famous, with POUILLY-LOCHÉ, POUILLY-VINZELLES, and SAINT-VÉRAN close equals. White Mâcon (Mâcon blanc) comes from a much larger area. The vineyards of BEAUJOLAIS are located principally in the department of the Rhône north of Lyon, and mark the southern limit of the Burgundy region. In all, Burgundy has about 76,600 acres of vineyard, most of them under their own APPELLATION CONTRÔLÉES.

Though soil and climate are largely responsible for Burgundy's excellent wines, the grape varieties used in making them are equally important. Burgundy's best red wines are usually made only from the Pinot Noir, especially in the Côte d'Or, where it gives full, fruity and vigorous wines. Although the Gamay is a secondary variety in the Côte d'Or, it thrives in the Beaujolais and there it

31

gives better wine than the Pinot Noir. The Chardonnay (or Pinot Chardonnay) is a noble variety grown nearly everywhere in Burgundy, where it gives the best white wines. Secondary white wines are made from the Aligoté.

Good, authentic Burgundy, despite its considerable fame, is a relatively rare wine. Grown in a cool inland climate, much of it comes from small scattered vineyards whose quality and output varies greatly from year to year. Thus, the more specific information indicated on the label, the better the wine, because its origins can be identified more precisely. This applies to all wines, but because of the diversity of the vineyards, it has special significance in Burgundy.

C

Cabernet Franc *(Cab′-air-nay Fronc)*: Fine red grape variety, widely cultivated in the BORDEAUX region. The Cabernet Franc is a close relative of the famous Cabernet Sauvignon, and shares many of its noble characteristics; as its wine is slightly softer, it is usually blended with Cabernet Sauvignon to give balance to Bordeaux wines. In the SAINT-ÉMILION and POMEROL districts of Bordeaux, it is called Bouchet. The Cabernet Franc is also grown in the LOIRE River valley, where it is known locally as Breton. Important new plantations have recently been made in California.

Cabernet Sauvignon *(Cab′-air-nay So′-vin-yawn)*: Premium red grape variety, one of the most important of several grape varieties used in blends to make the fine red wines of BORDEAUX, especially those of the

MÉDOC and GRAVES. Though it ripens fairly late and its yield is small, the wine that it gives has a great deal of finesse and concentration. When it is young, wine made from Cabernet Sauvignon has considerable astringency, which is lost as it ages. Such wines — especially from great vintages — are very long-lived.

Although Cabernet Sauvignon is not planted extensively in France outside of the Bordeaux region, it adapts well to different climates and is grown successfully in Chile, Australia, Italy, Argentina, and the United States. It is without much question America's finest red wine grape, and in the opinion of many experts, some recent California Cabernet Sauvignons rank with the world's best red wines. Over 26,000 acres have been planted in the state.

Cahors *(Kah-or')*: Fine full-bodied red wine, produced around the town of the same name in the Lot River valley, south-western France. Long a locally famous wine entitled to V.D.Q.S., Cahors was granted an APPELLATION CONTRÔLÉE in 1971, in recognition of the excellence of its wines and the improvement in their quality.

Cahors is made principally from the Malbec grape, also known as Cot or Auxerrois, which because of its considerable strength is usually blended with Merlot and Jurançon to soften it. Formerly the wine took years and even decades to mature, but recent changes in vinification allow it to be drunk much sooner.

The area under the appellation Cahors is immense — almost 100,000 acres — but not all of it is vineyards. Over 160,000 cases of wine are produced each year, suggesting the potential of this interesting old wine region.

34

Cailleret *(Ky'-uh-ray)*: French for "clot" or "curdle"; also the name of several vineyards in the CÔTE DE BEAUNE, Burgundy. The most famous is in the commune of VOLNAY and is known as Volnay Caillerets; made from the Pinot Noir grape, it is one of the best red wines of the Côte de Beaune.

There are also two other vineyards named Cailleret in PULIGNY-MONTRACHET and CHASSAGNE-MONTRACHET to the south; planted in white Chardonnay grapes, both vineyards are noted for their wine. The name Cailleret is said to originate from the Burgundians' humor, so bawdy that it can turn wine into vinegar.

Calabria *(Ka-la'-bree-ah)***:** The southernmost part of the Italian mainland — the "toe" of the Italian "boot." With its hot, dry climate, Calabria is primarily a producer of ordinary wines, but there are two exceptions. CIRÒ, a red, white or rosé wine, is rated D.O.C. GRECO DI GERACE, a rare sweet white wine made from Greco grapes, has been famous since Roman times. Calabria as a whole produces the equivalent of 12 million cases of wine a year.

Caldaro *(Cal-dar'-o)***:** Small town in the ALTO ADIGE region, northern Italy; also a lake (Lago di Caldaro) three miles to the south. Two D.O.C. wines may carry this name: Caldaro, a light red wine made from the Schiava grape, and Lago di Caldaro; the latter is apt to be somewhat finer. Because of Alto Adige's large German-speaking population, Caldaro and Lago di Caldaro may sometimes be called Kalterer and Kalterersee, respectively.

California: America's most important wine-producing state, both in terms of the volume of wine it produces (over 82% of the U.S. total) and its quality. Few areas in the world are as well-suited to the vine. There are over 646,000 acres of vineyards in California; about half are planted in table grapes or those used in raisin production, but new plantings during the past decade have focused on wine

- Calpella
- Ukiah

sonoma-mendocino

Cloverdale •
Asti •
Geyserville •
Healdsburg •
Windsor •
Santa Rosa •

- Calistoga
- St. Helen
- Ruther
- Oaki

Sonoma •

Novato •

San Rafael
•

San Francisco •

Pacific Ocean

Sa

Northern
California

See pages 188-189 for
central California wine districts

DA-SOLANO

• Sacramento

LODI-
SACRAMENTO

ba

Acampo•
•Lodi

LIVERMORE-
ALAMEDA

•Stockton

Livermore
•
•Pleasanton

• Tracy

•Mission San Jose

SANTA CLARA-
San Benito

ra• • San Jose
• Saratoga
tos•   • Morgan Hill
          • San Martin
          • Gilroy

nta Cruz

Watsonville • Hollister
          San Juan Bautista

• Salinas   • Paicines

grapes exclusively, and as these mature they steadily add millions of gallons to California's already prolific wine output. Annual wine production in California now exceeds 100 million cases.

California has had vineyards ever since Franciscan missionary settlers first planted them in the 18th century. Large-scale vineyard expansion began during the 1860s, but sustained growth did not occur until after World War II. Now California has become one of the world's foremost wine areas. Previously, most of California's wine production was sweet dessert wines — ''sherries'' and ''ports'' — with few dry table wines. Presently this trend is reversed, and public preference for table wines has been a major factor in the growth of the California wine industry.

There is also increasing emphasis in California on VARIETAL wines, named after the grape from which they are made. Most California wines used to bear GENERIC labels like ''burgundy'' and ''chablis'' because the wineries believed that consumers could not otherwise identify their products. Increasing public knowledge about wine has lead to widespread acceptance of varietal labeling for premium wines; generic labeling is currently used by many wineries to identify their less expensive products, and its use is much more restricted than it once was.

Qualitatively, there are two groups of California varietal wines. The ''premium varietals,'' which usually furnish the best and most costly wines, closely resemble the famous wines of Europe. They include Cabernet Sauvignon, Merlot and Pinot Noir for red wines; Chardonnay, Johannisberg Riesling, Pinot Blanc, Sémillon, Sauvignon Blanc and Gewürztraminer for white wines. The ''standard-varietals,'' which have a greater yield per acre and consequently produce less expensive wines, may occasionally be labeled generically. The reds are: Barbera,

Carignane, Gamay Beaujolais, Gamay, Petite Sirah and Zinfandel; white standard-varietals include Chenin Blanc, Grey Riesling, French Colombard, Green Hungarian, Sylvaner, and Ugni Blanc. Varietals used in making rosé wines are Grenache, Gamay, and Grignolino. California is no less famous for its sparkling wines or ''champagnes'' — the better ones are bottled-fermented according to the traditional French Champagne process, and are made from Pinot Noir, Chardonnay, or Pinot Blanc.

A series of promising new HYBRID varietals, made from a cross between two varietals, have proven especially well-suited to California's warmer wine regions. The more successful include Ruby Cabernet (red) and Emerald Riesling and Flora (white). Further information about each of these varietals appears under separate headings in this dictionary.

The principal fine wine regions of California include the ''North Coast Counties,'' located around the San Francisco Bay area between the Pacific Ocean and the Coast Range mountains, where some of the finest wines in the state originate. From north to south, the most important of the North Coast Counties are: MENDOCINO, SONOMA, NAPA, ALAMEDA, SANTA CLARA, and MONTEREY. Most of California's large-output wineries are situated in the important agricultural district of the Central Valley between Stockton and Fresno, and this warm region produces much of the nation's table grapes and raisins in addition to wine.

Leading California wineries with a national distribution of their products are listed alphabetically, by county. *Mendocino:* Cresta Blanca, Parducci. *Sonoma:* Buena Vista, Italian Swiss Colony, Korbel, Pedroncelli, Sebastiani, Simi, Sonoma Vineyards, Souverain of Alexander Valley. *Napa:* Beaulieu Vineyard, Beringer, Chappellet,

Christian Bros., Freemark Abbey, Heitz Cellars, Inglenook, Hanns Kornell, Charles Krug, Louis Martini, Robert Mondavi, Oakville Vineyards, Schramsberg Vineyards, Sterling Vineyards, Stag's Leap Wine Cellars. *Alameda:* Concannon. Wente Bros., Weibel. *Santa Clara:* Almadén, Paul Masson, Mirassou, San Martin. *Monterey:* Monterey Vineyard. *Central Valley:* Bear Mountain, East Side, Franzia, E. & J. Gallo, Guild, United Vintners. In addition, there are hundreds of smaller wineries whose output is restricted principally to local distribution.

Caluso Passito *(Ca-loo'-so Pah-see'-toe)*: Sweet white dessert wine made near the town of Caluso in PIEMONTE, northern Italy. To make the wine, white Erbaluce grapes are dried on indoor racks during the winter to concentrate their sugar, and in the following spring are made into wine. Caluso Passito, which is rated D.O.C., is not normally sold until it is five years old.

Campania *(Cam-pahn'-ee-ah)*: Wine region in southwest Italy, with an annual production equivalent to some 30 million cases of wine a year. Its principal city is the port of Naples; in the region's rich volcanic soil, the vine today is as abundant as it was in Greek and Roman times, and Campania's wines have strength and character.

Probably the best-known Campanian wine is LACRIMA CHRISTI, grown on the slopes of Mt. Vesuvius, which has long been famous; Lacrima Christi, which means ''Christ's Tears'', may be red, white or rosé. Equally renowned are the wines of ISCHIA, a picturesque little island in the Tyrrhenian Sea west of Naples. Ischia's good red, white and rosé wines are all rated D.O.C. The neighboring island of Capri to the south also produces a fine white wine of the same name, made from Greco grapes; TAURASI, a robust red wine made from Aglianico grapes, is grown

40

further inland. GRAGNANO, another red Campanian wine, is gaining in reputation. Though not rated D.O.C., the wines of RAVELLO, grown on a peninsula between Salerno and Capri, are popular in the U.S.

Canada: Canada's winters are too cold for grapes to grow in all but a few protected locations. Yet a fledgling Canadian wine industry was founded as early as 1811, and the country presently has over 24,000 acres of vineyards; domestic wine production doubled from 1960 to 1970.

Three-fourths of Canada's wine is made in the Niagara Peninsula between Lake Erie and Lake Ontario, where the lakes temper the cold north winds. Primarily LABRUSCA varieties (Concord, Catawba, etc.) are grown here, but on an experimental basis certain HYBRIDS like Chelois and de Chaunac have been successful. Vineyards have also been planted in Ontario and British Columbia. Recently, some promising results have been achieved from classic VINIFERA varieties (Pinot Noir, Chardonnay, etc.) that have been grafted onto frost-resistant rootstocks.

Cantenac *(Cahnt'-nack)*: Red wine commune in the HAUT-MÉDOC, north of BORDEAUX. Cantenac adjoins MARGAUX and its wines are entitled to this appellation; the commune is sometimes called Cantenac-Margaux. There are many famous wine estates or CHÂTEAUX; the ones that were officially ranked in the 1855 Bordeaux classification include Châteaux Brane-Cantenac, Kirwan, d'Issan, Cantenac-Brown, Boyd-Cantenac, Palmer, Pouget, and Prieuré-Lichine.

Cantina *(Can-tee'-na)*: Italian for "winery" or "cellar." A "cantina sociale" is a wine growers' cooperative.

41

Capsule: The seal over the mouth of a corked wine bottle. It may be made of lead or aluminum foil, or, most recently, plastic.

Carignan *(Car-een-yahn')*: Productive red grape variety, grown extensively in the French MIDI also in Algeria, Spain and California. Though not a noble variety, it is well-suited to warm climates, and generally produces sound, sturdy wines. In terms of total acreage, it is the most widely planted red grape variety in California, where it is called Carignane: 30,244 acres have been planted.

Case: A wooden or cardboard container of bottled wine, as prepared for shipment and distribution. A standard case contains 12 bottles of 25 oz. (73 cl.) each; this corresponds to 8.76 liters or 2.31 U.S. gallons. Other sizes are half-bottles (12.5 oz. or 37 cl.), which come 24 to the case, and magnums (50 oz. or 148 cl.), which come 6 to the case. In this dictionary, because bottle sizes vary, production statistics for different wine regions have been converted into cases, rather than bottles, for simplicity.

Cask: Rounded wooden vessels in which wine has traditionally been fermented and aged. The size of a cask varies by country and also by region, ranging from the diminutive *feuillette* of the CHABLIS region (equivalent to 15 cases) to the huge *Doppelstück* of the Rhine (equivalent to 275 cases). In BORDEAUX, the standard cask is the *barrique* (equivalent to 24 cases), which is similar to the *pièce* of BURGUNDY. Four barriques comprise a TONNEAU — the traditional measure of production in Bordeaux.

Of the various woods used for casks, oak is acknowledged to be the best, as it imparts an agreeable flavor to the wine. Recent experiments have shown that the type of oak used is highly important to the quality of the finished wine.

While wood casks are still the best containers in which to age fine wine, stainless steel fermenting tanks allow better temperature control and are rapidly replacing wood fermenting tanks in many parts of the world.

Cassis *(Cas-seese')*: Charming little seaport town in PROVENCE, southern France, on the Mediterranean coast; also the name of the wines made in its environs. An important fishing village, Cassis produces red, white and rosé wines, but the whites are the most famous. They are made principally from the Ugni Blanc grape, though other varieties may be used. The Cassis vineyards lie to the north of the town and extend over some 370 acres; average annual wine production amounts to over 57,000 cases, white wine accounting for about one-third of the total.

Cassis is also the name of a sweet liqueur made from blackcurrants, produced in the BURGUNDY region in France. It is mixed with a light white wine to make the popular aperitif KIR.

Castelli di Jesi *(Cas-stell'-ee dee Yay'-zee)*: Wine district in the region of MARCHE, central Italy, west of the town of Ancona. It is the principal production zone for the white wine VERDICCHIO, and many Verdicchios are labeled "Verdicchio dei Castelli di Jesi" to be distinguished from the less well-known "Verdicchio di Matelica," which is made south of the Castelli di Jesi region. Both wines are rated D.O.C.

Castelli Romani *(Cas-stell'-ee Ro-mahn'-nee)*: Italian for "Roman Castles"; also the general term for the many good white wines made in the hilly country to the south of Rome. Not all of them are exported or even bottled, but those that are usually are well-made and represent good value; they tend to be semi-dry or *abboccato*. The best and most famous is FRASCATI; notable Castelli Romani wines entitled to D.O.C. include COLLI ALBANI, Marino, Colli Lanuvini, Zagarolo,

43

and several others.

Catalonia *(Cat-ah-loon′-ya)*: Region in northeastern Spain, of which Barcelona is the principal city. Catalonia is spelled Cataluña in Spanish and its native language is Catalan; the limits of the region are said to be defined by the extent to which Catalan is spoken.

Catalonia has four principal wine districts. To the north of Barcelona is Alella, Spain's smallest wine region, located along the Mediterranean coast. Alella is known primarily for its many excellent white wines. Further south is the much larger Penedés region, the source of Codornieu — Spain's most famous sparkling wine, made in Villafranca del Penedés and bottle-fermented according to the traditional Champagne process. The Penedés also produces fine still white wines and sturdy reds.

Tarragona, both the name of a Catalonian province and an important city, produces a sweet fortified wine. The Priorato, a small mountainous region northwest of the city of Tarragona, is famous for its very rich, concentrated red wine.

Catawba *(Ca-taw′-ba)*: Native American pink grape of the species LABRUSCA, widely used to make wine and grape juice in the eastern United States, especially in the New York Finger Lakes district and Ohio. Named after the Catawba River in North Carolina, it was first cultivated in 1823 and quickly became a leading grape variety in several eastern states. It is also an important variety for sparkling wines.

Although technically a red grape, the Catawba is used to make red, white or rosé wines. It generally gives better white wine than red, and in making white Catawba wine the skins are removed prior to fermentation. White Catawba wine usually tends to be sweet or semi-sweet, with a characteristic flavor.

Cave *(Cahv)*: French for "cellar."

Cépage *(Say-pahj′)*: French for "grape variety." This term is often specified when several different grape varieties are employed in a vineyard — as is the practice in BORDEAUX.

Cérons *(Say-rawn′)*: White wine region of BORDEAUX, located north of BARSAC on the left bank of the GARONNE River. The neighboring districts of Podensac and Illats lie within the delimited region of Cérons. Like Barsac, Cérons produces sweet white wines made from Sauvignon Blanc, Sémillon and Muscadelle grapes — except that the wines of Cérons tend to be less sweet than most Barsacs. Some dry Cérons is also made. Cérons wines are well-known is France, and they are also increasingly popular in America. The leading estates or CHÂTEAUX include Châteaux Haut-Mayne, de Cérons, Lamouroux, Haut-Rat, and Madère.

Cesanese *(Chay-za-nay′-say)*: Red grape variety, grown extensively south of Rome in the region of LAZIO (Latium), Italy. The Cesanese yields a rich, full-bodied red wine that is Latium's best. There are three types of Cesanese: Cesanese del Piglio (dry), Cesanese di Olevano (semi-dry or *abboccato)*, and Cesanese di Affile (sweet). All three have recently been awarded a D.O.C. rating; the drier Cesaneses tend to be more popular.

Chablis *(Shab-lee′)*: Small town in northeastern France, in the department of the Yonne, Burgundy; also the name of its famous white wine. Although "chablis" is produced in many other parts of the world — this GENERIC name describing virtually any dry white wine regardless of origin — the true Chablis of France is relatively rare. There are approximately 10,919 acres of vineyard under this appellation in Chablis; only about

45

half are in full production, and output is often curbed by spring frosts. But a good Chablis ranks with the world's finest white wines.

Chablis may be produced from only one approved grape variety, the Chardonnay (which is called "Beaunois" in Chablis). The Chablis vineyards are located in 20 different communes on the banks of the Serein River, the central and most important being: Chablis, Maligny, La Chapelle-Vaupelteigne, Poinchy, Milly, Fyé, Chichée, and Fleys. The wines of Chablis are ranked according to quality:

— *Chablis Grand Cru.* The best Chablis, which is always identified by the names of seven vineyards: Bougros, Les Preuses, Vaudésir, Grenouilles, Valmur, Les Clos, and Blanchot. (La Moutonne, the proprietary name of a small vineyard parcel between Vaudésir and Les Preuses, is also rated Grand Cru but is relatively rare). Minimum alcoholic strength must be at least 11%; average production is about 45,000 cases.

— *Chablis Premier Cru.* This designation may appear by itself, or with a vineyard name added. (Note: Since 1966 several Premier Cru vineyards have been allowed to use the name of a more famous vineyard in close proximity. Though this usage is optional, many producers employ it, and in the following list the more famous vineyards are marked with an asterisk — subsequent names without asterisks are legally entitled to this name. The Premier Cru vineyards on the right bank of the Serein, near the Grand Crus, are considered superior.) *Right bank of the Serein:* Monts de Milieu*, Montée de Tonnerre*, Pied d' Aloup, Chapelot, Fourchaume*, Vaulorent, Côte de Fontenay, Vaupulent, L'Homme Mort, Vaucoupin*, Les Fourneaux*, Morein, Côtes des Près Girots. *Left bank of the Serein:* Vaillons*, Beugnons, Châtains, Séché, Les Lys, Montmains*, Les Forêts, Butteaux, Côte de Lechet*, Beauroy*,

Troesmes, Vosgros*, Vaugiraud, Mélinots*, Roncières, Les Epinottes. Minimum alcoholic strength must be at least 10½%; average production is about 180,000 cases.

— *Chablis*. Wine from the designated communes of Chablis, which is never identified with a vineyard name. In poor vintages, Grand Cru or Premier Cru Chablis may have to be declassified to this category if it does not meet minimum standards. Minimum alcoholic strength must be at least 10%; average production is about 350,000 cases.

— *Petit Chablis*. Lesser wine from the outermost vineyards near the district boundary; not always bottled or exported. Minimum alcoholic strength must be at least 9½%; average production is the equivalent of 100,000 cases.

Chai *(Shay)***:** French for a storage place for wine above ground, as opposed to a CAVE, or cellar, which is usually located underground.

Chalonnais *(Shall-lon-nay′)***:** Vineyard area in central BURGUNDY, France. The Chalonnais region (or Côte Chalonnaise) lies to the west of the city of Chalon-sur-Saône, from which its name is derived. The region is noted for its good red wines, made from the Pinot Noir, and fine white wines made from the Chardonnay; in addition some rosé and sparkling wine is also produced. There are four principal wine districts that are entitled to APPELLATION CONTRÔLÉE, which are, from north to south RULLY a producer of red and white wines, though the whites are better-known and amount to four-fifths of all the wine produced; MERCUREY, just to the south, famous for its red wines that are usually the best of the entire Chalonnais region; GIVRY, a source of equally good red and white wines, and finally MONTAGNY, the southernmost limit of the Chalonnais region, which is noted for its fine white wine.

47

Chambertin *(Shawm'-bear-tan)*: World-famous vineyard in the northern COTE DE NUITS, Burgundy. It has been producing wine for over 1,000 years and is rated Grand Cru (Great Growth) — the highest classification for a Burgundy. Planted entirely in red Pinot Noir vines, the Chambertin vineyard extends over 32 acres; another great vineyard, the CLOS DE BÈZE (which because of its close proximity, and the similarity of its fine wines, is called Chambertin-Clos de Bèze) adjoins it just to the north. Surrounding the two Chambertin vineyards are several others, also rated Grand Cru but considered to be not quite in the same class: LATRICIÈRES-CHAMBERTIN, CHARMES-CHAMBERTIN, MAZOYÈRES-CHAMBERTIN, MAZIS-CHAMBERTIN, CHAPELLE-CHAMBERTIN, GRIOTTE-CHAMBERTIN, and RUCHOTTES-CHAMBERTIN. Each of these vineyards has legally attached the name Chambertin to show their relationship to their noble neighbor, as has the town of Gevrey to the north, which since 1847 has been called GEVREY-CHAMBERTIN. All of these vineyards lie within the Gevrey-Chambertin commune.

A Chambertin from a fine vintage is one of Burgundy's very greatest red wines — sturdy and full-bodied, with considerable character. About 3,600 cases are made each year.

Chambolle-Musigny *(Shawm'-boll Moos'-een-ye)*: Picturesque little hillside town and wine commune in the CÔTE DE NUITS, Burgundy, with some 432 acres of vineyard. Chambolle-Musigny takes its name from the great vineyard MUSIGNY, one of Burgundy's best, which is rated Grand Cru (Great Growth); the commune's other Grand Cru, BONNES-MARES, is scarcely less famous. Two very fine Premier Cru (First Growth) vineyards, practically in the same class, are Les Amoureuses and Les Charmes, which lie close to Musigny. Chambolle-Musigny is renowned for its delicate and scented red wines made from the Pinot Noir, with the exception of a small amount of white wine, Musigny Blanc, which is made from the Chardonnay. Average annual production is about 74,330 cases.

Champagne *(Sham-pain')*: Of all the world's wines, Champagne is unquestionably the best-known, traditionally a beverage associated with festivity and gaiety. More precisely, Champagne is a uniquely French product, although its illustrious name has been borrowed by makers of sparkling wines all over the world, who use the same process.

Despite its world-wide fame, French Champagne comes from a rather small area in northeastern France, and is made by a slow, methodical process. While sparkling wines are made elsewhere in France, they are called "vins mousseux" (sparkling wines) and if they are made by the same process as Champagne, "méthode champenoise," but not Champagne.

The delimited area entitled to the appellation Champagne extends over 54,362 acres in the Marne River valley, within the departments of the Marne, Aube, Aisne and Seine-et-Marne. The department of the Marne is the most important area and produces 81% of all Champagne; it includes the famous "Champagne towns," Reims and Épernay, and has three principal vineyard areas. The northern section, which produces fine, full-bodied wines, is called the Montagne de Reims. The middle area, the Vallée de la Marne, lies on the right bank of the Marne River. Its vineyards have a southern exposure and yield soft, rounded wines. The southern area near Épernay is known as the "Côte des Blancs" because it is largely planted in white Chardonnay grapes; the Montagne de Reims and Vallée de la Marne are mainly planted in black grapes: Pinot Noir or Pinot Meunier, the only approved varieties.

Virtually all Champagne is white; a much lesser amount of still red and white wine, and pink Champagne, is made. Most of the white wines used in making Champagne come from black grapes; the Pinot Noir (or Pinot Meunier) grapes are pressed immediately after they are picked, yielding white juice (see BLANC DE NOIRS). A lesser amount of wine from Chardonnay is used, which is either blended with Pinot Noir to add finesse, or else is used exclusively on its own for especially light, delicate Champagnes (see BLANC DE BLANCS).

Each village in the Champagne district has been ranked according to the quality of its wines, by *crus* (growths). At harvest time, a committee of growers and merchants decides the price for one kilo of grapes, based on the quality of the vintage and market conditions. The highest-ranked villages, the Grands Crus, are rated 100%, which means that their grapes receive the full price. Next come the Premier Cru villages, rated 99% to 90%, which receive the corresponding fraction of the full price. Though lacking in finesse, the wines from the lesser communes are useful for adding strength to the blends. The towns rated Grand Cru (100%) are:

— *Montagne de Reims*: Beaumont-sur-Vesle, Mailly, Puisieulx, Sillery, Verzenay (Verzy: 99%).

— *Vallée de la Marne:* Ambonnay, Ay, Bouzy, Louvois, Tours-sur-Marne (Tauxières-Mutry: 99%).

— *Côte des Blancs*: Avize, Cramant (Le Mesnil-sur-Oger, Oger, and Oiry: 99%).

Most Champagne producers do not grow all their own grapes; instead, they buy direct from local vineyard owners who have holdings in the various communes. Each proprietor is paid according to the location of his holdings. When the grapes are taken to the presses, a record is kept of where they came from — this is vitally important later on, when the wines are blended.

At the harvest, the grapes are picked and the bunches examined so as to eliminate any unripe or sick berries (see ÉPLUCHAGE). They are then brought to the presses, and the expressed juice is taken to fermenting tanks where it turns into wine.

During the winter, Champagne is treated like any other still wine, but in the spring, when the process of blending or CUVÉE takes place, the Champagne process begins. Various blends are selected according to the "style" of the maker — which is the same each year — and are then given a precisely measured sugar and yeast solution: the LIQUEUR DE TIRAGE. This solution will ferment to produce alcohol and carbon dioxide gas, but because the wine is kept in tightly closed, heavy glass bottles, the gas is contained and the wine becomes sparkling. The bottles are then left in the chilly subterranean cellars to mature.

When the wines are ready for shipment, the sediment that was introduced during the secondary fermentation has to be removed. The process of removal is called REMUAGE. The bottles are placed in racks (*pupitres*) that can be tilted in order to collect the sediment at the cork. The bottles are given a slight twist periodically by skilled workmen, and after about 90 days all the sediment is collected on the cork, ready to be removed by the process of "disgorging" (DÉGORGEMENT). The bottles are then placed neck down into a freezing brine solution, and when uncorked, the sediment pops out in a frozen mass, leaving the wine perfectly clear.

Since some wine is lost during disgorging, this is replaced, along with another dose of sugar solution for shipment: the "shipping dosage" (LIQUEUR D'EXPÉDITION). Most Champagne is austerely dry, and the amount of shipping dosage relates to taste preferences

51

in the country where the wine will be shipped. *Nature,* the driest Champagne, theoretically receives no dosage at all, though in practice a little sugar *is* added; *Brut,* the next driest, receives less than 1½% dosage; *Extra Dry,* up to 3%; *Dry (Sec,* in French), up to 4%; *Demi-Sec,* up to 6%; and *Doux,* up to 10%. (Demi-Sec and Doux Champagnes are generally too sweet for the U.S. market, and are mostly shipped to Latin America.) The English have traditionally preferred drier Champagnes, and some Brut Champagnes are labeled "prepared for the English market" to indicate extreme dryness.

Vintages vary in Champagne as they do in many other fine wine regions, but because all Champagne is blended, vintage years do not mean as much as they do elsewhere; in addition, up to 20% of a wine from a specified vintage may legally be wine from other vintages. Following an exceptional harvest, a vintage may be declared by the producers during the process of *cuvée* in the spring, but because only a few years produce vintage Champagnes, only superior wine will bear a vintage date; the other wines will be blended into non-vintage Champagne, the most important commercial grade.

The following list identifies the major Champagne producers with a nation-wide U.S. distribution. There are hundreds of different Champagne producers, but not all export their wines outside of France. Leading firms *(maisons)* are: Ayala, Bollinger, Canard-Duchêne, A. Charbaut & Fils, Veuve Clicquot-Ponsardin, Deutz & Geldermann, Delbeck, Henriot, Charles Heidsieck, Heidsieck Monopole, Jacquesson, Krug, Lanson, Laurent-Perrier. Mercier, Moët & Chandon. G.H. Mumm, Pernier-Jouët, Piper-Heidsieck, Pol Roger, Pommery & Greno, Louis Roederer, Ruinart Père & Fils, and Taittinger.

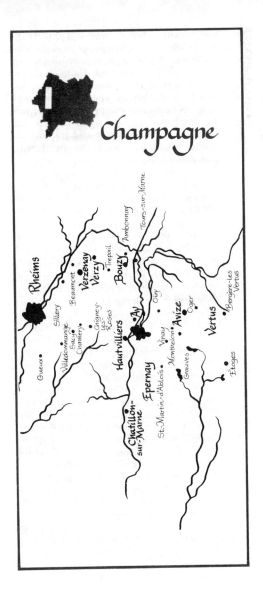

Champagne

Rheims
Gueux
Villedommange
Sacy
Chamery
Sillery
Beaumont
Chigny-les-Roses
Verzenay
Verzy
Trepail
Bouzy
Ambonnay
Tours-sur-Marne
Ay
Oiry
Hautvilliers
Vinay
Monthelon
Grauves
Avize
Oger
Bergère-les-Vertus
Vertus
Étoges
Epernay
St.-Martin-d'Ablois
Chatillon-sur-Marne

Champigny *(Shawm'-peen-ye)***:** Village in the LOIRE River valley, France, located southeast of SAUMUR in the district of ANJOU. Made from the Cabernet Franc grape, Champigny's fine red wines are Anjou's best. They are similar to the wines of CHINON upstream, except that Champignys are perhaps a bit sturdier. Because Champigny's vineyards extend into the region of Saumur, the wines are often labeled Saumur-Champigny.

Chapelle-Chambertin *(Sha-pell' Shawm'-bear-tan)***:** Famous vineyard in the northern CÔTE DE NUITS, Burgundy, rated Grand Cru (Great Growth). It extends over 13 acres, bounded on the west by the great CHAMBERTIN-CLOS DE BÈZE vineyard and on the south by GRIOTTE-CHAMBERTIN. Planted exclusively in Pinot Noir, Chapelle-Chambertin produces about 2,400 cases of excellent red wine annually.

Chaptalisation *(Shap-tally-zah'-see-yon)***:** The addition of sugar to grape must in order to increase the alcoholic strength of the wine. Chaptalisation (called *Gallization* in German) is named after a Frenchman, Dr. Jean Antoine Chaptal (1756-1832), minister of agriculture under Napoleon I, who wanted to simultaneously increase sugar beet acreage and improve the quality of wines made in years when the grapes do not ripen fully. It is a common practice in the making of red BURGUNDY wines, but the amount of sugar added may not exceed 3 kg. per hectoliter of must (6.6 lbs per 26.4 gallons). It is also permitted in BORDEAUX, though usually only in poor vintages. In Germany, sugaring of grape musts is performed regularly for ordinary wines (see TAFELWEIN, QUALITÄTSWEIN) but never for the best grades. Chaptalisation is not allowed in California, but it is permitted elsewhere in the U.S. where weather variations

54

could affect the quality and the quantity of wine.

Charbono *(Shar'-bo-no)*: Red wine grape, probably of Italian origin, which is grown primarily in the Napa Valley, California. The Charbono is very similar to the Barbera, and gives a robust, flavorful red table wine.

Chardonnay *(Shar'-doe-nay)*: Superior white wine grape, used in making the best white wines of Burgundy, France (see MONTRACHET, MEURSAULT, CHABLIS, and POUILLY-FUISSÉ) and for the BLANC DE BLANCS of CHAMPAGNE. Transplanted from its home ground, it has proved to be America's best white wine grape; excellent wines have been made from the Chardonnay, particularly in California where 11,500 acres have been planted: many of these rank with the world's greatest white wines. Compared with other grape varieties, the Chardonnay's yield is small and it does not grow well in all locations, but the wines that it gives have comparable finesse and elegance. While it is often called "Pinot Chardonnay," grape specialists (ampelographers) maintain that the Chardonnay technically is not a member of the Pinot family, and so it is more correct to simply call it Chardonnay.

Charmat (Bulk) Process: A method of producing sparkling wines more quickly than by the laborious process used in the French CHAMPAGNE region; also called "*cuve close.*" Still wine is introduced into closed tanks, where it is artificially aged before sugar and yeast is added to make the wine sparkling. No wines made by the Charmat process may be called Champagne in France, and U.S. law requires the label "Bulk Process" on any sparkling wines made by this method.

Charmes-Chambertin *(Sharm Shawm'-bear-tan)*: Excellent red wine vineyard in the northern CÔTE DE NUITS, Burgundy, rated Grand Cru (Great Growth). It adjoins MAZOYÈRES-CHAMBERTIN, another Grand Cru, and wines from the latter vineyard may legally be called Charmes-Chambertin; however, wines from the Charmes-Chambertin vineyard may not be labeled Mazoyères-Chambertin.

The name of both vineyards derives from the incomparable CHAMBERTIN vineyard, which borders Charmes-Chambertin to the west; LATRICIÈRES-CHAMBERTIN lies to the west of Mazoyères-Chambertin. Together, Charmes- and Mazoyères-Chambertin comprise some 78 acres and produce about 11,400 cases of fine, sturdy red wine annually.

Chassagne-Montrachet *(Sha-sign' Mon-rah-shay')*: Famous wine commune in the CÔTE DE BEAUNE, Burgundy; noted for its extremely fine white wines made from the Chardonnay grape, in addition to excellent reds made from the Pinot Noir. Chassagne-Montrachet adjoins PULIGNY-MONTRACHET to the north, and both communes are named after the magnificent MONTRACHET — the leading Grand Cru (Great Growth) white wine vineyard of Burgundy. Part of the scarcely less famous Grand Cru BÂTARD-MONTRACHET also lies in Chassagne-Montrachet; yet another Grand Cru, CRIOTS-BÂTARD-MONTRACHET, is exclusive to the commune. Two excellent vineyards, RUCHOTTES and CAILLERETS, produce fine white wine that is rated Premier Cru (First Growth).

There are about 860 acres of vineyard in Chassagne-Montrachet; despite its many famous white wines, the commune actually produces almost twice as much red wine as white — the most eminent red wine vineyards are MORGEOT, Clos St. Jean, and La Boudriotte. About 114,360 cases of wine are made in Chassagne-Montrachet annually.

Chasselas *(Shass'-la)*: Fine quality white table grape, used for wine in many parts of Europe. In northern France it gives light and attractive white wines, of which the best-known are POUILLY-SUR-LOIRE of upper Burgundy and CRÉPY of Savoy. In Germany the Chasselas is called GUTEDEL and it is widely grown in BADEN; in Switzerland near Lake Geneva it is called FENDANT in the canton of VALAIS and DORIN in the canton of VAUD, where it yields some of the best white wines of these regions.

Château *(Shot-toe')*: French for "castle"; specifically, in the BORDEAUX region, a wine estate in which a house (château) is associated with a vineyard. Under French law, the name of the château applies to the vineyard and the wines it produces, as well as the house (see CRU), but only if the vineyard and the house are mutually involved in wine production.

In many parts of Bordeaux the château is a residential building without wine-making facilities, normally separate from the winery and storage area — the CHAI. Wine that is bottled by the proprietor at the estate is said to be CHÂTEAU-BOTTLED.

Château-Bottled: In the BORDEAUX region, a wine made by an estate or CHÂTEAU that has been bottled directly at the property. The system of bottling wines at the château assures their authenticity through guarantee of origin. Elsewhere, wines bottled at the property are said to be ESTATE-BOTTLED; some indication of château-bottling should usually appear on the label of a superior Bordeaux wine. If the wine has been so bottled, it will be labeled "Mis en Bouteilles au Château" or "Mis du Château."

Château-Chalon *(Shot-toe' Shall'-lawn)*: Rare, exceptionally long-lived white wine from the JURA district, France. Chât-

57

eau-Chalon is not a CHÂTEAU-BOT-TLED wine, but derives its name from the town where it is produced. Made from the Savagnin grape, the wine is kept in cask for at least six years, and matures through the action of FLOR yeast — the same kind found in Spain's SHERRY district. The French term for this special kind of wine is ''vin jaune,'' and a unique bottle, the *clavelin,* is reserved exclusively for the vin jaunes of the Jura. Château-Chalon is a great rarity in the U.S. import trade, since less than 2,300 cases are produced annually.

Châteauneuf-du-Pape *(Shot-toe-nuff' dew Pop')***:** World-famous wine of the southern RHÔNE valley, France. Châteauneuf-du-Pape, which means ''new castle of the pope'' in French, was named after the papal residence at Avignon during the 14th century. The region was the first in France to enact laws relating to wine-making practices — a move that led to the APPELLATION CONTRÔLÉE laws promulgated in 1935.

The vineyards of Châteauneuf-du-Pape extend over some 6,600 acres in the department of Vaucluse. The coarse, pebbly soil retains the sun's heat to ripen the grapes fully, yielding a wine with the highest minimum alcoholic strength (12.5%) of any French wine. 99% is red, but a little white wine is also made. Up to 13 grape varieties may be blended together to make the red wine; the most important is Syrah, but Mourvèdre, Grenache, Picpoul and Cinsault are other leading varieties.

The best Châteauneuf-du-Pape is generally made on estates that bottle their own wine: Chateau des Fines-Roches, Château Fortia, Domaine de Mont-Redon, Château de la Gardine, Château de Vaudieu, etc. Typically, the region as a whole produces over 750,000 cases of wine annually.

Chavignol *(Shav'-een-yawl)***:** White wine commune in the upper LOIRE valley, near the village of SANCERRE. Planted exclusively in Sauvignon Blanc, Chavignol's vineyards lie within the area of Sancerre and are entitled to this appellation; in fact, one of the best Sancerre vineyards, Les Monts Damnés, is located in Chavignol.

Chénas *(Shay'-nass)***:** Red wine district in the BEAUJOLAIS region, extending over some 300 acres. Chénas is the smallest of the nine Beaujolais *crus* – those districts that generally make superior wine. Part of Chénas is included within the more famous area of MOULIN-À-VENT to the south; under its own appellation, Chénas annually produces over 76,600 cases of sturdy, full-bodied wine, among the slowest to mature of the Beaujolais.

Chenin Blanc *(Shay'-nan Blawn)***:** Excellent white wine grape, responsible for the famous white wines of the LOIRE River valley, France; these include VOUVRAY, SAVENNIÈRES, QUARTS DE CHAUME, and others. Wines made from the Chenin Blanc may be either dry or semi-dry, depending on autumn harvest weather and methods of vinification. Occasionally called Pineau de la Loire (or, incorrectly, white Pinot), the Chenin Blanc is also grown successfully in California, where almost 20,000 acres have been planted. It is a productive variety that gives fresh and attractive wines, frequently with an agreeable trace of sweetness.

Cheval-Blanc, Château *(Shev'-al Blawn')***:** Superb red BORDEAUX wine, from the district of SAINT-ÉMILION. Cheval-Blanc, which means "white horse" in French, is considered, along with Château AUSONE, the leading wine of Saint-Émilion and both wines are rated Premier Grand Cru (First Great Growth). The vineyard extends over about 80

59

acres, and production amounts to some 12,000 cases annually of fruity, scented and full-bodied red wine.

Chevalier-Montrachet *(Shev-al-yay′ Mon-rah-shay′)*: Superb white wine vineyard in the CÔTE DE BEAUNE, Burgundy, rated Grand Cru (Great Growth) — the highest rank for a Burgundy. Made from the Chardonnay grape, the wine of Chevalier-Montrachet is one of Burgundy's very best, often the equal of the magnificent MONTRACHET. The latter vineyard adjoins Chevalier-Montrachet further down the slope.

Chevalier-Montrachet's 18 acres of vineyard lie wholly within the commune of PULIGNY-MONTRACHET; production averages about 1,800 cases annually of very fine, scented and flavorful white wine.

Chianti *(Key-ahn′-tee)*: Famous wine from the region of TUSCANY, Italy; traditionally associated with the squat, straw-covered flask or FIASCO (plural: *fiaschi)* in which it has been bottled. The fiasco bottle used to be less costly than ordinary bottles, but because of higher labor costs it is now less frequently used. Regular bottles can be laid horizontally for storage, which fiaschi cannot, so the best Chiantis are normally not put into fiaschi.

Both red and white Chianti is made, although only red Chianti is entitled to D.O.C. and commercially the red is much more important. It is made from a blend of several grape varieties — normally the proportions are about 75% Sangiovese, 15% Canaiolo, and 10% white Trebbiano or Malvasia. The white grapes are added to make the wine less astringent and ready to drink sooner.

Less expensive grades of Chianti often have a faint sparkle, which results from the process of GOVERNO: a small amount of must from dried Colorino grapes is added to the new wine, causing a slight secondary fermentation which adds freshness. The Governo process is less frequently used for the best Chiantis, which are made to be drunk after some years of cask aging.

The D.O.C. region of Chianti includes the areas of Montalbano, Rufina, Colli Fiorentini, Colli Senesi, Colline Pisane, and Colli Arentini. The central and best part of the region lies to the south between the cities of Florence (Firenze) and Siena: Chianti CLASSICO. Chianti Classico extends over 31,200 acres, whereas the D.O.C. region in Chianti has 66,500 acres under vines.

The finer Chianti Classicos are generally shipped in brown bottles similar to those used for BORDEAUX wines. They are often accompanied by an official seal on the neck of the bottle, issued by the consortium for Chianti Classico (see CONSORZIO). A Chianti Classico will usually be slightly higher in alcohol than ordinary Chianti and possess greater aging potential; some select Chianti Classicos are among the finest wines of Italy.

Unfortunately, many wines made outside the limits of the Chianti region are given this famous name; rarely do they equal the authentic product of the classic Chianti production zone. There are, however, many California wineries that produce a wine called Chianti, similar in many ways to the Italian wine and often excellent.

Chiaretto *(Key-ah-rett′-o)***:** Fine Italian rosé wine produced on the western shores of Lake Garda (Riviera del Garda), in the region of LOMBARDY. Called Chiaretto del Garda, the wine is made principally from Gropello grapes and is rated D.O.C.; ideally it should be enjoyed when very young. Sometimes the term Chiaretto also applies to a light red wine.

Chile: Wine has been produced in Chile since the 16th century, but it was not until 1851 that French wine-makers first came to Chile to practice their trade, a move that precipitated

61

large-scale planting of vineyards in noble European grape varieties. With some 271,800 acres of vineyard, Chile is the second largest wine-producing country in Latin America, exceeded only by her eastern neighbor Argentina.

The climate is ideal for grape-growing in most of Chile between the 30th and 40th parallels. There are three principal regions where grapes are grown. In the north near Coquimbo, table grapes and raisins are produced under irrigation in a very dry climate. In the south near Valdivia, the climate is very humid and a lesser grape variety, the Pais, is grown primarily for use in brandy distillation. The central region near Santiago, the capital, has the greatest reputation for quality wines. It is cleaved by four rivers that course down from the Andes — Aconcagua, Maipo, Cachapoal, and Teno — each of which has vineyards on its fertile alluvial soil. One particularly fine wine region is the Maipo basin (Llano del Maipo) southwest of Santiago.

The best Chilean red wine is generally made from Cabernet Sauvignon, vinified according to the traditions of French immigrants from BORDEAUX, who also brought with them such noble varieties as Merlot, Malbec (often spelled Malbeck in Chile) and Petit-Verdot. Other good red wines are made from Pinot Noir and Barbera. White wine varieties include Sauvignon Blanc, Sémillon, Chardonnay and Riesling; the latter usually makes the best white Chilean wines and is normally shipped in squat BOCKSBEUTEL bottles.

Because of their very high quality and relatively low price, Chilean wines have been very popular on the U.S. market. Some are among the best wines made in Latin America.

62   **Chinon** *(Shee'-nawn)***:** Red wine district in the LOIRE River Valley, France, in the old province of TOURAINE. Made from the Cabernet Franc grape (locally called the Breton), Chinon is among the Loire valley's finest red wines. It is often drunk young but the best wines improve with some bottle age; they are sturdy and full-bodied, often with a scent of violets. Chinon's 2,000 acres of vineyard include the communes of Beaumont-en-Veron and l'Ille Bouchard; there are some 171,500 cases made each year.

Chiroubles *(Shee-roo'-bluh)***:** Red wine commune in the BEAUJOLAIS district, southern Burgundy, with some 650 acres of vineyard. Chiroubles is one of the nine Beaujolais *crus* — the regions that generally produce the best wine. Its vineyards adjoin FLEURIE to the east, and its scented and fruity red wines are similar; much Chiroubles is consumed directly from the cask during its first year and gains little with age, but a considerable quantity is bottled and exported. The equivalent of 111,000 cases is produced annually.

Chorey-Les-Beaune *(Shor'-ray Lay Bone')***:** Red wine commune of secondary importance, located to the north of BEAUNE, Burgundy, with some 400 acres of vineyard. Its wines may be sold either under the name Chorey-Les-Beaune or "CÔTE DE BEAUNE-VILLAGES."

Chusclan *(Shuss'-clawn)***:** Village in the southern RHÔNE River valley, France, located west of the city of Orange. Its red and rosé wines are entitled to the appellation CÔTES-DU-RHÔNE, and are usually labeled "Côtes-du-Rhône Chusclan."

Cinqueterre *(Chink'-way-tair'-ray)***:** Italian for "five lands"; specifically, five towns (Biassa, Corniglia, Monterosso, Riomaggiore, and Vernazza) located between the cities of Chiavari and La Spezia on the Italian Riviera, in the region of LIGURIA. The golden white wine of Cinqueterre has been famous since medieval times; it may be dry or quite sweet, depending on methods of vinification. In recognition of its long heritage of fine wines, Cinqueterre received a D.O.C. rating in 1973.

Cirò *(Chee'-ro)*: Small coastal town in the region of CALABRIA, southern Italy, with over 4,600 acres of vineyard. The fine red, white and rosé wines of Cirò are among Calabria's best, and are entitled to D.O.C. The reds and rosés are made from a local grape variety, the Gaglioppo, which yields full-bodied wines that age well. The whites are made from Greco Bianco; they are quite high in alcohol (over 13.5%) and like the reds are apt to be full-bodied.

Clairette *(Clair-rett')*: White wine grape grown extensively in southern France. There are three wines rated APPELLATION CONTRÔLÉE that are made from the Clairette: Clairette de Bellegarde, a soft, dry white wine produced south of the city of Nîmes in the department of Gard; Clairette de Die, a sparkling or semi-sparkling white wine to which some Muscat is normally added, produced southeast of the city of Valence in the RHÔNE River valley; and finally Clairette du Languedoc from the department of HÉRAULT, a full-bodied, golden white wine produced from semi-dried grapes. Though a few are exported, Clairettes are generally rare outside of their production zone.

Claret: A term used in English-speaking countries to designate light, dry red wines similar to those produced in BORDEAUX, France. The word *claret* originated from the medieval term "clairet," meaning either a light red wine or one to which some white wine was added. The English called clairet "claret," which has applied unofficially to Bordeaux wines ever since.

Legally, however, there is no precise definition for "claret"; this word is almost never seen on a bottle of Bordeaux wine, although in many other parts of the world it indicates a light, dry red wine.

Clarete *(Clar-ate'-ay)*: Spanish for "light red wine."

Classico *(Class'-ee-co)*: Italian for "classic"; when preceded by the name of a wine, it indicates that the wine comes from the central and best part of the region (CHIANTI Classico, SOAVE Classico, VALPOLICELLA Classico, etc.).

Classified Growth (French, *cru classé*): In BORDEAUX, France, a wine estate or CHÂTEAU that has been officially ranked or classified, based on the price of the wines and their reputation in the trade.

The first official Bordeaux wine classification took place in 1855 in preparation for the Paris Exposition of that year, and two wine districts — the MÉDOC and SAUTERNES — were officially classified into groups of CRUS (growths). Other leading wine regions of Bordeaux were classified about a century later. Owing to many changes that have taken place since the 1855 classification, a major revision in the near future remains a distinct possibility.

Climat *(Clee'-ma)*: French for "climate." In the region of the CÔTE D'OR in BURGUNDY, France, a climat is a single, specific vineyard or CRU (Growth), distinguished from its immediate neighbors. Each climat differs from others around it through variations in soil, exposure to the sun, the slope of the land, soil drainage, and suitability for certain grape varieties. Because of these subtle differences — and because Burgundy's vineyards are likely to be shared by a number of different proprietors — the Burgundians like to think in terms of climats rather than "vineyards."

65

CLONE •

Clone: A group of individual plants, reproduced asexually from a common ancestor. Selected clones of noble grape varieties can now be planted in many of the world's vineyards, resulting in a dramatic improvement in the quality of the wine.

Clos *(Clo):* French for "walled vineyard." In France, many good examples of a clos can be found in BURGUNDY, for monastical orders who tended the vineyards during the Middle Ages often built walls around their holdings. However, a number of clos exist outside of Burgundy. The use of the word "clos" is now restricted by French law to a specific vineyard, though it need not be surrounded by a wall.

Clos de Bèze *(Clo duh Bezz'):* World-famous vineyard in the northern CÔTE DE NUITS, Burgundy. The Clos de Bèze makes one of Burgundy's finest red wines, rated Grand Cru (Great Growth). It lies alongside the equally celebrated CHAMBERTIN vineyard and hence is officially called Chambertin-Clos de Bèze, although historically it is several centuries older than Chambertin. The vineyard is 37 acres large; about 5,800 cases of Chambertin-Clos de Bèze are produced each year.

Clos du Chapitre *(Clo dew Sha-peet'-ruh):* The name of two fine vineyards in the region of BURGUNDY, France. The first lies in the commune of FIXIN in the northern CÔTE DE NUITS; 11½ acres large, it produces a very good red wine rated Premier Cru (First Growth). The second is further south, located in the commune of VIRE near MÂCON; planted in white Chardonnay grapes, the vineyard makes an excellent white wine — one of the best of the Mâcon region.

66

Clos des Lambrays *(Clo day Lawm'-bray):* Excellent red wine vineyard in the commune of MOREY-ST. DENIS, in Burgundy's CÔTE

DE NUITS. Rated Premier Cru (First Growth), it is planted entirely in Pinot Noir grapes and extends over about 15 acres. Clos des Lambrays is the proprietary name for Les Larreys, as the vineyard is officially called; it lies adjacent to the famous CLOS DE TART vineyard and like the Clos de Tart it belongs to a single owner (see MONOPOLE). The wine of the Clos des Lambrays is an especially rich and fine red Burgundy.

Clos des Mouches (*Clo day Moosh'*): Celebrated vineyard in the CÔTE DE BEAUNE, Burgundy, extending over 61 acres within the commune of BEAUNE. The Clos des Mouches is planted in both red Pinot Noir and white Chardonnay grapes, although the red wine is better-known; it is a typical Beaune, graceful yet full-flavored. The rare *blanc* (white) Clos des Mouches is the exclusive property of the Burgundy shipper Joseph Drouhin, and is among the leading Côte de Beaune white wines.

Clos de la Perrière (*Clo duh la Pair-yair'*): Fine red wine vineyard in the commune of FIXIN, in the northern CÔTE DE NUITS, Burgundy. Planted in Pinot Noir, the vineyard's 12 acres produce what many experts regard as Fixin's best wine, rated Premier Cru (First Growth). There is an unrelated white wine vineyard in the commune of MEURSAULT to the south, in Burgundy's CÔTE DE BEAUNE, called "Clos des Perrières." Also rated Premier Cru, the wine is excellent but is not well-known on the U.S. market.

Clos de la Roche (*Clo duh la Rawsh'*): Outstanding red wine vineyard in the commune of MOREY-ST. DENIS, in the CÔTE DE NUITS, Burgundy. The Clos de la Roche is rated Grand Cru (Great Growth) and is one of Burgundy's best red wines; its qualities are similar to the great CHAMBERTIN produced nearby, which is much better-known. The

67

Clos de la Roche vineyard extends over some 38 acres; average annual production is about 4,500 cases of sturdy, full-bodied red wine.

Clos du Roi *(Clo dew Rwah')*: The name of two fine red wine vineyards in the CÔTE DE BEAUNE, Burgundy. The more famous of the two occupies about 25 acres in the commune of ALOXE-CORTON; it is officially part of the Grand Cru (Great Growth) vineyard CORTON and is usually sold as ''Corton-Clos du Roi.'' The other Clos Du Roi vineyard lies in the commune of BEAUNE to the south and is somewhat larger (34 acres); its similarly fine red wines, rated Premier Cru (First Growth), are among the best of Beaune.

Clos Saint-Denis *(Clo San Duh-nee')*: Excellent red wine vineyard in the CÔTE DE NUITS, Burgundy, rated Grand Cru (Great Growth). The name of this famous vineyard became legally associated with the town of Morey in 1927, in which it lies, which is now known as MOREY-SAINT-DENIS. The Clos Saint-Denis is some 16 acres large; production averages about 2,000 cases of fine, full-bodied red wine annually.

Clos Saint-Jacques *(Clo San Zhack')*: Outstanding red wine vineyard in the commune of GEVREY-CHAMBERTIN, in the northern CÔTE DE NUITS, Burgundy. Its wine, rated Premier Cru (First Growth), is similar to the Grand Cru (Great Growth) CHAMBERTIN, but the Clos Saint-Jacques vineyard is located some distance away from Chambertin on a different slope — hence the distinction in rank. Its 16 acres of vineyard are ideally located, and produce a fine, rich red Burgundy.

68   **Clos de Tart** *(Clo duh Tarr')*: Fine red wine vineyard in the CÔTE DE NUITS, Burgundy, rated Grand Cru (Great Growth). Its 18 acres of Pinot Noir vines lie in the commune of MOREY-ST. DENIS and adjoin BONNES-

MARES, another famous Grand Cru vineyard. The Clos de Tart is the exclusive property of J. Mommessin, a Burgundy shipper; the vineyard produces about 2,300 cases of excellent red wine annually.

Clos de Vougeot *(Clo duh Voo'-zho)*: World-famous red wine vineyard in the CÔTE DE NUITS, Burgundy. Originally the property of Cistercian monks prior to the French Revolution, the Clos de Vougeot presently consists of 125 acres planted in Pinot Noir vines — the largest vineyard in the Côte de Nuits. It produces red wine exclusively, rated Grand Cru (Great Growth), except for a small section planted in white Chardonnay grapes rated Premier Cru (First Growth): this is the rare Clos Blanc de Vougeot, the exclusive property of the Burgundy shipper L'Héritier-Guyot.

A venerable old building rising up in the heart of the vineyard, the Château du Clos de Vougeot is presently used for the banquets of the Confrérie des Chevaliers du Tastevin, Burgundy's wine fraternity, though wine is no longer made at the château. Today about sixty proprietors own different parts of the vineyard, and so the wines tend to vary more than most other Burgundies. At its best, a good Clos de Vougeot is one of Burgundy's best red wines — scented, complex, and with a glorious aftertaste. Currently some 16,000 cases of Clos de Vougeot are made each year; one should not confuse a Clos de Vougeot with lesser wines simply labeled VOUGEOT, which are pleasant but not in the same class.

Colares *(Co-lahr'-resh)*: One of the best red wines of Portugal, produced west of Lisbon near the town of Sintra. The vineyards of Colares border the Atlantic Ocean and are planted in unusually thin, sandy soil. Red Colares wine is produced from the Ramisco grape, which is said to have been imported from France, and after years of cask aging

69

becomes subtle and interesting. Some white Colares is made, but only in small quantities. Colares wines became quite famous during the 19th century, but the vineyards are very hard to work and the wines are now becoming rare.

Colli Albani *(Coll'-ee Ahl-bahn'-ee)*: Italian for ''Alban Hills,'' the fertile uplands 15 miles to the southeast of Rome, which have furnished wine for the capital since the days of the Roman Empire. Today, Colli Albani is the name of a dry or semi-dry white wine entitled to D.O.C., produced within six communes in the region of LAZIO (Latium). The wine is made principally from Malvasia and Trebbiano grapes; it is apt to be consumed directly from the cask when very young, but a considerable quantity is bottled and exported.

Colombard *(Coll'-um-bar)*: High-yield, good quality white wine grape grown in the Cognac district, France, where its pale and rather acidic white wines are used for brandy distillation. The Colombard produces better wine in warmer climates, and is grown extensively in California where it is called ''French Colombard''; there, its wine is light and fruity. Originally used principally in the making of GENERIC wines like ''chablis,'' it is now increasingly sold on its own as a good, inexpensive VARIETAL wine. Over 26,000 acres have been planted.

Color: The color of a wine indicates its age, concentration, and quality. The best way to assess a wine's color is to put it in a clear, stemmed glass that can be tipped easily, and hold it up to the light or against a white background. When viewed this way, the wine should be clear and brilliant.

70

Red and rosé wines derive their color from pigments in the grape skins that are dissolved by the alcohol produced during fermentation. Dark red wines contain more extracts, and are likely to be fuller in flavor. Light white wines from cool regions are palest in color; sweet white wines are usually darker in color than dry white wines, and are correspondingly darker when old.

During the aging process, the color of a wine changes through contact with oxygen (see OXIDATION). Initially oxidation helps mature the wine, but too much over too long a period of time is harmful. Exposure to heat will also damage a wine and make it change color.

Red wines are usually deep purple when young, then become brick-red when mature. When brownish-red, they are generally too old. White wines begin clear yellow or greenish, then turn golden with age. Brownish white wines are overly oxidized and unpleasant to drink. Rosé wines are pale pink when young, then develop a warm orange hue with age. An overly pronounced red or orange color in a rosé is a defect.

Combettes *(Cawm-bett')***:** Excellent white wine vineyard in the commune of PULIGNY-MONTRACHET, in Burgundy's CÔTE DE BEAUNE. Rated Premier Cru (First Growth), the Combettes vineyard extends over 16½ acres planted in Chardonnay, and produces racy white wines noted for their bouquet and finesse.

Commune *(Cawm'-yoon)***:** French for "township" or "parish"; a specific town or village and the surrounding land.

Complex: A complex wine has a multitude of pleasing flavors that are difficult to describe. Such a wine is exciting and very fine.

Concord: Native American red wine grape, named for the town of Concord, Massachusetts, where it originated. Of the species LABRUSCA, the Concord is widely grown in the eastern United States, the midwest, and Canada. It is an important table grape and makes good grape juice, but it has to be heav-

71

ily sugared to make wine; wine made from the Concord has a pronounced "foxy" (grapey) aroma and flavor, which many people nevertheless seem to enjoy. The most widely planted grape variety in New York State, the Concord is essential in the making of Kosher wines and also "Cold Duck" — a blend of champagne and sparkling burgundy.

Condrieu *(Cawn-dree-yuh')*: Rare and exquisite white wine of the RHÔNE River valley, France, produced south of the city of Vienne on the river's steep banks. The vineyards of Condrieu include the tiny Château-Grillet, only 4 acres large — the smallest vineyard in France with its own APPELLATION CONTRÔLÉE. A wine that is most enjoyable when young, Condrieu is made from the Viognier grape, a variety exclusive to the Rhône valley, which is also used in making the red CÔTE ROTIE produced just to the north. Condrieu is largely consumed locally and until recently very little was exported.

Consorzio *(Con-sorts'-ee-o)*: Italian for "consortium" or "guild": a regulatory agency for an Italian wine region that functions to oversee the region's wine production and set standards for quality. The most famous consorzio is probably that of CHIANTI, the "Consorzio Vino Chianti Classico," whose offices are in Florence. The Consorzio provides that its members identify their wines by a "Gallo Nero" (black rooster) seal banded on the neck of the bottle. The Gallo Nero indicates that the wines have been made by traditional methods and have passed rigorous tests before being released to the public. In existence since 1924, the Chianti Classico Consorzio has set the pace for fine wine standards in Italy, and its Gallo Nero is almost always an indication of superior quality.

Cooperative (French, *Co-oh'-pair-ah-teev'*): A winery owned and managed jointly by a number of different growers. Co-operatives are a convenient way for the smaller producers to share the cost of expensive wine-making equipment and also be in a better position to market their wines. For these reasons, cooperatives are increasing in number in Europe and the U.S.

Corbières *(Cor-be-yair')*: Wine region in southern France, extending over some 86,500 acres in the department of the AUDE. Corbières produces red, white and rosé wines under the V.D.Q.S. label; if they reach 12% alcohol they may be called Corbières Supérieur. The red Corbières are quite popular; made from Carignan, Grenache or Cinsault grapes, they are generally inexpensive and quite good. One of the best red Corbières, FITOU, has its own APPELLATION CONTRÔLÉE. The equivalent of over 6.8 million cases of Corbières is produced annually.

Cornas *(Cor-nahss')*: Fine, full-bodied red wine from the RHÔNE River valley, France. Made exclusively from the Syrah grape, Cornas is usually the sturdiest of the Rhône red wines and takes time to mature, but becomes distinctive with age. The steep, terraced vineyards of Cornas lie west of the city of Valence near the famous wine region of HERMITAGE, and the wines are similar; being less well-known, Cornas wines are often exceptional value. About 14,800 cases are produced each year.

Corsica: France's largest island, Corsica has had vineyards for centuries but the wines are not well-known on the U.S. market. Located in the Mediterranean Sea off the coast of Italy, Corsica acknowledges its proximity to Italy with many wines made from grape varieties indigenous to the Italian mainland: the most important are Vermentino, Aleatico, Genovesella and Moscato.

73

There are several APPELLATION CONTRÔLÉES in Corsica, all granted rather recently. ''Vin de Corse'' (Corsican Wine) is the most general; wines from more specific regions bear this label, followed by the name of the production zone. All apply to red, white or rosé wines. Patrimonio, one of the best rosés of Corsica, is produced in the north on the peninsula of Cap Corse; Coteaux d'Ajaccio, named for Ajaccio, Corsica's largest city, was with Patrimonio the first Corsican appellation contrôlée. Sartène in the southwest is famous chiefly for its strong and lively red wine; the coastal vineyards of Calvi lie near those of Patrimonio. While there are several others, they are not likely to be exported.

Cortese *(Cor-tay'-zay)*: White grape variety grown extensively in PIEMONTE, northern Italy. It gives fresh and attractive white wines best enjoyed in their youth; an especially good one is made around the town of GAVI and is called ''Gavi Cortese.'' Considered to be the best white wine of Piemonte, Gavi Cortese was awarded a D.O.C. rating in late 1974.

Corton *(Cor-tawn')*: Famous red wine of the CÔTE DE BEAUNE, Burgundy, produced near the little village of Aloxe, which has assumed the name of this illustrious vineyard to become ALOXE-CORTON. Rated Grand Cru (Great Growth), the noble red wine of Corton is the finest of the Côte de Beaune and the only Grand Cru red wine. The vineyard extends over 193 acres and combines a number of different parcels, each of which is legally entitled to the Corton APPELLATION CONTRÔLÉE; among the most famous are Corton-CLOS DU ROI, Corton-BRES-SANDES, Corton-Pougets, and Corton-Renardes. An exceptionally fine white wine of Aloxe-Corton, also rated Grand Cru, is called CORTON-CHARLEMAGNE. About

35,500 cases of Corton are produced annually.

Corton-Charlemagne *(Cor-tawn′ Sharlman′)***:** Outstanding white wine of the CÔTE DE BEAUNE, Burgundy, rated Grand Cru (Great Growth). Located in the commune of ALOXE-CORTON, the Corton-Charlemagne vineyard adjoins the equally famous red wine vineyard CORTON, and is planted exclusively in white Chardonnay grapes. Corton-Charlemagne is named after the great emperor Charlemagne (742-814 A.D.), who was one of its owners. It is one of Burgundy's very finest and rarest white wines; the vineyard extends over 61 acres, and production averages about 14,000 cases of superb, scented white wine annually.

Corvo di Casteldaccia *(Cor′-vo dee Cas-tell-datch′-ya)***:** Good red and white wines produced near the little town of Casteldaccia south of the city of Palermo, on the island of Sicily. While not rated D.O.C., the wines of Corvo di Casteldaccia are among Sicily's best and are internationally famous; the vineyards are owned by the estate of the Dukes of Salaparuta.

Côte *(Coat)***:** French for ''hill'' or ''slope''; the plural is *côtes*. In the wine regions, vineyards are likely to be located on slopes for proper drainage and optimum exposure to the sun.

Côte de Beaune *(Coat duh Bone′)***:** The southern half of Burgundy's CÔTE D'OR, the Côte de Beaune derives its name from the city of BEAUNE — the wine metropolis of Burgundy. Excellent red wines made from the Pinot Noir account for about four-fifths of the total annual production (about 800,500 cases); the exquisite white wines made from the Chardonnay are without peer anywhere in the world.

The Côte de Beaune consists of about

75

7,400 acres, blessed with the perfect combination of the right soil and exposure that makes great wines. The best of them, rated Grand Cru (Great Growth) under the French law of APPELLATION CONTRÔLÉE, are listed under separate headings in this dictionary (example: MONTRACHET). Next come wines rated Premier Cru (First Growth), a much larger group including most of the remaining classified vineyards, the most important of which also appear under separate headings (ex.: PULIGNY-MONTRACHET Les COMBETTES). Wine from unclassified vineyards within the Côte de Beaune communes is entitled to a communal appellation (ex.: Puligny-Montrachet); the quality of commune wines is more variable than the Grand or Premier Crus, but their quality standards are still among the highest in France. Wines that do not meet the minimum standards for their category — such as in a poor vintage or when there is overproduction — must be declassified (see BOURGOGNE).

The Côte de Beaune begins in the north near LADOIX-SERRIGNY and continues south for about 15 miles. It includes the major wine communes of ALOXE-CORTON, Beaune, POMMARD, VOLNAY, MEURSAULT, PULIGNY-MONTRACHET, CHASSAGNE-MONTRACHET, and SANTENAY. The secondary wine communes of the Côte de Beaune include PERNAND-VERGELESSES, SAVIGNY-LES-BEANUE, CHOREY-LES-BEAUNE, MONTHÉLIE, AUXEY-DURESSES, SAINT-ROMAIN, SAINT-AUBIN, Sampigny-Les-Maranges, Cheilly-Les- Maranges, and Dezize-Les-Maranges. Wines from the secondary communes may either be labeled after the name of the commune, or appear as CÔTE DE BEAUNE-VILLAGES.

Côte de Beaune-Villages *(Coat duh Boné Vil-lahj′)***:** A general term describing a wine or a blend of two or more wines from secondary communes within the CÔTE DE BEAUNE, Burgundy. Only red wines with a minimum of 10.5% alcohol are entitled to this appellation. The wines used for blending must be characteristic of their area of origin. Côte de Beaune-Villages wines are entirely different from those labeled "Côte de Beaune," which are ordinary wines produced in vineyards near Beaune but without right to that appellation.

Côte des Blancs *(Coat day Blawn')*: The southern portion of the French CHAMPAGNE country south of the city of ÉPERNAY, so named because it is planted in white Chardonnay grapes. Avize and Cramant are its two highest-ranked towns but Le Mesnil-sur-Oger, Oger, and Oiry also produce outstanding wines.

Côte de Brouilly *(Coat duh Broo-yee')*: The center of the red wine district of BROUILLY in the BEAUJOLAIS country, southern Burgundy. The middle of the Côte de Brouilly is a hill surrounded by vineyards, the Mont de Brouilly, at the top of which is a chapel that annually receives a pilgrimage prior to the harvest, in anticipation of a good vintage. Made from the Gamay grape, the wines of the Côte de Brouilly are similar to Brouilly's, with perhaps a bit more fruit and concentration. There are some 495 acres of vineyard; production averages about 87,000 cases of fine red wine each year.

Côte de Nuits *(Coat duh Nwee')*: The northern half of Burgundy's CÔTE D'OR, the Côte de Nuits is celebrated chiefly for its incomparable red wines made from the Pinot Noir — though there are a few isolated white wine vineyards planted in Chardonnay. The region takes its name from the medieval town of Nuits, the largest on the Côte, which is now called NUITS-ST. GEORGES. The total area

77

under vines in the Côte de Nuits is a scant, 3,460 acres.

Under the French law of APPELLATION CONTRÔLÉE, the greatest wines are rated Grand Cru (Great Growth). As an indication of the excellence of the Côte de Nuits vineyards, all but one of the 23 Grand Cru red Burgundies come from this region. Each Côte de Nuits Grand Cru is listed individually in this dictionary (example: CHAMBERTIN). The other leading vineyards in the Côte de Nuits are rated Premier Cru (First Growth), and can frequently produce some of the best Burgundies (Ex.: GEVREY-CHAMBERTIN CLOS SAINT-JACQUES). The unclassified vineyards in the Côte de Nuits produce wine entitled to a communal appellation, which in so renowned an area can still be very fine (ex.: Gevrey-Chambertin). When the wines do not meet minimum standards, they are declassified (see BOURGOGNE), but on the Côte de Nuits this is quite rare.

The Côte de Nuits begins a few miles south of the city of Dijon, and continues south past world-famous wine communes: Gevrey-Chambertin, MOREY-ST.-DENIS, CHAMBOLLE-MUSIGNY, VOUGEOT, FLAGEY-ÉCHEZEAUX, VOSNE-ROMANÉE, Nuits-St. Georges, and PRÉMEAUX. The secondary wine communes of the Côte de Nuits, located at the northern and southern extremes of the Côte, include FIXIN, Brochon, Prissy, Comblanchien, and Corgoloin. In the past, wine from the secondary communes received the appellation ''Vins Fins de la Côte de Nuits,'' but they are now labeled CÔTE DE NUITS-VILLAGES.

Côte de Nuits-Villages (*Coat duh Nwee Vil-lahj′*)**:** A general appellation for a wine or a blend of two of more wines from five secondary communes at the northern and southern extremes of the CÔTE DE NUITS, Burgundy. This new appellation replaces the former classification for red wines of at least 10.5% alcohol from communes whose wines share similar characteristics — "Vins Fins de la Côte de Nuits." While not representative of the best wines the Côte de Nuits has to offer, Côte de Nuits-Villages wines are generally inexpensive and often good value.

Côte d'Or *(Coat Dor)*: The "slope of gold," in French, the Côte d'Or is both an administrative region in France (department) and also the most famous wine region in BURGUNDY. It consists of a narrow strip of vineyard, located along a chalk-marl slope beginning south of the city of Dijon and continuing southwest for almost 30 miles. The Côte d'Or is divided into two principal sections: the northern part, the CÔTE DE NUITS, begins near the town of FIXIN and ends 12 miles south, near the town of PRÉMEAUX. The southern half, the CÔTE DE BEAUNE, begins near the town of ALOXE-CORTON and extends down to the village of SANTENAY some 15 miles to the south. There are two minor vineyard areas in the hilly country to the west, the "Hautes Côtes de Nuits" and the "Hautes Côtes de Beaune," but they produce lighter, less distinguished wines that are rarely exported.

Two noble grape varieties thrive in the Côte d'Or; while they are grown elsewhere, in few regions do they produce wines with such a high degree of finesse. Rich, robust reds are made from the Pinot Noir, while racy, scented whites are produced from the Chardonnay. In general, the Pinot Noir is predominant in the Côte de Nuits and the Chardonnay is more widely grown in the Côte de Beaune, though the Côte de Beaune actually produces more red wine than white and some white wine vineyards do exist in the Côte de Nuits.

Some vineyards in the Côte d'Or are superior to others, and have been classified by the French laws of APPELLATION CON-TRÔLÉE. Outstanding vineyards are rated Grand Cru (Great Growth); other leading vineyards, only slightly less celebrated, are rated Premier Cru (First Growth). Vineyards that have not been classified but lie within a delimited township or commune produce wine entitled to a commune appellation.

Some towns in the Côte d'Or have adopted a peculiar practice of adding their name to that of the most famous vineyard nearby. Thus the village of Aloxe in the Côte de Beaune is now ALOXE-CORTON. A few villages have not hyphenated their name because their vineyards are not as famous, but under the system one should always remember that "Aloxe-Corton" applies to any wine produced within that commune; Aloxe-Corton Les Chaillots to a particular vineyard rated Premier Cru; and CORTON to a single, outstanding vineyard rated Grand Cru. The Grand Crus never take the name of their commune and are always sold under their own name.

Over the years, many vineyards in the Côte d'Or were sold to different owners, and few vineyards presently belong only to one proprietor. Scores of different owners may have holdings in only one vineyard, which means that the wines will vary — even though they all come from the same source. Some owners sell their wines to a shipper (see NÉGOCIANT); others sell it themselves. A wine that is produced and bottled by the same person is said to be ESTATE-BOTTLED; the French equivalent is "Mis en Bouteilles au Domaine." Though estate-bottling is a key to authenticity in any wine region, it is particularly important in the Côte d'Or because of the fragmented nature of Burgundy's vineyards.

80

Côte Rotie *(Coat Ro-tee')***:** The "Roasted

Slope'' in French, Côte Rotie is a famous wine region in the northern RHÔNE River valley, France. The scented, slow-maturing red wine of Côte Rotie has been celebrated for nearly 2,000 years. It is produced near the town of Ampuis; the vineyard area includes the nearby commune of Tupin-et-Semons. Grown on steep, terraced vineyards, the Syrah grape produces four-fifths of the wine of Côte Rotie, with white Viognier constituting the remainder; the latter is used to soften the red wine and make it less astringent. Two principal sections of the Côte Rotie, the ''Côte Brune'' (Dark Slope) and the ''Côte Blonde'' (Fair Slope) are normally blended together to make the finished product. There are some 148 acres of vineyard, shared between many different proprietors; production averages about 22,900 cases annually.

Coteau *(Co-toe')*: French for ''hill'' or ''hillside''; the plural is *coteaux*.

Coteaux du Layon *(Co-toe' dew Lay-awn')*: White wine district in the region of ANJOU, on the lower LOIRE River, France. Named for the River Layon, a tributary of the Loire, the APPELLATION CONTRÔLÉE Coteaux du Layon includes the villages of Rochefort-sur-Loire, Beaulieu-sur-Layon, and Thouarcé. The famous wine regions of BONNEZEAUX and QUARTS DE CHAUME, noted for their sweet white wines made from late-picked Chenin Blanc grapes, are located within the Coteaux du Layon. The region as a whole extends over some 9,900 acres.

Côtes-Canon-Fronsac *(Coat Can'-nawn Frawn'-sack)*: Wine region located some 15 miles to the east of BORDEAUX, France, just west of the city of LIBOURNE. The APPELLATION CONTRÔLÉE Côtes-Canon-Fronsac may sometimes be abbreviated as Canon-Fronsac. Adjoining the area of CÔTES-DE-FRONSAC to the north, Côtes-

Canon-Fronsac lies closer to the Dordogne River, and takes its name from its most famous wine estate, Château Canon. Both regions are noted for their rich, slow-maturing red wines, not widely-known in the U.S. and still relatively inexpensive; the district produces over 125,800 cases of fine red wine each year. The leading wine estates include Châteaux Canon, de Brem, Gaby, Toumalin, and Junayme.

Côtes-de-Fronsac *(Coat duh Frawn′-sack)*: Red wine district situated to the east of BORDEAUX, near the city of LIBOURNE. Côtes-de-Fronsac is part of the region of Fronsac, though there is no APPELLATION CONTRÔLÉE called Fronsac; it lies to the north of the smaller district of CÔTES-CANON-FRONSAC and the wines are similar, though Côtes-Canon-Fronsac has the greater reputation. The leading Côtes-de-Fronsac wine estates (CHÂTEAUX) include Châteaux La Croix, La Dauphine, Rouet, des Tonnelles, and La Valade; production annually amounts to some 286,000 cases of full-bodied, slow-maturing red wine.

Côtes de Provence *(Coat duh Pro-vawnss′)*: Vineyard area in southern France near the Mediterranean Sea, in the old province of PROVENCE. The Côtes de Provence vineyards produce red, white and rosé wines entitled to the V.D.Q.S. seal; located in the present-day departments of Bouches-du-Rhône and Var, the region has been acclaimed primarily for its excellent rosés, sold in special amphora-shaped bottles. In some cases, finer wines will be sold as Côtes de Provence "Cru Classé" (classified growth), followed by the name of the vineyard, to indicate outstanding quality. Another V.D.Q.S. label from this region that is likely to be exported is Coteaux d'Aix-en-Provence.

The best wines from the Côtes de Provence area, however, are entitled to APPELLATION

82

CONTRÔLÉE and are always sold under their own names — these include CASSIS, known for its white wines; BANDOL, famous for its reds and rosés; and PALETTE, celebrated both for its red and white wines. The white wines of Bellet, produced north of Nice, are also famous but are rarely seen outside their production zone.

Côtes-du-Rhône *(Coat dew Rone')*: The general term for the red, white and rosé wines produced in the RHÔNE River valley, France. There are two principal areas of production: the northern Rhône district, between the cities of Vienne and Valence, in the departments of Drôme, Ardèche and Loire, and the southern Rhône district near the cities of Orange and Avignon, in the departments of Vaucluse and Gard. The total vineyard area extends over some 96,000 acres.

Côtes-du-Rhône is an APPELLATION CONTRÔLÉE for the fine, generally inexpensive wines produced throughout the entire Rhône region; if they come from a smaller area, whose wines are similar, they can be labeled "Côtes-du-Rhône-Villages." Better wines are made in delimited communes whose name is specified along with Côtes-du-Rhône: Côtes-du-Rhône CHUS-CLAN, Côtes-du-Rhone VACQUEYRAS, etc. The best wines of the Côtes-du-Rhône have their own appellation contrôlée and are sold under their own name. The northern Rhône includes world-famous wines like CÔTE-ROTIE, CONDRIEU, HERMITAGE, CROZES-HERMITAGE, CORNAS, SAINT-JOSEPH and SAINT-PÉRAY; the southern Rhône includes equally renowned wines of CHÂTEAUNEUF-DU-PAPE, TAVEL, LIRAC, GIGONDAS, and BEAUMES-DE-VENISE. Côtes de Ventoux, a large vineyard area in the southern Rhône region, has recently been granted an appellation contrôlée.

Cotnari *(Cot-narr'-ee)*: One of the best white

83

wines of Romania, Cotnari has been famous for centuries, although nowadays it is less well-known. Produced in the northeastern corner of the country near the city of Iasy, in the province of Moldavia, Cotnari is a fine, naturally sweet dessert wine made primarily from grape varieties indigenous to Romania — Grasa de Cotnari, Feteasca, and Tamîioasa. Scented and with a great depth of flavor, Cotnari is a distinctive and interesting dessert wine.

Crémant *(Cray'-mahn)*: French for a semi-sparkling wine; one that is not fully sparkling (see MOUSSEUX). Such wines obtain this slight effervescence occasionally when there is residual sugar and yeasts present after bottling.

Crépy *(Cray-pee')*: Light white wine produced south of Lake Geneva in northeastern France, near the town of Douvaine in the department of Haute-Savoie. Made from the Chasselas grape, Crépy is entitled to APPELLATION CONTRÔLÉE; more often than not it is faintly sparkling or *pétillant,* which makes it refreshing. There are about 148 acres of vineyard; some 22,900 cases are made each year.

Criots-Bâtard-Montrachet *(Cree'-o Bah'-tarr Mon-rah-shay')*: Fine white wine produced in the CÔTE DE BEAUNE, Burgundy, rated Grand Cru (Great Growth). Located in the commune of CHASSAGNE-MONTRACHET, the vineyard of Criots-Bâtard-Montrachet used to be part of the great BÂTARD-MONTRACHET, but the wines are now sold separately. A suave, scented white wine, Criots-Bâtard-Montrachet is relatively rare because of the vineyard's small size (3½ acres); production averages less than 600 cases a year.

Crozes-Hermitage *(Crows Air'-me-tahj)*: Good red and white wines produced in the northern RHÔNE River valley, France. Crozes-Hermitage is the APPELLATION CONTRÔLÉE for the wines made in 11 communes surrounding the famous vineyards of HERMITAGE; being sturdy and full-bodied, the wines are similar but generally lighter and less fine than Hermitage. About 90% of Crozes-Hermitage is red, made from the Syrah grape; the remainder is white wine produced from the Marsanne or Roussanne. Including Hermitage, the vineyards extend over some 1,230 acres; production averages over 100,000 cases annually.

Cru *(Crew):* French for "growth." Under the law of APPELLATION CONTRÔLÉE, a cru is a specific vineyard — and the wine that it gives — that has been classified according to its quality. When officially classified, the vineyard and the wine is said to be *cru classé*.

Cuvaison *(Kew-vay'-zawn):* From the French word *cuve,* meaning "tank": the essential practice of letting red wines ferment on their skins so as to extract color and tannin. The length of time required, or *cuvage,* is related to the degree of color and tannin desired.

Cuvée *(Kew-vay'):* From the French word *cuve,* meaning "tank": the contents of a vat of wine. There are three different meanings of cuvée, depending on the regions where this term is used. The first relates to the initial pressing of the juice from the grapes in the French CHAMPAGNE country — wine made from the first, light pressing is called "vin de cuvée," which will be superior to wine made from subsequent pressings. Another meaning of cuvée is the annual process of blending the finished wines to be made into Champagne. A third and rather ambiguous meaning of cuvée has until recently prevailed in BURGUNDY, where it referred to a vineyard and its wine. Since cuvée is by its very nature a cellar term and therefore not applicable to a vineyard, the APPELLATION CONTRÔLÉE law now designates Burgundy's vineyards by the more appropriate rating of CRU (growth). The greatest vineyards are called Grand Cru (Great Growth); other leading vineyards, Premier Cru (First Growth).

Cyprus: The third largest island in the Mediterranean Sea, Cyprus lies off the south coast of Turkey and wine constitutes over 7% of her exports. Most of the island is arid, but the lofty Troödos Mountains rise up in the west center to attract rainfall and provide an ideal setting for the vine; currently there are over 98,000 acres of vineyard.

Despite her close proximity to Turkey, Cyprus' ethnic and viticultural traditions are distinctly Greek. The Knights Templar settled in Cyprus in the 12th century, and their order at Limassol made a sweet, liquorous wine that later grew famous under the name Commandaria. This fine dessert wine is still made today, though in a somewhat different form. Cyprus also produces a wide variety of good red and white wine, and a large quantity of FORTIFIED WINES called "Cyprus sherry." Most wine for export is made by three large Limassol firms: Keo, Sodap, and Haggipavlu.

D

Dão *(Downg)*: Wine region in north-central Portugal, situated some 50 miles southeast of the city of Oporto. The town of Viseu is Dão's center, both viticulturally and economically. The hard, granitic soil produces good white wines and especially fine, full-bodied reds made from the same grape varieties used for making PORT. White Dão is best consumed young, but the red wine ages well and continues to develop for a decade or longer. Increasingly popular in the U.S., Dão is one of Portugal's best red wines and represents exceptional value.

Debröi Hárslevelü *(Deh-Broy'-ee Harsh'-level-yuh)*: Good quality white wine produced northeast of Budapest, Hungary, on the slopes of the Matra Mountains. Debroi Hárslevelu takes its name from the Hárslevelu grape, an indigenous variety, and may be either dry or semi-sweet, depending on the vintage.

Decant: To transfer the contents of one wine bottle to another container. Generally a glass wine decanter is used, though a clean, washed bottle may be substituted for a decanter.

The idea of decanting is twofold: aeration during the decanting process allows the wine to "breathe" and gain in bouquet; separation of the wine from its sediment will allow it to be served perfectly clear, without any harshness imparted by the sediment or the cloudiness it creates when stirred up.

Many red wines throw a sediment as they age, and have to be decanted; white wines can also be decanted, but as they are usually served chilled, directly from the bottle, most white wines do not benefit from decanting. To decant a wine that has sediment, stand it upright a day or so in advance so that the sediment collects at the bottom. Then, gently transfer the contents near a light source so that when sediment is seen trickling into the decanter, the operation can be stopped.

Dégorgement *(Day'-gor-zha-mawn)*: French for "disgorging": the process used in the French CHAMPAGNE country for removing sediment introduced by a secondary fermentation. After REMUAGE or "riddling," the sediment collects on the cork and is removed (disgorged) by placing the neck of the bottle in a freezing brine solution, and then allowing the frozen sediment to pop out under pressure when the bottle is opened.

Deidesheim *(Die'-dess-heim)***:** Fine wine area in the RHEINPFALZ (Palatinate), Germany. Located in the central portion of the Rheinpfalz called the Mittel-Haardt, Deidesheim's vineyards extend over approximately 950 acres and usually produce some of the finest white wines of the Rheinpfalz; the best of them are planted exclusively in Riesling. The leading vineyards or EINZELLAGEN are: Hergottsacker, Hohenmorgen, Leinhöhle, Grainhübel, Kieselberg, Letten, Paradiesgarten, and Maushöhle.

Delaware: Native American pink grape of the species LABRUSCA, named not for the state of Delaware (which presently has no bonded wineries) but the the town of Delaware, Ohio. Widely planted in New York State and Ohio, the Delaware is valuable both as a table grape and as an ideal wine grape, for it has a high sugar content when ripe. Though pink, it yields white juice, and is especially good for making sparkling wine.

Demijohn: An oversized wine container, usually in the form of a straw-covered glass flagon, with a capacity ranging from one to ten U.S. gallons. Inexpensive Spanish wines are often bottled in demijohns.

Demi-Sec *(Dem'-mee Seck')***:**French for "semi-dry"; officially, a grade of sweetness employed in the French CHAMPAGNE country. Like EXTRA DRY, this term is somewhat misleading because it really indicates a sweet Champagne with up to 6% sugar syrup solution added by the "shipping dosage" (LIQUEUR D'EXPÉDITION). Only those Champagnes labeled DOUX (sweet) are sweeter.

88

Denominazione di Origine Controllata

(Dee-nommy-nots-ee-oh'-nay dee Aw-ree'-gin-ay Cawn-trol-lah'-ta): Italian for "controlled denomination of origin," the law specifying approved place-names for Italian wines. Similar to the French laws of APPELLATION CONTRÔLÉE, the Denominazione di Origine Controllata (D.O.C.) laws were enacted in 1963 and have assisted a marked improvement in the quality of Italian wines. The words Denominazione di Origine Controllata on a wine bottle are an indication of superior quality.

The 1963 Italian wine law authorized three denominations:

— *Denominazione di Origine Semplice* (simple). Ordinary wines produced in Italy's traditional wine regions. No quality guarantee accompanies these wines.

— *Denominazione di Origine Controllata (controlled).* Quality wines originating from delimited wine regions, produced from approved grape varieties, and made by traditional practices. The vineyards producing D.O.C. wines are listed in an official register.

— *Denominazione di Origine Controllata e Garantita* (controlled and guaranteed). Particularly fine wines sold in bottles with less than 5 liters (1.32 gallons) capacity, bearing a government seal stating that the wines have conformed to certain standards.

In addition, the laws outline production limits, labeling practices and quality inspection procedures, and provide for penalties to violators.

Dessert Wine: In the U.S. wine trade usage, a wine that has been fortified (sherry, port, Angelica, etc.) by having brandy or spirits added to arrest fermentation, so that residual sugar remains. However, not all fortified wines are sweet, nor are all sweet wines fortified; a less ambiguous definition of a dessert wine would simply mean a sweet wine to be served with dessert. See FORTIFIED WINE.

89

Dézaley *(Day'-zuh-lay)*: Fine white wine region in the canton of the VAUD, western Switzerland, situated on the north shore of Lake Geneva east of the city of Lausanne. Planted in Chasselas grapes (locally called Dorin), the Dézalay vineyards produce some of Switzerland's best white wines; one particularly fine vineyard, the Clos des Abbayes, is the exclusive property of the city of Lausanne.

Dhron *(Drone)*: Attractive little town on the MOSEL River, Germany, located between PIESPORT and TRITTENHEIM. One of the oldest wine villages in Germany, Dhron is named after the Dhron River, a tributary of the Mosel, and the town's best vineyards lie along its banks. Dhron lies just to the north of NEUMAGEN, another famous wine village, and the community is called Dhron-Neumagen. The leading vineyards or EIN-ZELLAGEN are: Hofberger (also called Dhronhofberger), Engelgrube, Laudamusberg, Roterde, and Rosengärtchen.

Dienheim *(Deen'-heim)*: Town and vineyard area in the RHEINHESSEN region, Germany, located just south of OPPENHEIM. With well-exposed vineyards largely planted in Silvaner, Dienheim is one of the lesser-known wine towns of Rheinhessen and its wines are often exceptionally good value. There are over 900 acres of vineyard in Dienheim; the leading vineyards or EINZELLAGEN include: Falkenberg, Herrenberg, Kreuz, Paterhof, and Tafelstein.

D.O.C.: see DENOMINAZIONE DI ORIGINE CONTROLLATA.

Dolceacqua *(Dole-chay-ack'-wa)*: Italian for "sweet water"; a good red wine produced near the town of San Remo on the Italian Riviera, in the region of LIGURIA, Italy. Made from the Rossese grape, Dolceacqua may sometimes be called Rossese di Dolceacqua; the wine has been famous for centuries, and was awarded D.O.C. status in 1972.

Dolcetto *(Dole-chet'-toe)*: Red grape grown in the region of PIEMONTE, northern Italy, and the name of the good red wine that it produces. Fragrant and fruity, Dolcetto is usually the quickest to mature of the red Piemonte wines. Four areas that produce Dolcetto were granted D.O.C. status in 1974: Dolcetto di Diano d'Alba, Dolcetto d'Asti, Dolcetto delle Langhe Monregalesi, and Dolcetto d'Alba.

Dôle *(Dole)*: One of the best red wines of Switzerland, produced in the canton of VALAIS in the upper RHÔNE River valley. Dôle is made from both the Pinot Noir and Gamay grapes in equal proportions; sometimes Petite Dôle, made only from the Pinot Noir, is also produced. Generally quite full-bodied, Dôle has a deep, dark color, and ages well.

Domaine *(Doe-main')*: French for "wine estate." In the region of BURGUNDY, the estate may include vineyards owned in part or entirely by one owner. If the wines are bottled at the property by the owner, they are entitled to be labeled "Mis en Bouteilles au Domaine" (see ESTATE-BOTTLED). In BORDEAUX, the word domaine may be used as a property name for a wine, but only if the wine was actually produced on that property (see CHÂTEAU).

Dordogne *(Dor-doyn'-yuh)*: Major river in southwestern France; also the name of an administrative region or department. The Dordogne joins the GARONNE River north of the city of BORDEAUX to form the GIRONDE, a tidal estuary. Several wine regions are located further inland on the Dordogne; the most important are BERGERAC, MONBAZIL-LAC, and PÉCHARMANT. Closer to Bor-

91

deaux, the region of CÔTES-CANON-FRON-SAC also lies on the banks of the Dordogne.

Dorin *(Daw-ran')*: The local name for the white Chasselas grape in the canton of VAUD, Switzerland.

Dosage *(Doe-sahj')*: In the French CHAMPAGNE country, the process of adding an extra sugar solution, the LIQUEUR D'EXPÉDITION, to Champagnes before final corking and shipment. All Champagnes are very dry before the dosage, and the amount of dosage relates to customer taste preferences in the region where the wine is to be shipped. Normally, the dosage consists of a mixture of old wine, cane sugar and occasionally brandy, in a carefully measured solution. See CHAMPAGNE.

Doux *(Doo)*: French for "sweet." In the French CHAMPAGNE region, a wine labeled doux is always the sweetest (and usually not the best) Champagne that has received the maximum amount (8 - 10%) of sugar solution or DOSAGE prior to shipment. Doux Champagnes are popular in warm countries, but are relatively rare in the U.S.

Dry: The opposite of sweet. A dry wine contains only a little residual sugar; a sweet wine has considerable residual sugar. A wine becomes dry when all the sugar is completely fermented into alcohol.

Dubonnet *(Dew-bawn-nay')*: The proprietary name of a wine-based French apéritif to which plant extracts have been added, also manufactured under license in the U.S. in Fresno, California. Two types are produced: red Dubonnet, a semi-sweet wine, and white Dubonnet, which is drier.

Dürkheim *(Deerk'-heim)*: Vineyard town in the RHEINPFALZ (Palatinate) region, Germany, located in the central section known as the Mittel-Haardt. Because of its famous mineral spas, the town is officially called Bad

Dürkheim but the wines are known as Dürkheimers. With some 2,000 acres under vines, this is one of the largest wine communities in Germany. A considerable amount of red wine made from the Portuguiser grape is produced in Bad Dürkheim, but the white is superior — particularly if made from the Riesling — and accounts for 75% of the total. The most common vineyard names are Feuerberg, Hochmess and Schenkenböhl, but under the 1971 Wine Law these have become composite vineyards or GROSSLAGEN; the leading single vineyards (EINZELLAGEN) are: Fuchsmantel, Michelsberg, Fronhof, Abtsfronhof, Spielberg, Hochbenn, Herrenberg, Herrenmorgen and Rittergarten.

Є

Earthy: The unmistakable flavor of soil in a wine, usually caused by planting a vineyard in clayey or alluvial soil. If present to a marked degree, it can be most unpleasant. The French term for this is *goût de terroir;* in German it is called *Bodengeschmack.*

Échezeaux *(Esh'-shay-zo):* Fine red wine of the CÔTE DE NUITS, Burgundy, rated Grand Cru (Great Growth). The commune of FLAGEY-ÉCHEZEAUX in which it is produced is named after Échezeaux, though there is actually no vineyard of this name; wines labeled Échezeaux will come from about ten different vineyards extending over some 76 acres, whose wines are entitled to this famous appellation. The especially fine vineyard of GRANDS-ÉCHEZEAUX which lies nearby covers 22½ acres and is considered superior to Échezeaux, yet both wines are prized for their scent and delicacy. Production of both

93

Grands-Échezeaux and Échezeaux averages about 12,600 cases annually.

Edel *(Aid'-ll):* German for "noble"; when applied to wine, a very great one, with considerable class and substance. At least one German wine producer, when making a wine such as a BEERENAUSLESE from late-harvested grapes, prefers to call it "Edel-beerenauslese" in acknowledgment of its nobly sweet character.

Edelfäule *(Aid'-ll-foy-luh):* German for "noble mold," the fungus that collects on grape skins and concentrates the juice without rotting the grapes. See BOTRYTIS CINEREA.

Égrappage *(Eh-grap-pahj'):* French for "destemming," the process of removing the stalks from grapes before they are crushed and fermented, necessary to avoid an excess of tannin or astringency caused by the stalks. Formerly performed by hand, the process in many places is now carried out by a special machine, an *égrappoir,* which removes the stalks.

Egri Bikavér *(Eh'-gree Beek'-ah-vair):* Famous red wine produced near the town of Eger, Hungary, in the northeastern part of the country. Egri Bikavér, which means "Bull's Blood of Eger" in Hungarian, is made principally from a local red grape variety, the Kadarka, usually with some Pinot Noir and Merlot added. Generally rather full-bodied, Egri Bikavér ages well and is quite long-lived.

Einzellage *(Ein'-tse-log-uh):* German for "single vineyard." Under the 1971 German Wine Law, an Einzellage is an individual vineyard parcel at least 5 hectares (12 acres) large, located within a specific wine community or WEINBAUORT. The smallest geographical unit under the German Law, an Einzellage is a single, unbroken part of a composite vineyard or GROSSLAGE, and will usually produce superior wine.

Eiswein *(Ice'-vine)*: German for "ice wine," an unusual wine made from grapes that are pressed when still frozen. In late autumn, when the temperature falls below 21°F. during the night in the German vineyards, any unripe berries still on the vine will be completely frozen but the ripest berries will remain only partially frozen, owing to their higher sugar content. When these are pressed, the juice will be rich in sugar and extracts. Theoretically, an Eiswein can be made in all categories of QUALITÄTSWEIN MIT PRÄDIKAT, but in practice it is usually equivalent to a wine labeled AUSLESE. Usually made only once or twice a decade, Eisweins are very rare in the trade and are normally quite expensive.

Eitelsbach *(I'-tells-bock)*: Wine community in the RUWER region, Germany; since 1971 officially part of the district of TRIER. Eitelsbach is celebrated chiefly for its leading vineyard, the Karthäuserhofberg, which belonged to Carthusian monks during the Middle Ages and is now administered by Herr Werner Tyrell, president of the German Vintners Association. The property extends over 45 acres, and is divided into five sections or *lagen*: Kronenberg, Sang, Burgberg, Orthsberg, and Stirn; on the unusual little label the specific *lage* will be identified, preceded by the words "Eitelsbacher Karthäuserhofberg." In good vintages, the wines are prized for their bouquet and finesse.

Besides the Karthäuserhofberg, Eitelsbach has another fine vineyard or EINZELLAGE, Marienholz, which belongs to several different owners.

Eltville *(Elt'-villa)*: Important wine town in the RHEINGAU district, Germany; headquarters of the State Wine Domaine (Staatsweingut) in addition to the famous producers Langwerth von Simmern and Graf Eltz. There are 514 acres of vineyard, the best of them located behind the town away from the Rhine front. Though not considered the greatest of the Rheingaus, Eltville's wines are very consistent and charming, especially in great vintages; the leading vineyards (EINZELLAGEN) include: Sonnenberg, Langenstück, Taubenberg, Rheinberg, and Sandgrub.

Emerald Riesling: A HYBRID grape developed in 1946 by Dr. Harold Olmo of the University of California at Davis. Optimized to produce quality white wines in warm climatic regions, the Emerald Riesling is a cross between the Johannisberg Riesling (White Riesling) and the Muscadelle. In recent years it has proven quite successful, and its acreage — particularly in California's fertile Central Valley — is increasing.

Emilia-Romagna *(Eh-mee'-lee-ah Ro-mon'-ya)*: Wine region in central Italy, bounded in the north by the Po River and in the south by the Apennine Mountains. There are three principal wine areas in Emilia-Romagna: the first, near the city of Modena, is the center for the famous sparkling red wine LAMBRUSCO; further west, near the town of Piacenza, is the D.O.C. region of GUTTURNIO, a fine red wine; the southernmost part of Emilia-Romagna, near the little republic of San Marino, is renowned for a golden, semi-sweet white wine, ALBANA DI ROMAGNA, and a dry red, the Sangiovese di Romagna. Both wines are famous locally but the white seems to be better known in the U.S.

96

Entre-Deux-Mers *(Awn'-truh Duh Mair')*: French for "Between Two Seas"; specifically, an important wine district in the BORDEAUX region, France. The Entre-

Deux-Mers vineyards lie between the GARONNE and DORDOGNE Rivers east of the city of Bordeaux, hence the derivation of the name. There are few important wine estates or CHÂTEAUX in Entre-Deux-Mers, but a number of well-established wine cooperatives produce good dry white wines entitled to the appellation Entre-Deux-Mers; some red wine is made in the region, but it is only allowed the appellation Bordeaux. There are over 3,200 acres of vineyard; the equivalent of 686,000 cases of wine is made yearly.

Épenots *(Eh'-pen-no)*: Fine red wine vineyard in the commune of POMMARD, in Burgundy's CÔTE DE BEAUNE. One of Pommard's best vineyards, Épenots extends over 25 acres; Petits-Épenots, a larger vineyard nearby occupying 50 acres, is not considered to be in the same class, but both vineyards produce fine and graceful red wines, rated Premier Cru (First Growth). The vineyard plot continues into the adjoining commune of BEAUNE to the northeast, and there it is called Beaune Épenottes. This vineyard also produces good red wine, but the Pommard section is superior.

Épernay *(Eh'-pair-nay)*: City in the French CHAMPAGNE region, with a population of some 30,000. Situated in the Marne River valley, Épernay forms the northern extreme of the CÔTE DES BLANCS, a slope of vineyard largely planted in white Chardonnay grapes; Moët & Chandon, Pol Roger, Perrier-Jouët, Mercier, and A. Charbaut & Fils are important Champagne producers with offices in Épernay.

Épluchage *(Eh-ploo-shahj')*: A process employed in the French CHAMPAGNE country, by which grape bunches are carefully inspected after picking, and any sick or unripe berries discarded, before being taken to the press house and made into wine.

97

Erbach *(Air′-bock)*: Village in the RHEINGAU district, Germany, with 470 acres of vineyard. Erbach is renowned primarily for a single vineyard, the MARCOBRUNN. Planted in Riesling vines near the Rhine River front, this remarkable vineyard used to be called "Marcobrunner," but since the enactment of the 1971 German Wine Law its wines are called "Erbacher Marcobrunn."

Besides Marcobrunn, Erbach has other superior vineyards or EINZELLAGEN, the most famous being: Siegelsberg, Schlossberg, Steinmorgen, Michelmark and Hohenrain.

Erben *(Airb′-en)*: German for "heirs." When preceded by a proper name, this indicates that the estate's wines are sold under the original family name, and that the estate is managed by the present generation.

Erden *(Aird′-en)*: Small wine village on the MOSEL River, Germany. Celebrated for its excellent wines, Erden lies on the right bank of the Mosel, and its best vineyards or EINZELLAGEN face south on an extraordinary steep slope; the most famous is Treppchen ("little staircase," in German), but Prälat, Busslay and Herrenberg also produce good wine. There are some 200 acres of vineyard in Erden, most of them planted in Riesling.

Erzeuger-Abfüllung *(Air-tsoy′-ger Ab′-foolung)*: German for "Producer Bottling." Authorized under the German Wine Law of 1971, Erzeuger-Abfüllung replaces "Original-Abfüllung," which is no longer allowed on a German wine label. It indicates that the wine has been ESTATE-BOTTLED by a single producer, and not by a shipper. "Aus Eigenem Lesegut," which means "From the Producer's Own Harvest," means essentially the same thing, and may also appear in connection with Erzeuger-Abfüllung.

Escherndorf *(Esh'-shern-dorf)*: Wine village in the region of FRANKEN (Franconia), Germany with some 195 acres of vineyard, most of them planted in Silvaner and Riesling. Escherndorf is one of Franken's leading wine communes; its wines are traditionally shipped in the squat BOCKSBEUTEL bottle native to the region. The most famous vineyards (EINZELLAGEN) are: Lump, Berg, and Fürstenberg.

Estate-Bottled: A term signifying that a wine was produced and bottled by the same person, and not sold in bulk to a shipper. By guaranteeing origin and authenticity, estate-bottling usually indicates a superior wine.

In the region of BORDEAUX, France, an estate-bottled wine is said to be CHÂTEAU-BOTTLED. In BURGUNDY, an estate-bottled wine is officially labeled "Mis en Bouteilles au Domaine" (Domain-Bottled) or "Mis en Bouteilles à la Proprieté" (Bottled at the Property). These terms are sometimes accompanied by the English translation on the same label.

Some French wines, however, seem to be estate-bottled when in fact they are not; thus the terms "Mis en Bouteilles dans Nos Caves" (Bottled in Our Cellars) "Mis en Bouteilles dans la Région de Production" (Bottled in the Region of Production) and "Mis en Bouteilles par les Vignerons" (Bottled by the Wine-Growers) legally do not mean estate-bottled in French. "Produced and Bottled," written in English on a French wine label, likewise does not mean estate-bottled. While the wines may be quite acceptable, their labels officially do not mean what they imply.

Elsewhere, the 1971 German Wine Law authorizes the term ERZEUGER-ABFÜLLUNG to indicate estate-bottling, and in California, an estate-bottled wine by law must be made exclusively from grapes grown by the proprietor.

Est! Est! Est!: Good white wine produced in the region of LAZIO, Italy, north of Rome near the town of Montefiascone. Tending to be semi-dry, Est! Est! Est! is made chiefly from Trebbiano and Malvasia grapes, and is rated D.O.C.

Estufa *(Esh-too'-fa)*: The process by which the wines of MADEIRA are heated slowly, at high temperature, so as to take on a caramel color and characteristic flavor.

Etna *(Et'-na)*: Fine red, white and rosé wines produced in 20 communes on the slopes of Mount Etna, Sicily, a volcanic peak 10,741 ft. high. Sometimes spelled Aetna, the wines of Etna are among Sicily's best, and are entitled to D.O.C. The whites, called Etna Bianco, are made from a local grape variety, the Carricante; the reds and rosés are produced principally from the Nerello. Some particularly fine Etna reds can improve for a decade or more.

Extra Dry (French, *Extra-Sec*): A grade of sweetness employed in the French CHAMPAGNE region. Though a wine labeled Extra Dry will be fairly dry, this term usually does not mean what it implies; Champagnes labeled BRUT are actually drier than Extra Dry. Officially, an Extra Dry Champagne contains between 1 and 2% sugar solution from the LIQUEUR D'EXPÉDITION (shipping dosage) added before shipment.

100

F

Fass *(Fahss)*: German for "barrel" or "cask," a term used most frequently in the

Rhine region. Officially, a Fass has no specific capacity; the *Halbstück* of 600 liters (68.6 cases) is the preferred cask size in the RHEINGAU.

Faugères *(Fo-zhair')*: Wine region in the department of HÉRAULT, southern France, north of the city of Béziers. Both red and white wines entitled to the V.D.Q.S. seal are produced in Faugères; the reds, made from Carignan and Grenache grapes, are superior. Generally well-made and inexpensive, the wines of Faugères are becoming popular in the U.S.

Fendant *(Fawn'-dawn)*: The local name for the Chasselas grape in the canton of VALAIS, Switzerland.

Fermentation: The conversion of grape sugar to ethyl alcohol and carbon dioxide by the action of yeasts, which use an enzyme, ZYMASE, to convert the grape sugar by a complex series of biochemical reactions. Fermentation usually stops when 14-15% alcohol is reached, but a different process, MALOLACTIC FERMENTATION, occurs in some wines after the initial fermentation takes place.

Fiasco *(Fee-ass'-co)*: Italian for "flask"; specifically, the squat, straw-covered flask in which the wines of CHIANTI and ORVIETO have traditionally been bottled. The plural is *fiaschi*.

Filtration: The process of clarifying a wine by passing it through a filter. A wine filter is usually constructed of several porous layers sandwiched together, through which the wine is pumped under pressure.

Besides removing sediment that might make the wine cloudy, filtration is helpful in removing yeast, bacteria and other unwanted substances so as to stabilize the wine and protect it from spoilage. Essentially an ab-

101

sorption process, filtration should not be confused with FINING, a technique by which colloidal substances are added to the wine to remove particles in suspension.

Finger Lakes: Important wine region in NEW YORK STATE, named for four lakes: Canandaigua, Keuka, Seneca, and Cayuga. The first two lakes are the most significant in terms of leading wineries and total vineyard acreage; Widmer, Taylor, Pleasant Valley Winery, Gold Seal, Bully Hill and Vinifera Wine Cellars are representative Finger Lakes wineries.

Fining: The addition of a precipitating agent (fining agent) to a wine in order to remove small, suspended particles. When the fining agent is added, the particles cling to it and settle to the bottom; the clarified wine is subsequently transferred to another container.

Called *collage* in French, fining is traditionally performed with colloidal fining agents such as egg whites, isinglass, gelatin, or even ox-blood, but nylon powder and bentonite are often substituted nowadays. Traditionally performed at least six months after the vintage, fining assists in stabilizing wines prior to bottling. It is an older method than FILTRATION, but it is equally helpful in removing suspended particles; many wineries presently use both fining and filtration in order to render their wines free of sediment.

Fino *(Fee'-no)*: The palest and driest kind of SHERRY, which has matured through the action of FLOR yeast.

Fitou *(Fee'-too)*: Excellent red wine produced in the region of CORBIÈRES, in the department of AUDE, France. The Fitou vineyards are planted chiefly in two red grape varieties, Carignan and Grenache, which must constitute at least 75% of the wine. One of the best wines of Corbières, Fitou is entitled to APPELLATION CONTRÔLÉE; by law it

102

must be aged in cask for two years prior to sale. Generally inexpensive, Fitou is often excellent value; about 183,000 cases are produced annually.

Fixin *(Feex'-san)*: Red wine commune in the CÔTE DE NUITS, Burgundy. The most northerly village of consequence in the Côte de Nuits, Fixin lies just to the north of GEVREY-CHAMBERTIN and its best wines show a close similarity to those of that famous commune. Fixin's three most important vineyards are rated Premier Cru (First Growth); they include CLOS DE LA PERRIÈRE, CLOS DU CHAPITRE, and Les Hervelets. There are about 106 acres under vines in Fixin; production averages about 10,000 cases annually.

Flagey-Échezeaux *(Flah-zhay' Esh'-shay-zo)*: Town in the CÔTE DE NUITS, Burgundy, named after the great red wine ÉCHE-ZEAUX, rated Grand Cru (Great Growth). Another Grand Cru vineyard, GRANDS-ÉCHEZEAUX, is considered to be even better, and usually produces one of Burgundy's very finest wines. The vineyard commune of Flagey-Échezeaux lies just to the north of VOSNE-ROMANÉE, and most of its wines are usually sold as Vosne-Romanées, as there is no Flagey-Échezeaux APPEL-LATION CONTRÔLÉE. Some 150 acres of vineyard lie within the commune boundaries.

Fleurie *(Flur-ree')*: Wine village in the BEAUJOLAIS district, southern Burgundy, and its fine red wine. Officially one of the nine Beaujolais *crus* (growths), those areas that generally produce the best Beaujolais, Fleurie is one of the most famous *crus*. The wine is prized for its early-maturing, fruity qualities — hence the name, which means "flowery." There are 1,729 acres of vineyards in Fleurie; annual production amounts to some 292,700 cases.

103

Flor *(Floor)*: Spanish for "flower"; specifically, a special kind of yeast, *Mycodermi vini,* found only in certain wine regions — most notably, the SHERRY and MONTILLA districts of Spain, and in the JURA, France. The yeast collects as a thick film on the surface of the wine in the cask and protects it from oxidation; in addition, it imparts an agreeable taste, which is characteristic of the best dry FINO Sherries. In the United States, sherries that have been made by the action of flor yeast are often called "flor sherries," to distinguish them from ordinary sherries that have been "baked" by exposure to high temperature, without the beneficial action of flor yeast.

Flora: A white HYBRID grape variety, recently developed by Dr. Harold Olmo of the University of California at Davis. Made from a cross between the Gewürztraminer and the Sémillon, the Flora combines many desirable characteristics of both varieties. Several California wineries have already produced VARIETAL wines from the Flora, and the grape also appears to be well-suited to the making of sparkling wines.

Folle Blanche *(Fall Blawnsh')*: White wine grape, known under several different names. Because of the low alcoholic strength and high acidity of its wines, the Folle Blanche used to be the principal grape variety in the French Cognac district, but now comprises less than 3% of the total vineyard acreage because of its susceptibility to various diseases. Known under the name Picpoul, the Folle Blanche is widely grown in the Armagnac district and in other parts of southern France, where it makes light dry wines; one of the best, Picpoul de Pinet, is rated V.D.Q.S. In the lower LOIRE River valley, the Folle Blanche is called Gros Plant; another wine rated V.D.Q.S., Gros Plant du Pays Nantais, is produced near the city of Nantes and is occasionally exported.

On a limited basis, the Folle Blanche has found a good environment in California; there, its inherently high acidity is lessened, and it is used either for sound and generally inexpensive still white wines, or in blends for better-than-average sparkling wines.

Forst: Famous wine town in the RHEINPFALZ (Palatinate) region, Germany, with some 495 acres of vineyard. Forst is located on a rare basalt outcropping, and largely for this reason, its vineyards are among the most valuable in the Rheinpfalz. Three-fourths of the best sites are planted in Riesling, and in good vintages especially ripe, scented wines are made. The leading vineyards (EINZELLAGEN) are: Kirchenstück, Jesuitengarten, Ungeheuer, Freundstück, Elster, Musenhang, and Pechstein.

Fortified Wine: A wine to which brandy has been added, either to arrest fermentation so as to retain sweetness, or to increase the alcoholic content. Examples of fortified wines include SHERRY, PORT, and MADEIRA. U.S. law does not allow wines of this type to be labeled "fortified wine," and so they must be called DESSERT WINES.

Fracia *(Frach'-ee-ah)*: Red wine from the VALTELLINA district, in the region of LOMBARDY, northern Italy. Produced near the town of Sondrio on the Adda River, Fracia is made from the Nebbiolo grape, which is called Chiavennasca locally. The wine is full-bodied but graceful, and ages well.

France: The wines of France are world-renowned for their quality and variety. Wine is one of France's most valuable agricultural products, and about one Frenchman in seven is a member of the wine industry. France's

105

vineyard area is prodigious: over 3 million acres are planted in vines.

Although a heritage of quality wines has endured for centuries in France, fine wines actually make only a small contribution to the total annual production. Well over four-fifths of all French wine is sold in bulk for everyday consumption, and much of this *vin ordinaire* is not even bottled. Many Americans are unaware that, despite France's reputation for fine food and wines, the average Frenchman is not apt to be a gourmet or a wine connoisseur, although he does consume almost 30 times as much wine every year as his American counterpart.

VINEYARD ACREAGE
IN FRANCE,
BY DEPARTMENT

01 Ain: 8,154
02 Aisne: 1,977
03 Allier: 9,884
04 Alpes de Hautes-Pyrénées: 5,930
05 Alpes (Hautes-): 3,707
06 Alpes-Maritimes: 2,718
07 Ardèche: 56,833
08 Ardennes: 25
09 Ariège: 4,201
10 Aube: 5,436
11 Aude: 279,223
12 Aveyron: 14,085
13 Bouches-du-Rhône: 64,246
14 Calvados: 0
15 Cantal: 138
16 Charente: 86,485
17 Charente-Maritime: 108,724
18 Cher: 8,896
19 Corrèze: 4,478
20 Corse: 74,130
21 Côte d'Or: 19,768
22 Côtes-du-Nord: 0
23 Creuse: 2
24 Dordogne: 74,130

25 Doubs: 247
26 Drôme: 39,536
27 Eure: 2
28 Eure-et-Loir: 20
29 Finistère: 0
30 Gard: 217,448
31 Garonne (Haute-): 37,065
32 Gers: 88,956
33 Gironde: 266,868
34 Hérault: 412,657
35 Ille-et-Vilaine: 2
36 Indre: 14,826
37 Indre-et-Loire: 42,007
38 Isère: 16,062
39 Jura: 4,695
40 Landes: 33,359
41 Loir-et-Cher: 39,536
42 Loire: 11,861
43 Loire (Haute-): 1,977
44 Loire-Atlantique: 59,304
45 Loiret: 4,201
46 Lot: 22,239
47 Lot-et-Garonne: 44,478
48 Lozère: 988
49 Maine-et-Loire: 61,775
50 Manche: 0
51 Marne: 35,335
52 Marne (Haute-): 741
53 Mayenne: 0
54 Meurthe-et-Moselle: 1,236
55 Meuse: 247
56 Morbihan: 0
57 Moselle: 494
58 Nièvre: 3,212
59 Nord: 0
60 Oise: 2
61 Orne: 0
62 Pas-de-Calais: 0
63 Puy-de-Dôme: 9,884
64 Pyrénées-Atlantique: 15,567
65 Pyrénées (Hautes-): 8,649
66 Pyrénées-Orientales: 163,086
67 Rhin (Bas-): 13,591
68 Rhin (Haut-): 15,814

69 Rhône: 46,949
70 Saône (Haute-): 741
71 Saône-et-Loire: 27,181
72 Sarthe: 2,471
73 Savoie: 7,413
74 Savoie (Haute-): 988
75 Paris: 2
76 Seine-Maritime: 0
77 Seine-et-Marne: 247
78 Yvelines: 0
79 Sèvres (Deux-): 14,826
80 Somme: 0
81 Tarn: 61,775
82 Tarn-et-Garonne: 37,065
83 Var: 145,789
84 Vaucluse: 126,021
85 Vendée: 32,123
86 Vienne: 32,123
87 Vienne (Haute-): 247
88 Vosges: 494
89 Yonne: 6,672
90 Belfort: 0
91 Essone:
92 Hauts-de-Seine: PARIS
93 Seine-St. Denis: SUBURBAN
94 Val-de-Marne: ZONES
95 Val-d'Oise:

TOTAL: 3,064,264

Yet the French government is keenly aware that the fame of French wine is founded on quality and not quantity, and strict controls are enforced over the sale of wine. As vineyards and climates vary substantially throughout France, it is important to know where the wines are produced. Enacted in 1935, the laws of APPELLATION CONTRÔLÈE (controlled place-name) not only protect the consumer from wine frauds, but through guarantee of origin and authenticity, the laws assure that the buyer gets exactly what he pays for. The appellation contrôlée laws are enforced by the Institut National des

108

Appellations d'Origine (I.N.A.O.), a governmental agency, and the laws are periodically reviewed and amended as needed.

France's wine laws have several quality levels. The most basic has no geographical designation — the wine is merely graded by its alcoholic content. Some is sold under a brand name *(vin de marque):* a good deal is actually blended with foreign wine to give it strength.

The regional wines *(vins de pays)* are on a higher quality level. In 1974 the French government authorized 44 regions from which *vins de pays* could originate. The wines are labeled according to their place of origin and the name of the department (administrative region) where they were made. This provides some information for the French consumer, but only a few *vins de pays* have been exported to the U.S.; most of them are consumed in local restaurants or taverns.

Considerably more significant on the export market are the ''Vins Délimités de Qualité Supérieur'' (V.D.Q.S.), which must be made from approved grape varieties having a restricted yield per acre. The quality of some V.D.Q.S. wines is quite high, and the law provides that certain outstanding wines can be raised to the highest quality category: appellation contrôlée.

Appellation contrôlée wines include all of the most famous wines of France. The scope of this category is such that it delimits vineyards ranging from thousands of acres in size down to tiny plots of only an acre or less. A new feature of the appellation contrôlée law enacted in 1975 was a mandatory testing and laboratory analysis of the wines, plus an official declaration of the maximum yield per acre established by a regional professional wine committee. Few countries have passed such comprehensive wine laws.

Vineyards grow in most of France, but not everywhere. An invisible barrier winds

109

France

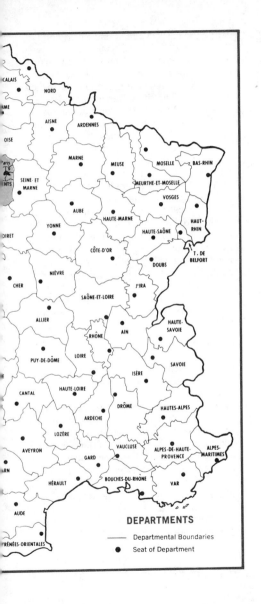

DEPARTMENTS

— Departmental Boundaries

● Seat of Department

across France above the Loire River; north of this "limit of the vine," centuries of experience have determined that no quality wines can be produced. But south of this barrier, vineyards abound in most regions where they are suited. The more important wine areas include: CHAMPAGNE, the source of the world's most renowned sparkling wine; ALSACE, near the German border, where many good white wines are made; BURGUNDY, the home of some of the world's most famous red and white wines; the RHÔNE River valley, with its noble red wines prized for their strength and finesse; PROVENCE, with its excellent rosé wines; the MIDI to the south, providing most of France's ordinary wines; BORDEAUX, traditionally one of France's most famous wine regions, and the LOIRE River valley, with a whole chain of quality vineyards following its course across France. An indication of the wide range of excellent French wines can be appreciated by their extensive representation in this dictionary.

Franken *(Frank'-en)*: German for "Franconia," an important wine region (ANBAUGEBIET) in the upper Main River valley, Germany. There are some 7,700 acres of vineyard in Franken, most of them planted in white grape varieties. Some of the best wines of Franken are made from the Silvaner — normally a secondary variety in other parts of Germany—and the wines are traditionally shipped in the squat, green BOCKSBEUTEL bottles native to Franken. The region's center is the city of WÜRZBURG, which has the most famous vineyards, but the neighboring villages of ESCHERNDORF, IPHOFEN and RANDERSACKER are equally acclaimed for their wines. Franken normally produces over 2.2 million cases of wine annually.

Frascati *(Fras-cah'-tee)*: Fine white wine

from the region of LAZIO (Latium), Italy, produced south of the city of Rome. Made chiefly from Malvasia and Trebbiano grapes, Frascati is one of the best wines of the CASTELLI ROMANI district. Three types are produced: dry, semi-dry, and *cannellino* (sweet); the dry is more popular in the U.S. The wine has been famous since the days of the Renaissance, and is rated D.O.C.

Frecciarossa *(Frech-ya-ross'-ah)***:** Italian for "red arrow," the proprietary name for red, white and rosé wines produced near the town of Casteggio in the region of LOMBARDY, Italy. Frecciarossa is made by the estate of Dr. Giorgio Odero, who labels the red *(rosso)* "Grand Cru," the white *(bianco)* "La Vigne Blanche," and the rosé "St. George."

Free Run: The free-flowing wine after fermentation, as opposed to the solid residue or POMACE. After the free run wine is drawn off, the pomace can be pressed to extract PRESS WINE, which contains more tannin and coloring. Called *vin de goutte* in French, free run wine usually makes up four-fifths of the total volume of fermented wine.

Normally, free run wine is superior to press wine and many producers bottle it separately, but press wine is often blended with free run wine for a balanced product.

Freiherr *(Fry'-hair)***:** German for "baron." The nobility still own many wine estates in Germany, and this term occasionally appears on a German wine label.

Freisa *(Fray'-za)***:** Red wine grape grown extensively in PIEMONTE, northern Italy; also the name of its wine. One of the best of Piemonte's lesser-known wines, Freisa may be either dry or semi-sweet, and is sometimes slightly sparkling or *frizzante*. Two Freisa wines bear the D.O.C. seal: Freisa di Chieri (usually the best and most famous), produced east of the city of Turin in the Monferrato

113

Hills, and Freisa d'Asti. A third, Freisa delle Langhe, has not yet received D.O.C. status.

Friuli-Venezia Giulia *(Free-oo'-lee Ven-etts'-ee-ah Julia)*: Wine region in the extreme northeast corner of Italy, bordering Austria and Yugoslavia. Friuli-Venezia Giulia produces a great variety of wines; not many are exported, but some are excellent value. There are several D.O.C. wines; the most famous is Collio Goriziano (or Collio), a golden, dry white wine. Collio may be produced from several varieties; the most important is occasionally indicated on the label. Colli Orientali del Friuli, another D.O.C., comes from the eastern hills of Friuli in the province of Udine; this district is famous for Picolit, a rare and exquisite sweet white wine. The region's third D.O.C. is Grave del Friuli, named for the region of Grave between the towns of Udine and Pordenone. The average annual production for the region as a whole is over 14 million cases of wine.

Frizzante *(Fritz-sahn'-tee)*: Italian for "semi-sparkling"; said of some Italian wines that are occasionally bottled early, allowing a slight secondary fermentation to develop.

Fronsac *(Frawn'-sack)*: Town in the BORDEAUX region, France, located on the DORDOGNE River. The fine, sturdy red wines of Fronsac are not well-known, but are among the best values in Bordeaux wines. They are not labeled Fronsac, however, as there is no APPELLATION CONTRÔLÉE of that name. See CÔTES-CANON-FRONSAC and CÔTES-DE-FRONSAC.

Frontignan *(Frawn'-teen-yawn)*: French wine region and town on the Mediterranean coast, north of the city of Sète. Frontignan is famous for its golden sweet wine made from the Muscat Doré grape, called Muscat de Frontignan. Officially rated APPELLATION CONTRÔLÉE, Muscat de Frontignan is a

FORTIFIED WINE to which brandy is added to arrest fermentation and retain sweetness; its minimum alcoholic strength is 15%. Bottled with a special seal, the wine is similar to SHERRY, and is very popular in France as an apéritif. The Frontignan vineyards extend over 865 acres; three-fourths of the annual production of 228,700 cases is produced by the Frontignan wine cooperative.

Fuder *(Foo'-der)*: German for "barrel" or "cask." Originally a Fuder was a tun (tonne), an old measure of cooperage; nowadays it is an oak cask used in the MOSEL region, with a capacity of 1,000 liters (114 cases).

Funchal *(Foon'-shal)*: The largest town on the island of MADEIRA, and the headquarters of the Madeira wine trade, where the shippers' offices (lodges) are located.

Furmint *(Foor'-mint)*: The grape variety grown in the TOKAY district, Hungary, and in other Hungarian wine regions.

Fürst *(Foorst)*: German for "prince."

G

Gaillac *(Guy'-yak)*: Wine region in southwestern France, located around the town of the same name in the department of Tarn. There are two Gaillac APPELLATION CONTRÔLÉES, Premier Côtes de Gaillac and Gaillac, which apply to red, white or rosé wines. It is primarily the sweet or semi-sweet wines of Gaillac, which are occasionally made sparkling *(mousseux)*, that have made the region famous. Sparkling Gaillacs may be produced either by the Champagne process or by merely bottling the wine early, when residual sugar and yeast are still present. The total area under vines in Gaillac is 2,700 acres; production amounts to the equivalent of 228,700 cases of wine annually.

Gamay *(Gam-may')*: Red wine grape grown extensively in the BEAUJOLAIS district, southern Burgundy. The zesty, generous red wines that it gives are prized for their quick-maturing, fruity qualities. There are several varieties of Gamay, some of which give red juice; the *Gamay Noir à jus blanc,* which gives white juice, is the only one permitted to grow in the Beaujolais. This grape does not produce good wines in the CÔTE D'OR to the north, although it is often used in blends with the Pinot Noir, which are called "Bourgogne Passe-Tout-Grains" (see BOURGOGNE). The Gamay is also grown in other parts of France and in Switzerland.

The Gamay is planted widely in northern California, but its wines are generally not as successful as in its native Beaujolais. California wines labeled "Gamay Beaujolais" usually are superior to those labeled Gamay, and more closely typify the Beaujolais style, but grape specialists (ampelographers) have recently determined that the Gamay Beaujolais grown in California is not related to the Gamay, but is actually a clone or sub-variety of the Pinot Noir.

Gambellara *(Gam-buh-larr'-ah)*: Light white wine produced in the region of VENETO, northeast Italy. The D.O.C. region of Gambellara lies east of the city of Verona, and adjoins the more famous white wine district of SOAVE; the wines are similar and are made from identical grape varieties, but Gambellara is generally a lighter wine and is much less well-known.

Garganega *(Gar-ga'-nay-ga)*: White grape variety used in making the wines of SOAVE, and other good white wines of northern Italy.

Garonne *(Gar-rawn')*: Major river in south-

116

western France, drawing its source in the foothills of the Pyrénées and draining into the GIRONDE estuary north of the city of BORDEAUX. The wine regions of GRAVES, SAUTERNES, and Premières Côtes de Bordeaux lie near the Garonne.

Gattinara *(Got-tee-nar'-rah)*: Excellent red wine produced in the region of PIEMONTE, northern Italy. Made from the Nebbiolo grape, Gattinara is one of the very finest Italian red wines—rich, pungent, and slow to mature. It is produced in the section of Piemonte known as the Novara Hills, just southwest of Lake Maggiore; in this district, the Nebbiolo is also known locally as the Spanna, and sometimes a bottle of Gattinara will be labeled Spanna. Gattinara must be aged at least four years before being sold; about 29,000 cases are produced annually.

Gavi *(Gah'-vee)*: Little town in the region of PIEMONTE, northern Italy, famous for its white wine. See CORTESE.

Geisenheim *(Guy'-zen-heim)*: Town and wine region in the western portion of the RHEINGAU district, Germany. The location of a famous school of viticulture, Geisenheim has several good vineyards planted in Riesling, though not many of its white wines are widely known outside of Germany. The entire Geisenheim commune officially has over 1,000 acres suitable for cultivation, though only about half are presently under vines. The leading vineyards (EINZELLAGEN) are: Rothenberg, Mäuerchen, Kläuserweg, Mönchspfad, Kilzberg, Fuchsberg, and Schlossgarten.

Gemeinde *(Ge-mine'-duh)*: German for "community" or "municipality," a delimited township and the surrounding land. This term is roughly equivalent to the French COMMUNE.

117

Generic *(Jen-nair'-ick)*: A wine labeled according to a particular class or type, as opposed to place of origin. Under U.S. labeling law, a generic wine is named after a wine region that has ceased to have any significance of geographical origin—chablis, sauterne, champagne, etc. Originally these names were used by American winemakers to label their products, for lack of better names. But since many nations have codified wine laws restricting the use of place names, there has been considerable pressure on the U.S. to prohibit generic labeling. This could only come about with great difficulty, however, since these names are in such widespread use.

In the U.S. wine trade nowadays, a generic wine usually falls into the lower quality categories, and most wineries prefer to use VARIETAL labeling for their premium wines, specifying the grape variety used. However, U.S. law permits generic labeling for any wine, so long as the true place of origin is clearly indicated on the label.

Germany: Since the days of Rome, Germany has produced wines that have won worldwide acclaim. Today, fine German wines dominate the world market. Germany exports more wines to America than to any other country, and the U.S. imports more white wines from Germany than any place else. Most German wines sold in the U.S. are moderately-priced, blended wines sold under a brand name, such as LIEBFRAUMILCH. Yet Germany's 220,000 acres of vineyard produce wines unmatched for their quality and variety. 85% of all German wines are white; the rather light reds are mostly consumed locally and few are exported.

118

A German wine label is generally quite informative. Besides the producer's name and the vintage year, the label usually indicates the town where the wine was made, and if the wine is superior, the name of the vineyard. The town and vineyard name are always specified together, in that order (ex.: Piesporter Goldtröpfchen, Rauenthaler Baiken).

Because the vine is near its northern limit in Germany, vintages vary considerably in this cold climate. Many German wines are made each year with sugar added (see CHAPTALISATION), which is authorized by law. If this were not allowed, there would be very little German wine available for sale.

Since 1971, German wines have been produced and sold under new laws, and the authorities hope that the new legislation eliminates some of the confusion of the past. The 1971 German Wine Law recognizes three basic classes of wines. The first, TAFELWEIN (table wine), is the most ordinary. German Tafelwein is usually produced in bulk and sold in large containers; very little is exported. QUALITÄTSWEIN (quality wine) is much more significant on the export market, and it includes two groups. All Qualitätswein must originate from officially designated wine-growing regions (ANBAUGEBIETE). The lowest category is Qualitätswein bestimmter Anbaugebiete or Q.b.A. (quality wine from designated wine regions), to which sugar may be added. When released, the wine is given an official certification number (Amtliche Prüfungsnummer), indicating that it has met minimum standards.

The best German wines are made from fully-ripened grapes that need no addition of sugar: QUALITÄTSWEIN MIT PRÄDIKAT (quality wine with special attributes). All of Germany's best wines belong to this group (see KABINETT, SPÄTLESE and AUSLESE). Each category of Prädikat wines has legal minimum MUST WEIGHT standards for ripeness and sugar content (see chart on accompanying page), and all Prädikat wines are tasted by an impartial professional committee before they are released for sale.

119

German wines owe their distinctive characteristics to several grape varieties. Although not the most widely planted variety, the Riesling is by far the best, and gives racy, scented white wines. The Silvaner is also an important producer, especially in southern regions. The Müller-Thurgau, a cross between the Riesling and Silvaner, is gaining in acreage as it combines many desirable characteristics of each. Good wines are also made from the Gewürztraminer and the Ruländer; a recent Riesling/Silvaner cross, the Scheurebe, shows great promise.

Most of the best German vineyards are located near rivers, for in this northern climate a river has a modifying effect on temperature changes. The vineyards also tend to have a southerly exposure, so that they receive as much sunshine during the day as possible.

Of the eleven designated German Anbaugebiete, four border the Rhine River, one of Europe's most important waterways. Probably Germany's most famous wine district is the RHEINGAU, extending west from Hochheim to Assmannshausen. Produced mostly from the Riesling, Rheingau wines are characteristically ripe and full-flavored, particularly in great vintages. To the south is the RHEINHESSEN district, better known for Liebfraumilch than the other outstanding wines it produces. Away from the Rhine to the south is the RHEINPFALZ (Palatinate), Germany's largest wine region; its center, the Mittel-Haardt, is particularly renowned for its wines. The MITTELRHEIN, Germany's most northern wine region, extends south from Bonn to Bingen; many good wines are made, but only a few are exported. The same applies to the HESSISCHE BERGSTRASSE, Germany's smallest wine region, located between the cities of Heidelberg and Darmstadt.

Two important tributaries of the Rhine, the MOSEL and NAHE Rivers, also have top qual-

ity vineyards. The Mosel in turn has two tributaries, the SAAR and the RUWER Rivers, which have exceptional wine districts; the designated Anbaugebiet is Mosel-Saar-Ruwer. These wines are prized for their scent and delicacy; Nahe wines, not well-known in the U.S., are similar to the Rheingaus. The little district of the AHR, to the north, produces some of Germany's best red wine from the Spätburgunder (Pinot Noir).

The three remaining districts are all further

south. BADEN, the most southerly, extends along the French border north from Lake Constance (Bodensee). Its wines are steadily gaining in reputation. To the northwest, WÜRTTEMBERG produces a wide variety of red, white and rosé wines, but not many are exported. FRANKEN (Franconia), located around the city of Würzburg, is noted for its sturdy white wines shipped in the squat, green BOCKSBEUTEL bottles native to the region.

The color of the traditional, fluted German wine bottle varies by region. Mosel-Saar-Ruwer wines are always shipped in green bottles; Rhine wines are shipped in brown bottles. Bocksbeutel bottles are always green in Germany.

	AHR	BADEN	FRANKEN	HESSISCHE BERGSTRASSE	MITTELRHEIN	MOSEL-SAAR-RUWER	NAHE	RHEINGAU	RHEINHESSEN	RHEINPFALZ	WÜRTTEMBERG
KABINETT											
Riesling	70	75	76	73	70	70	70	73	73	73	72
Müller-Thurgau & Silvaner		72	76				73		73	73	72
All other whites	73	75	76	73	73	73	76	73	76	76	75
All reds	73	78	80	78			76	80	76	76	75
SPÄTLESE											
Riesling	76	85		85	76	76	78	85	85	85	85
Ruländer/Traminer	80	88	90	85	81		85	85	85	85	85
All other whites	80	85	85	85	80	80	82	85	85	85	85
All reds	85	91	90	90	80		90	90	90	90	88
AUSLESE											
Riesling	83	98	100	95	83	83	85	95	92	92	95
All other whites	88	101	100	100	88	88	92	100	95	95	95
All reds	88	101	100	105			100	105	100	100	95
BEERENAUSLESE											
All varieties	110	124	125	125	110	110	120	125	120	120	124
TROCKENBEERENAUSLESE											
All varieties	150	150	150	150	150	150	150	150	150	150	150

MINIMUM ÖCHSLE READINGS (MUST WEIGHT) FOR GERMAN WINES

This chart, derived from the 1971 German Wine Law, shows the legal minimum Öchsle readings for each category of Qualitätswein mit Prädikat. It gives an idea of the amount of sunshine each wine region (Anbaugebiet) normally receives, as well as the grape varieties grown in each region. Note that in the north it is more difficult to make an Auslese; the minimum Öchsle readings are equivalent to a Spätlese in the south.

Gevrey-Chambertin *(Jev'-ray Shawm'-bair-tan):* Famous town and red wine commune in the northern CÔTE DE NUITS, Burgundy, since 1847 named after the great CHAMBERTIN vineyard, rated Grand Cru (Great Growth). The equally fine CLOS DE BÈZE vineyard alongside is also named after Chambertin, and is known as Chambertin-Clos de Bèze officially. Other Grand Cru vineyards in Gevrey-Chambertin include LATRICIÈRES-CHAMBERTIN, CHARMES-CHAMBERTIN, MAZOYÈRES-CHAMBERTIN, MAZIS-CHAMBERTIN, CHAPELLE-CHAMBERTIN, GRIOTTE-CHAMBERTIN, and RUCHOTTES-CHAMBERTIN, though these are considered to be in a somewhat lower class. There are several good vineyards of nearly equal quality, rated Premier Cru (First Growth), the names of which are preceded by Gevrey-Chambertin. The most notable include CLOS SAINT-JACQUES, Veroilles, Gazetiers, Estournelles, and Aux Combottes. Wine not produced from a classified vineyard but from a plot within the Gevrey-Chambertin commune is entitled to a commune appellation. There are 506 acres of vineyard in Gevrey-Chambertin; average annual production amounts to some 114,300 cases of red wine, there being no Gevrey-Chambertin appellation allowed for white wines.

Gewürztraminer (German, *Ge-vertz'-tram-me'-ner;* French, *Gevoorts'-tram-me-nair'*): Fine white grape variety, grown widely in Germany and in Alsace, France. Its name means "spicy Traminer" in German, and it is an especially selected strain of the Traminer; its wines have a particularly pronounced bouquet and a characteristically full flavor. Because the Gewürztraminer is recognizably superior to the Traminer, it was recently decreed that no more Alsatian wines are to be labeled Traminer — this distinction being reserved for the Gewürztraminer —

123

although the Traminer is still grown in other parts of the world. Transplanted, the Gewürztraminer has proven very successful in California, and many recent California Gewürztraminers compare favorably with better French and German wines; over 2,600 acres have been planted.

Ghemme *(Gemm'-ay)*: Excellent red wine from the region of PIEMONTE, northern Italy, produced in the northern section of Piemonte known as the Novara Hills. Made primarily from the Nebbiolo grape, usually with an admixture of Bonarda or Vespolina added, Ghemme is a powerful, full-bodied red wine that ages well; by law it must attain at least 12% alcohol. The D.O.C. region of Ghemme covers a relatively small area, however, and production amounts to less than 9,000 cases annually.

Gigondas *(She'-gawn-das)*: Wine region in the southern RHÔNE River valley, France, situated in the department of Vaucluse. Gigondas recently received an APPELLATION CONTRÔLEE rating, primarily on the merits of its excellent and sturdy red wines, though rosés and whites are also produced. The area lies just to the northeast of the famous CHÂTEAUNEUF-DU-PAPE region and the wines are similar, though being less well known, Gigondas wines are apt to be considerably less expensive. The equivalent of about 343,000 cases of wine is produced annually in Gigondas.

Gironde *(She'-rawnd)*: Tidal estuary formed by the confluence of the GARONNE and DORDOGNE Rivers north of the city of BORDEAUX, France; also the name of a department or administrative region. The vineyards of the MÉDOC lie on the left bank of the Gironde; opposite, on the right bank, lie the vineyards of BOURG and BLAYE.

Givry *(She′-vree)***:** Wine region in the CHALONNAIS district, Burgundy. One of Burgundy's lesser known regions, Givry produces red and white wines from the Pinot Noir and Chardonnay; the reds are particularly acclaimed. Certain outstanding vineyards in Givry have been rated Premier Cru (First Growth) under the law of APPELLATION CONTRÔLÉE; they include: La Baraude, Clos Saint-Pierre, Clos Saint-Paul, Clos Salomon, and Cellier aux Moines. About 22,900 cases of Givry are produced annually, reds accounting for about four-fifths of the total.

Governo *(Go-vair′-no)***:** The process of adding a small amount of concentrated must made from dried Colorino grapes to the new wine in the CHIANTI region, Italy. The must ferments and causes a small addition of carbon dioxide to form in the wine, giving it a slight sparkle and added freshness. The process of governo is normally reserved for ordinary Chiantis and is not usually performed on the best wines.

Graach *(Grock)***:** Little town on the MOSEL River, Germany, with some 250 acres of vineyard. Made from the Riesling grape, the fine wines of Graach are among the Mosel's best, especially in dry years, for the soil consists of thick slate that retains moisture. The leading vineyard (EINZELLAGE) is Himmelreich, but there is one excellent Graach wine from a vineyard owned by the von Kesselstatt family, JOSEPHSHOF, which is not sold as a Graach but is called Josephshöfer. Other good Graach vineyards include Abtsberg and Domprobst.

Graf *(Grof)***:** German for "earl" or "count."

Gragnano *(Gran-yan′-no)***:** Village located some 20 miles to the southeast of Naples, Italy, in the region of CAMPANIA; also a light red wine of the same name. Often faintly sparkling or *frizzante,* Gragnano is a pleasant local wine to be drunk young.

Grand Cru *(Grawn Crew'):* French for "Great Growth," a wine from an officially classified vineyard (see CRU). As authorized by the laws of APPELLATION CONTRÔLÉE, the usage of this term varies in the fine wine regions of France. In BURGUNDY, a Grand Cru is the very highest rating, applying only to rare and distinguished wines. In BORDEAUX, there are several different categories of Grand Cru, depending on the region. In the MÉDOC district, a Grand Cru applies only to those vineyards classified in 1855, which are divided into five groups of *crus.* In SAINT ÉMILION to the east, a Grand Cru defines a classified vineyard, but officially not one of the best; the finest wines are rated Premier Grand Cru (First Great Growth).

Further north, in ALSACE, a new government decree enacted in 1975 provides that the term Grand Cru shall apply only to wines of at least 11% alcohol made from "noble" grape varieties (Gewürztraminer, Riesling, Pinot Gris, and Muscat) grown in the central and best portion of the Alsatian vineyards. In the French CHAMPAGNE region, a Grand Cru rating applies not to a wine but to the vineyards of a particularly famous village, whose grapes fetch a maximum price each year.

Grande Réserve *(Grawn Ray-zairv'):* In ALSACE, France, a wine that has reached a minimum of 11% alcohol. Formerly this term was roughly interchangeable with GRAND CRU (see above), but use of the latter designation has now been more restricted.

126 **Grands-Échezeaux** *(Grawns Esh'-shay-zo):* Outstanding red wine produced in the CÔTE DE NUITS, Burgundy, rated Grand Cru (Great Growth). Located in the commune of FLAGEY-ÉCHEZEAUX, the vineyard of

Grands-Échezeaux consists of 22½ acres planted in Pinot Noir that adjoin those of ÉCHEZEAUX, also rated Grand Cru but not considered to be quite as fine. A good Grands Échezeaux is typically very scented and graceful, with a good deal of finesse, and many experts consider it one of Burgundy's very best red wines.

Graves *(Grahv)***:** French for "gravel"; specifically, a fine wine region located near the city of BORDEAUX, France, on the left bank of the GARONNE River. Graves derives its name from the gravelly soil that dominates the region; both red and white wines of fine quality are made in Graves, though more white is produced than red and it tends to be better-known. The northern portion of the Graves region includes the adjoining communes of Pessac, Talence, Léognan, Villenave, Cadaujac and Martillac, each of which has several famous wine estates or CHÂTEAUX. Probably the best-known château in Graves is HAUT-BRION in the commune of Pessac, which produces some of Bordeaux's finest red and white wines, but Graves has a wealth of other fine wine estates, which were officially classified in 1953: (In the following list, châteaux that produce both red and white wines are marked with an asterisk.) Bouscaut*, Carbonnieux*, Domaine de Chevalier*, Couhins, Fieuzal*, Haut-Bailly, La Mission-Haut-Brion, La Tour-Martillac*, La Tour-Haut-Brion, Laville-Haut-Brion, Malartic-Lagravière*, Olivier*, Pape-Clément, and Smith-Haut-Lafitte*. The Graves region as a whole extends over 6,000 acres.

Greco di Gerace *(Gray'-co dee Jair-rach'-ee)***:** Golden, sweet white wine produced near the town of Gerace in the region of CALABRIA, southern Italy. Made from the Greco grape, Greco di Gerace has been famous since the days of Rome, but has not yet received a D.O.C. rating.

Greece: Ancient Greece was one of the birthplaces of viticulture. Wine figures heavily in classical Greek poetry, and was considered a gift of the gods. Today, Greece's warm Mediterranean climate is especially well-suited to grape-growing; in addition to wine, table grapes and raisins are other important products. Currently, Greece has over 420,000 acres planted in wine grapes.

Many Americans associate Greek wines with retsina, or resinated wine, which is white or rosé wine to which pine resin is added during fermentation. The custom of resinating wines dates back to ancient times, when it was thought to give the wines longevity, but retsina wines actually age poorly and should be drunk when very young. To many, retsina is an acquired taste, but it is an ideal accompaniment to Greek food. It is mostly produced around the city of Athens, and is made from the Savatiano grape. The Roditis grape is mostly used for rosés.

The most important vineyard area in Greece is the Peloponnesus in the south, where 33% of the country's wine is produced. The little town of Monemvasia on the Mirtoan Sea, famous for its sweet wine, gave its name to Malvasia (Malvoisie), a sweet grape which is now grown all over the world. The Peloponnesus is also the original home of Mavrodaphne, a dark-colored, sweetish red wine that is one of Greece's most famous.

The Greek islands also produce celebrated wine. The Muscat of Samos is a famous, golden sweet wine made from late-harvested grapes. The islands of Crete and Santorin are also noted for their wines. On the mainland, the areas of Thessalia and Macedonia primarily produce red wine, much of which is used in blending.

Most Greek wines exported to the U.S. are

produced by large private firms like Cambas and Achaia-Clauss, whose headquarters are in the city of Patras on the Peloponnesus. Their brand names of "Castel Danielis," "Demestica," "Santa Helena" and "Pendeli" are well-known in the trade.

Green Hungarian: White wine grape grown in the cool coastal districts of California. Despite its unusual name, the origins of the Green Hungarian are uncertain. It has a rather neutral flavor, and for this reason it is most often used for blending, but occasionally some pleasant, light white wines are made and sold under its VARIETAL name.

Grenache *(Gren-nash′)*:Sweet pink grape, used in blends to make the famous red wine of CHÂTEAUNEUF DU-PAPE and on its own to make the fine rosés of TAVEL and LIRAC. The Grenache is also grown in Spain's RIOJA district (where it is called Garnacha), and is the leading variety. Transplanted to California, the Grenache produces some of the best American rosé wines, usually under its VARIETAL name.

Grèves *(Grev)*: Fine red wine vineyard in the commune of BEAUNE. in Burgundy's CÔTE D'OR. Considered to be one of the best in Beaune, the Grèves vineyard consists of 78 acres planted in Pinot Noir, and regularly produces very distinguished wine rated Premier Cru (First Growth). A small quantity of particularly fine wine called "Beaune Grèves de l'Enfant Jesus" is produced exclusively by the Burgundy shipper Bouchard Père et Fils.

Grey Riesling: White wine grape grown in many parts of California. Despite its name, it is not a Riesling but another, unrelated variety known in France as Chauché Gris. The Grey Riesling gives pleasant, rather light white wine, especially when planted in cool climates, but it should not be confused with the true Riesling of Germany, called Johannis-

129

berg Riesling or White Riesling in California.

Grignolino *(Grin-yo-leen'-o):* Good red wine grape grown in the region of PIEMONTE, northern Italy; also a wine of the same name. Wine made from the Grignolino is characteristically light in color, but it is full-flavored. Two superior areas where it is made, Asti and Monferrato, were recently awarded a D.O.C. rating.

Important new plantations of Grignolino have also been made in California, and the wines are very similar to their Italian counterpart.

Grinzing *(Grintz'-ing):* Light, fresh white wine produced north of the city of Vienna, Austria, in the suburb of Grinzing. Made primarily from the Grüner Veltliner grape, Grinzing is very charming when consumed young, and is usually drunk during its first year in many Viennese wine taverns *(Weinstuben),* although it is also exported.

Griotte-Chambertin *(Gree-ot' Shawm'-bear-tan):* Excellent red wine vineyard in the northern CÔTE DE NUITS, Burgundy, located in the commune of GEVREY-CHAMBERTIN. Officially rated Grand Cru (Great Growth), Griotte-Chambertin is named after the great CHAMBERTIN vineyard, which lies nearby. It is celebrated for its full, rich red wines, but the vineyard is rather small (13½ acres) and production rarely exceeds 1,000 cases annually.

Gropello *(Gro-pell'-o):* Red wine grape grown on the shores of Lake Garda in the region of LOMBARDY, northern Italy. The Gropello is the principal grape variety used for the wines of CHIARETTO; light red wines and rosés are also made from the Gropello in other parts of Lombardy.

Gros Lot *(Gro Lo):* Productive red grape grown in the lower LOIRE River valley,

France, where it is used to produce the ordinary rosés of ANJOU. Also known as the Grolleau, the Gros Lot is usually vinified to retain some residual sugar.

Gros Plant *(Gro Plawn')*: The local name for the Folle Blanche grape in the lower LOIRE River valley, France. One distinguished wine produced near the city of Nantes, Gros Plant du Pays Nantais, has a V.D.Q.S. rating.

Grosslage *(Gross'-log-uh)*: German for "collective site." Under the 1971 German Wine Law, a Grosslage is a collective or composite vineyard, made up of a number of different individual vineyards (EINZEL-LAGEN) within a sub-region or BEREICH. It replaces the former generic sites *(Gattungs-lagen)*, which were used for regional wines.

A Grosslage frequently extends over several different wine villages whose vineyards, soil and climate are judged similar; its size may range from 125 acres to over 3,000 acres. While Grosslage wines will rarely be the best a producer has to offer, they represent a more marketable alternative for the producer in several ways. A Grosslage name may be better-known to the consumer than an Einzellage (ex.: Niersteiner Gutes Domthal vs. Niersteiner Orbel); a producer may also choose to de-classify wine from an Einzellage and sell it in blends as a Grosslage; this allows him to offer it at a lower price, which is advantageous for the consumer since Grosslage wines can be produced in all categories of QUALITÄTSWEIN.

A LIST OF MOST FREQUENTLY USED GROSSLAGEN

131

GROSSLAGE	ANBAUGEBIET	OTHER VILLAGES INCLUDED IN GROSSLAGE
Bernkasteler Badstube	Mosel-Saar-Ruwer	none
Bernkasteler Kurfürstlay	Mosel-Saar-Ruwer	Brauneberg, Lieser, Veldenz, Wintrich

GROSSLAGE	ANBAUGEBIET	OTHER VILLAGES INCLUDED IN GROSSLAGE
Deidesheimer Hofstück	Rheinpfalz	Rupperstberg, Ellerstadt, Meckenheim
Dürkheimer Feuerberg	Rheinpfalz	Kallstadt, Ellerstadt, Gonnheim
Forster Mariengarten	Rheinpfalz	Deidesheim, Wachenheim
Hattenheimer Deutelsberg	Rheingau	Erbach
Hochheimer Daubhaus	Rheingau	Kostheim, Wicker, Florsheim
Ihringer Vulkanfelsen	Baden	Bickensohl, Bötzingen, Endingen
Johannisberger Erntebringer	Rheingau	Geisenheim, Mittelheim, Winkel
Kreuznacher Kronenberg	Nahe	Bretzenheim, Hargesheim
Kröver Nacktarsch	Mosel-Saar-Ruwer	none
Niersteiner Auflangen	Rheinhessen	none
Niersteiner Gutes Domthal	Rheinhessen	Nackenheim, Dalheim, Friesenheim
Niersteiner Rehbach	Rheinhessen	Nackenheim
Niersteiner Spiegelberg	Rheinhessen	Nackenheim
Oppenheimer Krötenbrunnen	Rheinhessen	Dienheim, Alsheim, Guntersblum
Piesporter Michelsberg	Mosel-Saar-Ruwer	Neumagen-Dhron, Trittenheim
Rauenthaler Steinmächer	Rheingau	Eltville, Martinsthal, Nierderwalluf
Rüdesheimer Burgweg	Rheingau	Geisenheim, Assmannshausen, Lorch
Rüdesheimer Rosengarten	Nahe	Braunweiler, Roxheim, Weinsheim
Schloss Böckelheimer Burgweg	Nahe	Bad Münster, Nierderhausen, Norheim
Trierer Römerlay	Mosel-Saar-Ruwer	Kasel, Avelsbach, Waldrach, Mertesdorf
Ürziger Schwarzlay	Mosel-Saar-Ruwer	Erden, Enkirch, Traben-Trarbach
Wachenheimer Schenkenböhl	Rheinpfalz	Bad Durkheim
Wehlener Munzlay	Mosel-Saar-Ruwer	Graach, Zeltingen
Wiltinger Scharzberg	Mosel-Saar-Ruwer	Ayl, Kanzem, Ockfen, Oberemmel
Winkeler Honigberg	Rheingau	Mittelheim
Zeller Schwarze Katz	Mosel-Saar-Ruwer	Senheim, Kaimt, Merl

Grumello *(Grew-mell'-o)*: Sturdy red wine produced in the VALTELLINA district, in the region of LOMBARDY, northern Italy. Made from the Nebbiolo grape, which is called Chiavennasca locally, Grumello is one of the Valtellina's best wines. It is slow to mature and can live for decades.

Gumpoldskirchner *(Goom'-polds-keersch'-ner)*: One of the best white wines of Austria, produced near the town of Gumpolds-kirchen south of the city of Vienna. Gumpoldskirchner is made primarily from the Grüner Veltliner and the Spätrot (Rot-gipfler), which can produce luscious sweet wines when harvested late. Very popular in Vienna, Gumpoldskirchner was formerly exported only rarely, but some very fine wines have recently been shipped to the U.S.

Gutedel *(Goot-aid'-l)*: The German name for the Chasselas grape, which is grown primarily in the MARKGRÄFLERLAND district in the region of BADEN. Wines made from the Gutedel tend to be characteristically mild with low acidity, and are most agreeable when consumed young.

Gutturnio *(Goo-toor'-nee-o)*: Light red wine produced in the hills south of the city of Piacenza, in the region of EMILIA-ROMAGNA, Italy. Made from Barbera and Bonarda grapes, Gutturnio was one of the region's first wines to receive a D.O.C. rating. Its full name is Gutturnio dei Colli Piacentini.

H

Haardt *(Hart)*: Chain of hills in southern Germany, geologically an extension of the Vosges Mountains in France. The Haardt essentially defines the entire RHEINPFALZ (Palatinate) region; it is divided into three sections: in the south, the Ober-Haardt; in the center, the Mittel-Haardt, and in the north, the Unter-Haardt. The Mittel-Haardt is the most famous for its wines.

133

Halbstück *(Halb'-shtook)*: Wine cask with a

capacity of 600 liters (68.6 cases), used in Germany's RHEINGAU region either as a unit of sale in the trade or, formerly, as an offering at an auction.

Hallgarten *(Hahl'-garten)*: Village and wine community in the RHEINGAU district, Germany, with some 500 acres of vineyard, mostly planted in Riesling. An upland commune where the Rheingau reaches its highest point, Hallgarten is distinguished by its full-flavored wines, often the most pronounced of the entire Rheingau. The leading vineyards (EINZELLAGEN) are: Schönhell, Jungfer, Würzgarten, and Hendelberg.

Haro *(Ha'-ro)*: Little Spanish town on the Ebro River, the center of the RIOJA wine trade.

Hattenheim *(Hot'-en-heim)*: World-famous wine village in the RHEINGAU district, Germany, located on the banks of the Rhine River. Hattenheim has 494 acres under vines; its fine wines are distinguished by their grace and elegance. A portion of the great MARCOBRUNN vineyard extends into Hattenheim from neighboring ERBACH, but under the 1971 German Wine Law all of the wine must be labeled Erbacher Marcobrunn. At a higher elevation, the renowned STEINBERG vineyard lies in its entirety within the Hattenheim commune, but all the wines are only sold as Steinbergers. Besides these two vineyards, Hattenheim has several other fine vineyards or EINZELLAGEN; the most famous are: Nussbrunnen, Mannberg, Wisselbrunnen, Engelmannsberg, Pfaffenberg, and Schutzenhaus.

Haut-Brion, Château *(Oh-bree-awn')*: Famous BORDEAUX wine estate, located in the region of GRAVES. Owned by C. Douglas Dillon, an American banker, Château Haut-Brion regularly produces some of Bordeaux's best wines and was the only red wine château

134

outside the MÉDOC region to be included in the 1855 Bordeaux classification. The vineyard consists of 104 acres, most of which are planted in red grape varieties (Cabernet, Merlot), but a small amount of rare white (blanc) Haut-Brion is also made. Annual production averages about 11,000 cases of the red wine; less than 900 cases of the white.

Haut-Médoc *(Oh May-dawk′)*: The central and best portion of the MÉDOC region, north of the city of BORDEAUX. Virtually all of the red wine estates (CHÂTEAUX) that were officially classified in 1855 are located in the Haut-Médoc; for regional wines, Haut-Médoc is also an APPELLATION CONTRÔLÉE, and wines bearing this name will usually be superior to those labeled ''Médoc,'' which normally come from the less favored Bas-Médoc region in the north. The Haut-Médoc district includes the outstanding wine communes of SAINT-ESTÈPHE, PAUILLAC, SAINT-JULIEN, and MARGAUX.

Hectare *(Heck′-tar)*: Metric measure of area, equivalent to 10,000 square meters or 2.471 U.S. acres. For simplicity, hectares have been converted to acres throughout this dictionary.

Hectoliter *(Heck′-toe-liter)*: Metric measure of volume, equivalent to 100 liters or 26.4179 U.S. gallons. A hectoliter is also abbreviated as ''hecto.'' In this dictionary, for simplicity, production statistics specified in hectoliters have been converted into cases of 2.31 U.S. gallons each.

Hérault *(Air-ro′)*: Department or administrative region in southern France, located on the Mediterranean coast. A part of the MIDI district, the Hérault is France's largest vineyard area: over 400,000 acres are currently in production. Most of the land is given over to ordinary grape varieties for use in bulk wine production and VERMOUTH bases, but

135

there are a few notable wine regions; the sweet Muscat wines of FRONTIGNAN and LUNEL are world-famous, and the many good red wines of FAUGÈRES and the MINERVOIS are increasingly important in the export trade, being inexpensive and good value.

Hermitage *(Air'-me-tahj)*: Famous wine of the northern RHÔNE River valley, France, produced near the ancient town of Tain, which has assumed its name to become Tain-l'Hermitage. Some good white Hermitage is produced from Roussanne or Marsanne grapes, but the more plentiful red Hermitage is superior, and it is world-renowned. Made primarily from the Syrah grape, usually with a small amount of white grapes added for finesse, Hermitage is one of the most fruity and full-bodied Rhône wines and is exceptionally long-lived. There are 376 acres entitled to the APPELLATION CONTRÔLÉE Hermitage; the area is surrounded by the region of CROZES-HERMITAGE, which produces similar but slightly less distinctive wines. Traditionally, the Hermitage vineyards are divided into little parcels called *mas,* but few of these names appear on labels today and many so-called *mas* are actually trade names. About 40,000 cases of red and white Hermitage are produced annually.

Hessische Bergstrasse *(Hessis'-shuh Bairg'-strass-uh)*: The smallest wine region or ANBAUGEBIET in Germany, located on the right bank of the Rhine River north of the city of Heidelberg. The region is only about 700 acres large, and Hessische Bergstrasse wines were formerly sold along with those of BADEN before the region was officially delimited in 1971; Bensheim, Heppenheim, Zwingenberg and Auerbach are its most important towns. Hessische Bergstrasse wines are rarely seen on the export market, but the region makes some good white wines from the Riesling; total annual production is approximately 230,000 cases.

Hochheim *(Hawk'-heim)***:** Village and wine region in the most eastern portion of the RHEINGAU district, Germany, with some 470 acres of vineyard. Hochheim is located on the River Main, a tributary of the Rhine; its fine white wines are celebrated for their characteristic mellowness. Long popular in England, the wines of Hochheim lent their name to the nickname ''Hock,'' a word that now describes Rhine wines in general. The two most famous vineyards or EINZELLAGEN are Kirchenstück and Domdechaney (the latter means ''deanery,'' a name that also applies to an outstanding Hochheim producer, Domdechant Werner'sches Weingut); other fine vineyards include: Stielweg, Hölle, Stein, Hofmeister, Berg, Reichesthal, and Herrnberg. The Königin Viktoria Berg vineyard, named after Queen Victoria of England, is the exclusive property of the Neus company in Ingelheim.

Hogshead: A cask of varying capacity, used for wines, spirits and beers. It applies generally to the *barrique* of BORDEAUX and the pièce of BURGUNDY, each of which hold about 225 liters (25 cases), but the hogshead cask used for sherry, port and whiskey is somewhat larger. The name hogshead is said to derive from *oxhoft,* an old Germanic word, and ordinary casks were called hogsheads during the Middle Ages.

Hospices de Beaune *(Awss'-peace duh Bone')***:** A charity hospital located in the city of BEAUNE, Burgundy, built in 1443 by Nicholas Rolin, chancellor to the duke of Burgundy. The Hospices derives most of its revenues from the wines it sells, produced from a number of fine vineyard holdings throughout the CÔTE DE BEAUNE. Following each year's vintage, the Hospices sells its new

137

wines at an auction traditionally held on the third Sunday of November, and the prices paid for them are a fairly accurate gauge of Burgundy prices for that year's vintage; the quantity also indicates the size of production. The Hospices' holdings consist of about 136 acres planted in both red and white grapes, and typically about 600 casks *(pièces)* of wine are offered at auction, equivalent to approximately 15,700 cases.

All Hospices de Beaune wines are indicated by the name of the original donor who bequeathed the vineyard to the Hospices: Nicholas Rolin, Guigone de Salins, Charlotte Dumay, Docteur Peste, Dames de la Charité, Jehan Humblot, etc. There are some quality differences between them, depending on the location of the holdings, but in general most Hospices de Beaune wines are well-made. They are not inexpensive, but the buyer is assured that the premium he pays contributes to a worthy cause.

Hungary: The many fine wines of Hungary are more significant on the U.S. market than those of any other eastern European country. Hungarian wines have been famous for centuries, though nationalization of the wine industry following World War II has definitely improved their overall quality. The export of quality Hungarian wines is now in the hands of Monimpex, the state export monopoly, whose central cellars are in Budafok, south of the city of Budapest. Monimpex selects only quality wines for export and stamps each bottle with a government seal of authenticity, with the result that most Hungarian wine shipped to the U.S. is generally quite sound.

Hungarian wines normally take the name of the district where they were grown, plus the grape variety. They are characteristically full-flavored —robust reds *(Vörös)* and sturdy whites *(Fehér)* are ideal complements to the spicy national cuisine. Commercially the most important wine region in Hungary is the Great Plain *(Alföld)*, extending over much of the middle half of the country with over 284,000 acres planted in vines. But Hungary's finest wines are produced from vineyards at higher elevations, such as those at TOKAY in the extreme northeast of the country. The most famous Hungarian wine district, Tokay makes a luscious, golden sweet wine from the Furmint, a native variety that is also used to make dry wines. The red Kadarka is Hungary's other leading native grape. It is used for the wines of Eger, produced on the slopes of the Mátra Mountains to the west of Tokay. Eger is celebrated for EGRI BIKAVÉR ("Bull's Blood of Eger"); several other good wines are also made there. Many wine-lovers maintain that VILLÁNY in the south produces the best red wine of Hungary, made from the Nagyburgundi (Pinot Noir). Szekzárd, to the north—and Hajós, in the Alföld—are other leading red wine areas.

70% of all Hungarian wines are white. The most widely-grown white wine grape, Olaszrizling (or Wälschriesling), is used for ordinary wine. The Hárslevelü, named for the odd lime shape of its leaves, gives a superior white wine, of which DEBRÖI HÁRSLEVELÜ is an outstanding example, Leányka, another important white grape, is grown in many wine regions—most successfully in Eger. Hungary has the largest lake in Europe, Lake Balaton; on its north shore an extinct volcano, Mount Badacsony, rises up to provide a perfect location for the famous vineyards of BADACSONY. Two particularly good white wines, Badacsonyi Kéknyelü and Badacsonyi Szürkebarát, are among Hungary's most flavorful. The towns of Somló and Mór to the north are other leading white wine areas; the former is famous for its Furmints and Rizlings, the latter for Ezerjó.

Hybrid: In viticulture, a cross between two

different kinds of grapes or vines, usually accomplished by seedlings rather than cuttings, which is the normal way that vines are propagated in the world's vineyards. A common example of a hybrid is a cross between a European species, Vitis VINIFERA, and an American species, Vitis LABRUSCA; years of experiments in France and the U.S. resulted in hybrids such as Seyve-Villard, Chancellor Noir, Seibel, Couderc, Baco Noir, Foch, de Chaunac, Aurora, and others. Not all hybrids produce wines with ideal characteristics, but their chief advantage lies in resistance to cold and disease, making them desirable in many regions in the U.S.

New grapes can also be produced from crossing two varieties of vinifera. In conjunction with the science of CLONES, botanists now seek to perfect "super grapes" made from crossing two noble varieties, which have been specially adapted to specific areas or climates. A well-known example is the Müller-Thurgau, a cross between the Riesling and the Silvaner that is primarily grown in Germany; other successful crosses include such varieties as Scheurebe (also a Riesling/Silvaner cross), Siegerrebe, Kerner, Optima, Emerald Riesling, Ruby Cabernet, etc. The latter two were developed in California to produce quality wines in warm climatic regions.

Hydrometer: An instrument used to measure the amount of sugar in grape musts (see MUST WEIGHT), based on the principle that a sugar solution has a higher density or specific gravity than water. Grape must hydrometers are usually calibrated to indicate the amount of sugar present in grams per 100 grams of solution. The Brix or Balling scale hydrometer is in general use in the U.S.; in Germany and Switzerland, the ÖCHSLE scale is preferred.

I

Ihringen *(Ear'-ring-en)*: Little town west of the city of Freiburg in the region of BADEN, Germany, with some 740 acres of vineyard. Located in the section of Baden known as the KAISERSTUHL, Ihringen is famous for its fine white wines made from the Ruländer (Pinot Gris) grape, among Baden's best. The leading vineyards (EINZELLAGEN) are Castellberg, Kreuzhalde, Fohrenberg, Steinfelsen, Schlossberg and Winklerberg; one excellent vineyard, the Doktorgarten, is owned by the wine estate of Blankenhornsberg.

Impériale *(Em-pay'-ree-ahl')*: An oversize wine bottle occasionally used in the BORDEAUX district, with the capacity of eight ordinary bottles.

Inferno *(In-fair'-no)*: Outstanding red wine produced in the VALTELLINA district, in the region of LOMBARDY. Made from the Nebbiolo grape, which in the Valtellina is called Chiavennasca, Inferno is the most renowned of the robust Valtellina wines, slow to develop but with impeccable balance at maturity.

Ingelheim *(Ing'-el-heim)*: Town and wine region in the RHEINHESSEN district, Germany, with over 1,000 acres of vineyard. Located on the left bank of the Rhine River and facing the village of JOHANNISBERG, Ingelheim is one of the few regions in Germany that specialize in the making of red wines; some white wine of slightly lesser quality is also made. Kaiserpfalz is the best-known wine name in Ingelheim, but it is important to know that this is a composite vineyard or GROSSLAGE; the leading single vine-

141

yards (EINZELLAGEN) are: Horn, Pares, Rheinhohe, Burgberg, and Hollenweg.

Iphofen *(Ip'-hawf-en)*: One of the leading wine villages of the district of FRANKEN (Franconia), Germany. Its 306 acres of vineyard are mostly planted in Silvaner; the wines are shipped in the squat BOCKS-BEUTEL bottles native to the Franken region. The vineyards or EINZELLAGEN include: Julius-Echter-Berg, Kronsberg, and Kalb.

Ischia *(Isk'-ee-ah)*: Picturesque little island west of the city of Naples in the region of CAMPANIA, Italy, famous for its good red and white wines rated D.O.C. Certain select Ischian white wines produced in better vineyards are called Ischia Bianco Superiore.

Israel: Wine has been produced in the Palestine region since the dawn of history. The vine suffered under centuries of Moslem rule, but in the 1880s under the direction of Baron Edmond de Rothschild, large-scale vineyard plantings were begun and a developing wine industry sprang up in Israel; with independence in 1948 success was assured.

Israel's mediterranean climate is hot and semi-arid, but modern techniques produce quality wines that rival many others from cooler climates. The new method of drip-flow irrigation introduced in Israel is now in wide use in many parts of the world, and while Israel's vineyards were originally planted in ordinary high-yield varieties, today a trend is developing towards premium wines made from better varieties such as Cabernet Sauvignon, Sauvignon Blanc, Sémillon and Chenin Blanc. Currently there are over 13,000 acres of vineyard planted in wine grapes.

Israel's vineyards are scattered, but many lie near the coast. The largest and most famous is located at Richon-le-Zion to the south of Tel Aviv; another leading area is to the north, at Zichron-Jacob. Together, these two areas produce over 75% of Israel's wine. Their Kosher products are made under Rabbinical supervision, and the U.S. is an important market.

A majority of Israeli wine exported to the U.S. is marketed by the Carmel Wine Co., which offers many good wines. The lower quality grades are not given GENERIC names such as ''chablis'' because Israel respects the Madrid Convention, restricting these names to the original location. Instead, brand names like ''Adom Atic'' and ''Avdat'' are used. A wide range of good VARIETAL table wines is offered, and ''The President's Sparkling Wine,'' bottle-fermented by the traditional Champagne process, is internationally famous.

Italy: Italy is truly a paradise of vineyards. Wine is produced in every part of the country, from the arid barrens of Sicily to the precipitous alpine slopes in the north. With a winemaking heritage dating back 2,000 years, Italy is the largest supplier of wine to America; the total increases each year. By a comfortable margin, Italy is the world's largest wine-producing country, and she is also the world's foremost wine exporting country.

The variety of Italian wines dazzles the imagination. Scores of different grape varieties are grown throughout the country; many indigenous varieties are grown nowhere else in the world. The average Italian considers wine-drinking a natural part of everyday life, yet most Italians do not trouble themselves with the quality of the wines they drink. Much wine is not even bottled, and is usually and properly consumed before its first year.

For centuries, wine-making in Italy was performed mainly by tradition handed down by father to son, and only recently has science

143

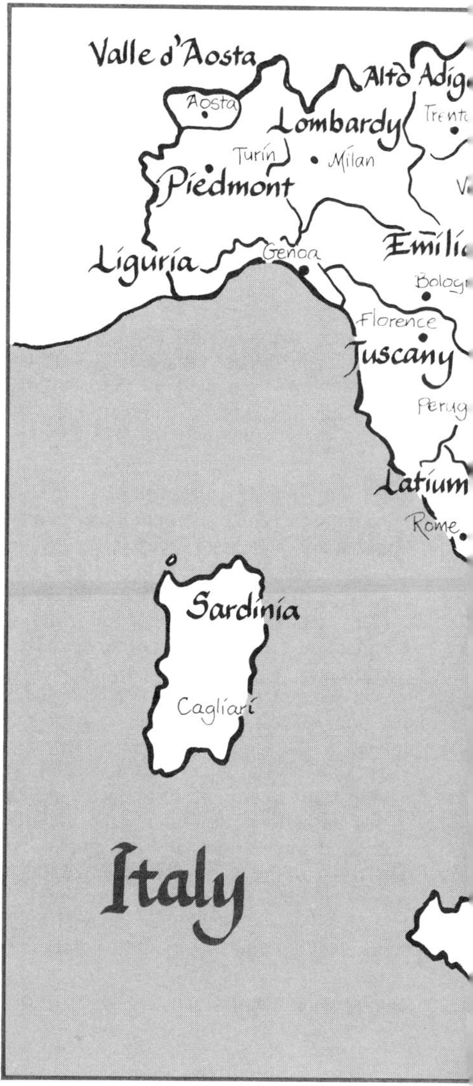
Valle d'Aosta
Aosta
Lombardy
Turin
Milan
Piedmont
Liguria
Genoa
Bologna
Florence
Tuscany
Latium
Rome
Sardinia
Cagliari
Italy

tino

Friuli-Venezia Giulia

• Udine

:to

nagna

Ancosta

Marches

bria

L'Aquila

Abruzzo Molise

Campobasso

ampania

Naples

Rari

Apulia

Potenza

Basilicata

Calabria

Reggio di Calabria

e

cily

played an important role in improving the quality of Italian wines. For this reason, the overall quality of Italian wine exports in the past was very uneven. Italian wines were symbolized by the wickered *fiasco* flask of the CHIANTI region: pleasant to drink when young, but hardly anything great. But following Italy's membership into the European Common Market, in 1963 the Italian government took steps to codify wine legislation by enacting the DENOMINAZIONE DI ORIGINE CONTROLLATA (D.O.C.) laws, which outlined specific place-names and delimited viticultural districts according to the best sites. In practice, only potentially fine wines are entitled to a D.O.C. rating, and an inspection period is required before D.O.C. status is officially granted. Excellent and even great wines were of course produced in Italy long before the D.O.C. laws were enacted, but not many of them ever left the country. In the past decade, the overall quality of Italian wines shipped to the U.S. has unquestionably improved, and much of the improvement can be attributed to the D.O.C. laws.

The simplest category of D.O.C. is *simplice* (simple), for ordinary wines without a quality guarantee. The next category, *controllata* (controlled), is the most important; it includes all of Italy's leading wines. The highest category, *controllata e garantita* (controlled and guaranteed), provides a government quality guarantee issued after an official examination of the wine by qualified experts. The last category is presently only in limited application, and few wines have been shipped with this label. But the fact that such provisions exist is indicative of the serious approach towards quality wines in Italy.

An additional quality control is the national network of *consorzi* (consortiums), which are voluntary organizations that set quality standards for wines of various regions. The most famous is that of the Chianti Classico region, which came into being nearly forty years before the D.O.C. laws were enacted. The *consorzi* have their own seals that are affixed to wine bottles, in addition to a red seal issued by the Italian government which attests that every drop of wine in that bottle is a product of Italy.

In general, Italy's finest wines are produced in the north, particularly red wines made from the Nebbiolo grape; the leading white wine grape is the Trebbiano. The region of PIEMONTE (Piedmont) is particularly noted for its sturdy red wines, of which BAROLO, BARBARESCO and GATTINARA rank with the world's best. The Nebbiolo also is used for the fine, slow-maturing reds of the VALTELLINA district to the east. The *Spumante* of ASTI is the most famous Italian sparkling wine.

The VENETO region to the southeast, near the city of Venice, produces SOAVE, VALPOLICELLA and BARDOLINO, probably the best-known Italian wines in the U.S. To the south is the EMILIA-ROMAGNA region, famous primarily for its sparkling red LAMBRUSCO that is very popular in the U.S. The region of TUSCANY is well-known for Chianti, but the fine red wines of BRUNELLO DI MONTALCINO and VINO NOBILE DI MONTEPULCIANO are equally acclaimed. The region of MARCHE gives the fine white wine VERDICCHIO, and UMBRIA to the southwest is noted for ORVIETO, another good white. The Rome region is praised for its light white wines, of which FRASCATI and other wines of the CASTELLI ROMANI district are well-known. The region of CAMPANIA near Naples is famous for LACRIMA CHRISTI and GRAGNANO; further south, three noteworthy red wines are made: SAN SEVERO in APULIA, AGLIANO DEL VULTURE in the Basilicata region, and CIRÒ from CALABRIA are already making a name for

147

themselves in the U.S. import trade.

No discussion of Italian wines would be complete without the fine FORTIFIED WINES of MARSALA, produced on the island of Sicily. Sicily as a whole, and the island of Sardinia, are expanding their vineyard acreage and increasing their production of quality wines.

J

Jerez *(Hair-eth′)*: Town in Andalusia, Spain, located north of the city of Cadiz; its full name is Jerez de la Frontera. The wines of Jerez have been called ''sherries'' since the Middle Ages.

Jeroboam: An oversized wine bottle used in the fine wine regions of France. The jeroboam of BORDEAUX has a capacity of five ordinary bottles; in the French CHAMPAGNE district, a jeroboam is equivalent to four regular bottles. No Champagnes are ever aged in jeroboams, however; they are decanted from smaller bottles following the process of DÉGORGEMENT.

Johannisberg *(Yo-hahn′-nis-bairg)*: World-famous wine village in the RHEINGAU district, Germany, with some 450 acres of vineyard. The villages is renowned principally for its leading wine estate, Schloss Johannisberg (see JOHANNISBERG, SCHLOSS), one of the Rheingau's most famous, but Johannisberg has several other fine vineyards or EINZELLAGEN: Klaus, Vogelsang, Hölle, Mittelhölle, Hansenberg, Goldatzel, and Schwarzenstein. Johannisbergers are typically among the best wines of the Rheingau, but it is important to know that under the 1971 German Wine Law, Johannis-

148

berg is also the name of a sub-region or BEREICH, and a wine labeled "Bereich Johannisberg" is simply a regional wine made anywhere in the Rheingau—in all likelihood, not from a vineyard in Johannisberg itself. To be sure of getting the best, one should look for an estate-bottled wine (ERZEUGER-ABFÜLLUNG) from a leading producer.

Johannisberg is also the name used in Switzerland for a wine made from the Sylvaner grape, most often in the canton of VALAIS.

Johannisberg Riesling *(Yo-hahn'-nis-bairg Reese'-ling)*: Name given in California to the true Riesling of Germany (also called White Riesling), to distinguish it from other grapes grown in California that, despite their name, are unrelated. Such varieties include: Franken Riesling (Sylvaner), Grey Riesling, Emerald Riesling and Main Riesling.

The Johannisberg Riesling in California generally gives rather different and drier wines than in Germany, but under the right conditions it can ripen fully in a late harvest under the action of the "noble mold" (BOTRYTIS CINEREA) to make what are unquestionably the best sweet wines of California. 8,300 acres have been planted throughout the state.

Johannisberg, Schloss: Outstanding wine estate in the RHEINGAU district, Germany, producing some of the most famous wines in the world. The estate consists of about 87 acres planted in Riesling, located on a high slope overlooking the Rhine River; the wines are prized for their scent and concentration. Since 1816 the Schloss has belonged to the von Metternich family, but vines have been grown on the property since 871 A.D.

The estate bottles its fine white wines under two different labels: the regular label bears the von Metternich coat of arms against a plain background; the much rarer Schloss

149

label, formerly used to indicate a private reserve or *Cabinet,* is a colored engraving showing a view of the Schloss from across the Rhine. Because the two labels have different colored capsules, the various quality categories and their markings are as follows:

REGULAR LABEL

	Capsule	*Color*
QUALITATSWEIN b.A.	Gelblack	yellow
KABINETT	Rotlack	red
SPATLESE	Grünlack	green
AUSLESE	Rosalack	pink
BEERENAUSLESE	Rosa-Goldlack	gold with pink stripe
TROCKENBEERENAUSLESE	——	——

SCHLOSS LABEL

	Capsule	*Color*
QUALITATSWEIN b.A.	——	——
KABINETT	Orangenlack	orange
SPATLESE	Weisslack	white
AUSLESE	Himmelblaulack	sky blue
BEERENAUSLESE	Blau-Goldlack	gold with blue stripe
TROCKENBEERENAUSLESE	Goldlack	gold

In addition, some sparkling wine is made under the label of Fürst von Metternich Prädikats-Sekt.

Josephshof *(Yo'-zefs-hof)*: One of the best vineyards in the MOSEL River valley, Germany. The Josephshof is officially located in the village of GRAACH, yet the wines are not sold as Graachs but under the name of Josephshöfer. Owned exclusively by the von Kesselstatt Company, a leading shipper headquarted in Trier, the vineyard consists of 25 acres planted in Riesling, and regularly produces some of the Mosel's best wines—typically full-flavored and very fine.

Juliénas *(Jule-yay'-nahss)*: Wine region in the BEAUJOLAIS district, southern Burgundy; also the name of its fine red wine. Officially classified as one of the *crus* (growths), which regularly produce outstanding Beaujolais, Juliénas is one of the better ones, usually with a characteristic firmness that makes it relatively slow to mature. There are currently 1,125 acres of vineyard; average annual production is about 206,000 cases of fine red wine.

Jura *(Shur'-ra)*: Mountain range, administrative region (department) and wine region in eastern France, near the Swiss border. The Jura was formerly a large, important wine region, but today there are less than 2,000 acres of vineyard—a fraction of the former total. Its light red, white and rosé wines are not well-known outside the region, but are noted for their quality and variety. Commercially the most important wines are those of ARBOIS, in particular the sturdy rosés; traditionally the rare CHÂTEAU-CHALON, legally required to age six years in cask, is the most famous Jura wine. Another wine, L'Etoile, is equally celebrated but is extremely rare.

Jurançon *(Shur-awn-sawn')*: Wine region in southwest France near the Spanish border, south of the city of Pau. Three grape varieties — Courbu, Gros Manseng and Petit Manseng — are used to make the fine white wines of Jurançon. The vineyards are planted on the slopes of the Pyrénées, and the grapes are often harvested in the late autumn when overripe to make luscious sweet wines; unfortunately, because of high production costs, these excellent wines are now becoming rare. A much larger quantity of less distinguished dry white wine is now produced. The vineyard area of Jurançon extends over about 1,250 acres; average annual production is approximately 171,500 cases.

151

K

Kabinett *(Kab-ee-nett′)*: German for "cabinet." Under the 1971 German Wine Law, Kabinett is the most basic grade of QUALITÄTSWEIN MIT PRÄDIKAT (Quality Wine with Special Attributes). Kabinett derives from *Cabinet,* a term coined in the 19th century by the Duke of Nassau for his special wine reserves at KLOSTER EBERBACH in the RHEINGAU district. The 1971 Wine Law provides that only the spelling Kabinett may be used, and that this term indicates a wine made solely from ripe grapes that have not received any addition of sugar.

The legal minimum MUST WEIGHT requirements for Kabinett vary by area, but in general a Kabinett is the least expensive and driest wine in the *Prädikat* categories that a producer has to offer. See QUALITÄTSWEIN.

Kadarka *(Kah′-dark-ah)*: Red grape variety grown in Hungary and Romania. It is the principal variety used to make EGRI BIKAVÉR, perhaps Hungary's best-known red wine.

Kaiserstuhl *(Kuy′-zer-shtool)*: A hilly volcanic outcropping in the region of BADEN, southern Germany. The Kaiserstuhl (which means "emperor's seat" in German) is part of the BEREICH (sub-region) Kaiserstuhl-Tuniberg. With the exception of Endingen, its northern slopes generally do not yield any wines of great distinction; the southern slopes, particularly the vineyards of IHRINGEN, Achkarren, Bötzingen and Bickensohl, often produce the best white wines of Baden, especially if planted in Ruländer (Pinot Gris).

152

Kallstadt *(Kahl'-shtat)*: Noted wine village in the RHEINPFALZ (Palatinate) region, Germany, with 715 acres of vineyard. Kallstadt lies just to the north of DÜRKHEIM, and its fine wines are similar but are not well-known outside Germany. The leading vineyards (EINZELLAGEN) include: Annaberg, Horn, Kirchenstück, Kreidkeller, Kronenberg, Nill, and Steinacker.

Kalterersee *(Kahl'-ter-rer-zay')*: German for CALDARO, a lake located in the region of ALTO ADIGE, northern Italy. This spelling may sometimes be found on wine labels destined for markets where German is spoken.

Kanzem *(Kahnt'-zem)*: Noted wine village in the SAAR River valley, Germany, with some 300 acres of vineyard — nearly all of them planted in Riesling. The fresh white wines of Kanzem, usually a bit more full-bodied than others of the Saar, closely rival those of WILTINGEN just to the east. The leading vineyards (EINZELLAGEN) include: Altenberg, Hörecker, Schlossberg, and Sonnenberg.

Kasel *(Kah'-zel)*: Little village on the RUWER River, Germany, with 215 acres of vineyard. The largest wine community or *Weinbauort* in the Ruwer district, Kasel is famous for its fine white wines made from the Riesling. The most famous vineyard (EINZELLAGE) is Nies'chen, but Kehrnagel, Herrenberg, Hitzlay, Paulinsberg and Timpert can also produce memorable wines.

Keller: German for "cellar."

Kelter: German for "wine press."

Kiedrich *(Keed'-rich)*: Celebrated wine village in the RHEINGAU district, Germany, with 430 acres of vineyard; most of them planted in Riesling. Often one of the outstanding Rheingau villages in hot years, Kiedrich

153

boasts several fine vineyards or EINZELLAGEN: Gräfenberg, Sandgrub, Wasseros (or Wasserrose), and Klosterberg.

Kir *(Keer)*: Refreshing wine apéritif, made with a light, dry white wine and a little crème de cassis liqueur. The classic formula calls for a Bourgogne Aligoté and crème de cassis from Dijon. It is named for the late Canon Félix Kir, former major of the city of Dijon, whose favorite drink it was.

Klevner *(Clayv'-ner)*: The local name for the Pinot Blanc grape in the region of ALSACE, France. In BADEN, Germany, under the spelling *Clevner*, this term applies to the Traminer grape.

Kloster Eberbach *(Klaws'-ter Eh'-ber-bock)*: Historic medieval monastery in the RHEINGAU district, Germany, located in the commune of HATTENHEIM. The Kloster was constructed in the 12th century by Cistercian monks, who later planted a walled vineyard nearby: the famous STEINBERG. The Kloster Eberbach presently belongs to the German State, and has been preserved as a wine museum. The Kloster is the location for the annual wine auctions held by the Staats-weingut in Eltville, and bottles that have been sold there at auction often bear a small seal stating: "Ersteigert im Kloster Eberbach" (auctioned at Kloster Eberbach).

Königsbach *(Ker'-nigs-bock)*: Wine village in the RHEINPFALZ (Palatinate) district, Germany, located just to the south of RUPPERTSBERG. Although excellent, the wines are not well-known outside of Germany. The vineyards (EINZELLAGEN) include: Idig, Jesuitengarten, Ölberg, and Reiterpfad.

Kosher Wine: By definition, a wine used for sacramental purposes during Jewish religious services. According to Rabbinical law, all

Kosher wine must be pure, unmixed, and produced under strict Rabbinical supervision. There are no restrictions on the type of grape or grapes that go into making it, though in the U.S. most Kosher wines are usually made from the Concord, with cane sugar added to give it characteristic sweetness.

Krems: One of the most famous wine towns in Austria, located in the WACHAU district on the Danube River west of the city of Vienna. A picturesque old village, Krems is noted for its fine white wines made from the Rheinriesling and Grüner Veltliner grapes.

Kreuznach *(Kroytz'-nock)*: City on the NAHE River, Germany; the largest Nahe wine commune and the center of its wine trade. Because of its famous mineral spas, it is officially called Bad Kreuznach. Its vineyards are among the Nahe's best, but it is important to know that under the 1971 German Wine Law, Kreuznach is also the name of a sub-region or BEREICH, and that a "Kreuznacher" without a vineyard name is merely a regional wine that could come from dozens of villages within the Kreuznach Bereich. To be sure of getting the best, one should specify one of the leading Kreuznach vineyards or EINZELLAGEN: Narrenkappe, Mönchberg, Hinkelstein, Brückes, Krötenpfuhl, Kahlenberg, St. Martin, and Kauzenberg. Vineyards from neighboring villages have recently been incorporated into the Kreuznach municipality, with the result that the area under vines is now in excess of 2,700 acres.

Kröv *(Kruhv)*: Little village on the MOSEL River, Germany; also occasionally spelled Cröv. It has achieved considerable fame on account of a comic name given to one of its vineyards, Nacktarsch, which means "naked bottom." The wines bear a label showing a small boy being spanked, with his trousers down, in punishment for drinking in the wine cellar.

The 1971 German Wine Law authorized Nacktarsch to be the name of a composite vineyard or GROSSLAGE, and while Kröv has six vineyards or EINZELLAGEN (Burglay, Herrenberg, Kirchlay, Letterlay, Paradies, and Steffensberg), the Grosslage name will usually be used because it is better-known.

L

Labrusca *(La-broos'-ca)*: A species of grape vines native to the American continent; its full name is *Vitis labrusca*. Grown chiefly in the eastern United States, labrusca grape varieties are quite different from the European or East Asian species, Vitis VINIFERA. Concord, Delaware, Catawba, Ives, Noah, Niagara, and others are common examples of labrusca grape varieties.

Lacrima Christi *(La'-creem-ah Kreest'-ee)*: Italian for "Christ's Tears"; specifically, a golden white wine produced on the southern slopes of Mt. Vesuvius near the city of Naples, in the region of CAMPANIA, Italy. A little red wine is also made. Lacrima Christi has been famous for centuries, but has not yet received a D.O.C. rating; its name has often been used freely by producers outside of the original region, for their white wines.

Ladoix-Serrigny *(La-dwah' Serr-een-yee')*: Secondary wine commune with about 340 acres of vineyard in the CÔTE DE BEAUNE, Burgundy, adjoining the commune of ALOXE-CORTON. Very little wine is marketed under the name Ladoix-Serrigny, as most producers prefer to label their wines under the name CÔTE DE BEAUNE-

VILLAGES, which is allowed by law. The best wines are generally sold either as CORTON or CORTON-CHARLEMAGNE.

Lafite-Rothschild, Château *(La-feet' Rawt'-shield)*: Perhaps the most famous red wine of BORDEAUX, and one of the most celebrated wines in the world. The Lafite vineyard is many centuries old; it takes its name from the de Rothschilds, a French family of bankers who have owned the property since 1868. The vineyard lies in the MÉDOC district within the commune of PAUILLAC; the area under vines is approximately 200 acres, and production annually averages about 20,000 cases of especially elegant and refined claret, officially rated Premier Cru (First Growth).

Lage *(Log'-uh)*: German for "location" or "site," a term used in connection with an officially delimited vineyard. Under the 1971 German Wine Law, an EINZELLAGE denotes an individual vineyard of at least 12 acres in size; a GROSSLAGE is composed of a number of different Einzellagen.

Lagrein *(La-grine')*: Red grape variety grown in the regions of TRENTINO and ALTO ADIGE, northern Italy; used for light red wines and rosés.

Lalande-de-Pomerol *(La-lawnd' duh Pawm-uh-roll')*: Secondary red wine district in the BORDEAUX region, located north of the commune of POMEROL. The many good wines of Lalande-de-Pomerol are similar to Pomerols, but are usually not quite as fine; the leading wine estates (CHÂTEAUX) include: Bel-Air, de la Commanderie, Moulin-à-Vent, Perron, Canon-Chaigneau, and Garraud.

157

Lambrusco *(Lom-bruce'-co)*: Famous red sparkling wine produced near the city of Modena in the region of EMILIA-ROMAGNA,

Italy. Lambrusco is made from a grape of the same name in three designated communes: Sorbara, Grasparossa, and Salamino, each of them rated D.O.C. By law the sparkle in a Lambrusco must come from natural fermentation — any addition of carbon dioxide is forbidden. Lambrusco is a light, refreshing and usually inexpensive red wine; ideally, it should be drunk young.

Languedoc *(Long-uh-dock')*: Old French province, now divided up into five smaller administrative regions or departments: Lozère, Gard, HÉRAULT, AUDE, and Pyrénées-Orientales. The Hérault, Aude and Gard are, in that order, the three largest wine-producing departments in France; most of their output is ordinary wine, either used for VERMOUTH manufacture or for blending purposes, but there are a few exceptions, such as the fine Muscat of FRONTIGNAN and the good red wine of FITOU. See CLAIRETTE, CORBIÈRES, and MINERVOIS.

Latour, Château *(La-tour')*: One of the very greatest red wines of BORDEAUX, officially rated Premier Cru (First Growth). Named for an ancient fortress ·that still stands on the property, the Latour vineyard consists of some 150 acres of choice land located in the commune . of PAUILLAC in the MÉDOC district; annual · production averages about 16,000 cases of very distinguished red wine — initially hard and slow to develop, but with incomparable excellence at maturity. The estate also produces a second wine from young vines called Les Forts de Latour, which is somewhat less expensive.

Latricières-Chambertin *(La-treese-yair' Shawm'-bear-tan)*: World-famous red wine vineyard in the northern CÔTE DE NUITS, Burgundy, rated Grand Cru (Great Growth). The Latricières-Chambertin vineyard extends over 17½ acres planted in Pinot Noir, and shares practically the same ideal soil and exposure as the great CHAMBERTIN vineyard, which lies alongside it. About 2,600 cases of especially rich and full-bodied red Burgundy are produced each year.

Lavaux *(La-vo')***:** Wine district in the canton of VAUD, Switzerland, located on the north shore of Lake Geneva. Some of Switzerland's best white wines made from the Dorin (Chasselas) grape are produced in Lavaux, particularly those of DÉZALEY and SAINT-SAPHORIN.

Lazio *(Lots'-ee-o)***:** Italian for "Latium," the region surrounding the city of Rome. Its vineyards have furnished wine for the capital since the days of the Roman Empire, and are most famous for their fresh white wines that are best consumed when quite young. One of the most famous of all Italian white wines is EST! EST! EST!, made to the north of Rome around the village of Montefiascone. To the south, the many excellent white wines of the CASTELLI ROMANI region — FRASCATI, COLLI ALBANI, Marino, and Colli Lanuvini — are also renowned and have officially been granted D.O.C. status. A good Lazio red wine is CESANESE, produced near the town of Frosinone. The Lazio region as a whole typically produces in excess of 57 million cases of wine, mostly white.

Lees: The residue or gross sediment thrown off by a wine soon after it is made. Most fine wines are allowed to age in cask following vinification, and when most of the lees have settled to the bottom of the cask, the clarified wine is siphoned off into another container during the process of RACKING.

Léognan *(Lay'-own-yawn)***:** Wine commune in the region of GRAVES, located south of the city of BORDEAUX. Léognan has the highest concentration of classified vineyards of any Graves commune; the top wine estates

159

(CHÂTEAUX) are: Domaine de Chevalier, Haut-Bailly, Carbonnieux, Malartic-Lagravière, Olivier, and Fieuzal.

Libourne *(Lee-boorn′)*: City in southwest France, located on the DORDOGNE River twenty miles to the east of the city of BORDEAUX. Libourne is the center of the wine trade for such notable regions as SAINT-ÉMILION, POMEROL, CÔTES-CANON-FRONSAC, CÔTES-DE-FRONSAC, and others.

Liebfraumilch *(Leeb′-frow-milsch)*: German for "milk of the Blessed Mother," a trade name for a mild, blended white wine that has become one of the most widely-used German wine terms. The name Liebfraumilch is said to derive from the Liebfrauenstift vineyard near the city of Worms in the RHEINHESSEN district, but as the vineyard is only 26 acres large, it could hardly supply the millions of gallons of white wine annually sold as Liebfraumilch.

Following official sanction in 1910, many different wines were sold quite freely under the name Liebfraumilch. The 1971 German Wine Law outlined the legal requirements for wines of this type: all wines sold as Liebfraumilch must meet the minimum standards for QUALITÄTSWEIN, and be the exclusive product of vineyards in the Rhine region. No indication of the grape varieties used may appear on the label, nor any of the specific categories of QUALITÄTSWEIN MIT PRÄDIKAT, but the wines must be sound and are subject to an official inspection before they are released for sale.

Wine experts usually disparage Liebfraumilch, perhaps excessively, but they do maintain (with some justification) that to buy Liebfraumilch is to disregard other fine wines of the Rheinhessen region — especially the pure, unblended wines that are characteristic of their area of origin.

160

Liguria *(Lee-goor'-ya)*: One of Italy's smaller wine regions, situated along the Italian Riviera. Its economic and geographic center is the city of Genoa. Although not many of Liguria's wines are exported, they have been famous for centuries — particularly the sweet white wine of CINQUETERRE, which was considered the best Italian wine during the Renaissance; the red DOLCEAQUA, made from the Rossesse grape, is also acclaimed.

Lillet *(Lee-lay')*: The proprietary name for a French wine-based apéritif produced in Bordeaux. In its most usual form it is white and semi-dry, although a less well-known red Lillet is also produced.

Limoux *(Lee-moo')*: City in southern France near the ancient fortress of Carcassonne, in the department of AUDE. It is known chiefly for a locally famous, semi-dry white sparkling wine, Blanquette de Limoux, which has an APPELLATION CONTRÔLÉE rating.

Liqueur d'Expédition *(Lee-kerr' Dex-pay-deese'-syon)*: French for "shipping dosage," a mixture of cane sugar, wine, and sometimes brandy, added to wines in the French CHAMPAGNE district following the process of disgorging (see DÉGORGEMENT) before the wines are marketed. The amount of shipping dosage determines the sweetness of the Champagne. See DOSAGE.

Liqueur de Tirage *(Lee-kerr' duh Teer-rahj')*: French for "bottling dosage," a solution of pure cane sugar mixed with yeasts, added to the wine in the French CHAMPAGNE district so that a secondary fermentation occurs in the bottle, producing a sparkling wine. An essential step in the Champagne process, the bottling dosage is precisely calculated so that just the right degree of sparkle is achieved.

161

Lirac *(Lee'-rack)*: Wine region in southern

France, near the city of Avignon in the department of Gard. Lirac lies just to the north of TAVEL, and like Tavel is celebrated for its excellent rosés made from the Grenache grape, though because they are not as well-known, Liracs are usually less expensive. Some red and white wine of lesser quality is also made in Lirac. The equivalent of some 172,500 cases of wine is produced annually.

Listrac *(Leese'-trac)***:** Wine commune in the HAUT-MÉDOC district, north of the city of BORDEAUX. Though there are no classified growths (CRUS) in Listrac, there are a number of good estates or CHÂTEAUX that regularly produce fine red wine, entitled to the appellation Haut-Médoc and rated *cru bourgeois supérieur*. Leading estates include Châteaux Fourcas-Hosten, Fourcas-Dupré, Lestage, Sémeillan- Mazeu, and Pierre-Bibian.

Loire *(Lwahr)***:** One of France's principal rivers, originating in southern Burgundy and winding across the country for some 600 miles to its mouth in the Atlantic Ocean. An area rich in scenery and history, the Loire valley is also an immense vineyard area. For simplicity, the chief wine regions can be divided into three: upper, middle, and lower Loire.

The upper Loire produces white wines almost exclusively, from the Sauvignon Blanc and Chasselas grapes. The vineyards of POUILLY-SUR-LOIRE and SANCERRE are world-famous. The middle Loire or TOURAINE, around the city of Tours, produces some of the best red wines of the Loire from the Cabernet Franc grape; excellent examples are CHINON and BOURGUEIL. Fine white wines from the Chenin Blanc grape are also a Touraine specialty, such as those produced in VOUVRAY and MONTLOUIS. The lower Loire, between the cities of SAUMUR and Nantes, includes the district of ANJOU,

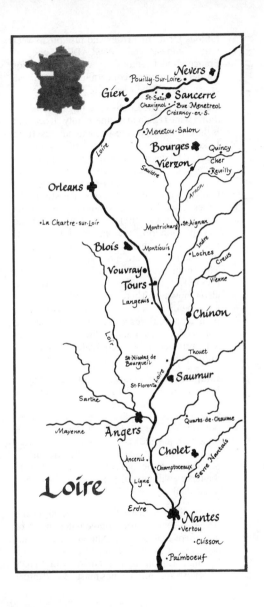

famous for its fine rosés and luscious, sweet white wines, and MUSCADET, one of France's most famous dry white wines. For further information concerning each of these areas, consult their separate headings.

Lombardy: The English spelling of *Lombardia,* a wine region in northern Italy. Its capital is the city of Milan; the area extends east from Lake Maggiore to Lake Garda (Lago di Garda), the largest lakes in Italy. Lake Garda is the source of some attractive light red and white wines, of which LUGANA (white) and CHIARETTO (red) are famous. The sturdy red wines made from the Nebbiolo grape in the VALTELLINA district to the north, near the city of Sondrio, are among Italy's best. Further south, the FRECCIAROSSA wines of the Odero estate are internationally famous. The numerous wines of the OLTREPÒ PAVESE region in the province of Pavia are also renowned. There are several other smaller wine districts in Lombardy — Botticino, Franciacorta, Barbacarlo, etc. — but they are not well-known outside the region. Total wine production is the equivalent of some 24 million cases a year.

Loupiac *(Loop'-ee-ack):* White wine region in the BORDEAUX district, on the right bank of the GARONNE River near the region of SAUTERNES. Loupiac forms the northern portion of the SAINTE-CROIX-DU-MONT region, and likewise specializes in sweet white wines made from the Sémillon, Sauvignon Blanc and Muscadelle, similar to Sauternes but generally heavier and less distinguished.

Ludon *(Loo'-dawn):* Wine commune in the HAUT-MÉDOC district, immediately north of the city of BORDEAUX. Although Ludon has one excellent estate or CHÂTEAU, La Lagune, Ludon is not an APPELLATION CONTRÔLÉE and its wines must be sold under

164

the appellation HAUT-MÉDOC. Besides La Lagune, there are several other lesser estates in Ludon: d'Aggasac, Lafitte-Canteloup, Pommies-Aggasac, d'Arches, and Nexon-Lemoyne.

Lugana *(Loo-gahn'-nah)*: Light, dry white wine produced near Lake Garda (Lago di Garda) in the region of LOMBARDY, northern Italy. One of the better Lake Garda white wines, Lugana is made from the Trebbiano grape, and is rated D.O.C.

Lugny *(Loon-yee')*: Village in the MÀCON district, Burgundy, famous for its good white wines made from the Chardonnay grape, which are entitled to the appellation Mâcon-Lugny.

Lunel *(Loo-nell')*: Town and wine region on France's Mediterranean coast, near the city of Nîmes in the department of HÉRAULT. Lunel lies 20 miles to the east of FRONTIGNAN, and likewise is celebrated for its sweet FORTIFIED WINE made from the Muscat grape, though Lunel is smaller and less important.

Lussac-Saint-Émilion *(Loo'-sack Sahnt Eh-meel-lyon')*: Red wine commune of secondary importance in the BORDEAUX district, officially part of the region of SAINT-ÉMILION. Lussac lies about 8 miles to the north of the village of Saint-Émilion; the soil is quite different and the wines are generally less fine, but many are quite good and represent excellent value.

Luxembourg *(Lukes'-em-boorg)*: The Grand Duchy of Luxembourg has about 3,000 acres of vineyard in the upper Moselle River valley, before the river flows into Germany and is called MOSEL. Light white wines are made from the Müller-Thurgau (Riesling x Sylvaner), Traminer, Riesling, and Ruländer grapes. The east-facing slopes of the Moselle

165

in certain villages — most notably, Remich, Grevenmacher, Ehnen, Wintringen, Wasser-billig, and Wormeldange — can produce some good wines, but few of them are seen on the U.S. market.

M

Mâcon *(Mah-cawn')*: City in southern BURGUNDY, an important center for the wine trade. Mâcon is also an APPELLATION CONTRÔLÉE for red, white and rosé wines produced in the region around the city; the region is called MÂCONNAIS in French. Usu-ally inexpensive and good value, the Mâcon wines — particularly the fresh, engaging whites — are very popular. They have several quality categories: Mâcon blanc (white), Mâcon rouge (red), and "Pinot Char-donnay-Mâcon," the latter indicating the grape variety from which the wine was made, applies to wines produced anywhere in the Mâcon region. "Mâcon" or "Mâcon Supérieur" indicates wines produced in the *arrondissement* (township) of Mâcon, a much smaller area. The word "Mâcon," followed by the name of the commune where the wine was made, applies to more distinctive white wines; these are also known as "Mâcon-Villages." Particularly outstanding white Mâcon-Villages wines are made in the areas of LUGNY and VIRÉ.

Mâconnais *(Mah-cawn-nay')*: Wine region in southern Burgundy, France, surrounding the city of MÂCON in the department of Saône-et-Loire. The Mâconnais extends southwards from the village of Sennecy-le-Grand down to the BEAUJOLAIS district; the region is celebrated for its fine white wines made from the Chardonnay grape, although some red Mâcon of lesser quality is also made from the Gamay. By far the most famous Mâconnais wine is POUILLY-FUISSÉ, produced in four communes southwest of Mâcon; surrounding Pouilly-Fuissé are the similarly fine regions of POUILLY-VINZELLES and POUILLY-LOCHÉ. A new appellation created in 1971, SAINT-VÉRAN, includes several villages near these areas but without right to their appellation. The total vineyard area in the Mâconnais region extends over some 7,400 acres; the average production is in excess of 1 million cases of wine a year, 66% of it white.

Madeira: Island in the Atlantic Ocean, located some 360 miles off the coast of Morocco; also the name of its wines. Under Portuguese control since 1419, Madeira has been famous for its wines for over 400 years. But in the beginning, Madeira wine was acidic and rather harsh. During the mid-18th century brandy was first added to the wines to strengthen them for long sea voyages, but it was found that the sea voyage itself — with constant motion and exposure to tropical heat seasoning the wines — improved their flavor. Later, Madeira wine-makers discovered how to duplicate the effects of the sea voyage with the process of *estufa,* by which the wines are exposed to high temperatures in special warming ovens over a period of 4-5 months, giving them a caramel color and characteristic flavor. Madeira became a national drink in colonial America because the island was Portuguese-controlled and the wines could be carried on American ships. But the Madeira trade with the U.S. declined during the 19th century and is no longer as important today as it once was; western Europe is a more significant market for Madeira than the U.S. Currently, there are about 3,700 acres of vineyard on the island, supplemented by others on nearby Porto Santo island.

Like SHERRY, Madeira is a fortified wine, made with the addition of brandy and blended by the same process used in the Sherry district: the SOLERA system. In Madeira, following fortification and completion of the estufa process, the wines are gradually blended over a period of time with wines from many vintages. In most cases, a vintage date on a bottle of Madeira indicates the date the solera was begun, not the actual age of the wine. Although vintage Madeiras from exceptional years were made at one time, very few have ever been exported.

The different types of Madeira are identified by grades of sweetness, which relates to when the wine is fortified. Sweet Madeiras receive an addition of brandy before the estufa process; the dry wines are allowed to ferment out first, fortification taking place after the estufa process. When all steps are completed, however, the alcoholic content in each case will be the same (18-20%).

The driest Madeira is generally SERCIAL, a scented, pale gold wine made from the Sercial grape — believed to be the same as Germany's Riesling. Grown on Madeira's highest slopes, Sercial is harvested later than other grapes as it is the last to ripen. Being dry, Sercial makes a fine apéritif.

VERDELHO, a slightly darker wine than Sercial, is also a shade sweeter. At one time, an especially light and fragrant blend of Verdelho was known under the trade name RAINWATER and used by a shipper named Habisham in Savannah, Georgia. Today, Rainwater has become a GENERIC name for a fairly light, dry Madeira; the term is now in the public domain.

The next sweetest Madeira is BUAL (or Boal), which, because of its residual sugar, is best served as a dessert wine. The sweetest, richest and fullest of all Madeiras is MALMSEY, made from the Malvasia (Malvoisie) grape that English buyers originally pronounced as "Malmsey."

The port city of Funchal is the center for the Madeira wine trade, where the shippers' offices or "lodges" are headquartered. Leacock, Cossart Gordon, Rutherford & Miles, Blandy's, Welsh Bros., and Henriques & Henriques are among the more important Madeira shippers.

Maderization: The chemical deterioration of a wine, caused either by poor storage or from exposure to heat. Maderization is particularly objectionable in white and rosé wines, causing them to turn brown and take on an unpleasant flat flavor. The word is derived from the wines of MADEIRA, which have a characteristic dark color.

Primarily a process of OXIDATION, maderization gradually occurs in all wines but is most evident when white wines are consumed when too old. Once maderization takes place, the process is irreversible.

Madiran *(Ma-dee-rawn')*: Robust red wine produced in southwest France in the department of Hautes-Pyrénées. One of France's lesser-known wines, Madiran is made from a local grape variety known as the Tannat, usually with some Cabernet Sauvignon added. The wine is particularly rich and full-bodied; not much is exported, but the area has considerable potential.

Magnum: A large wine bottle with the capacity of two ordinary bottles. Besides having extra capacity, a magnum is quite functional: wines age more slowly in large bottles, and fine wines from especially great vintages are often at their best when served from magnums.

Málaga *(Ma'-la-ga)*: Sweet, dark-colored wine produced in southern Spain near the city of Málaga on the Mediterranean coast. Formerly known as "Mountain," the wines of

169

Málaga were popular centuries ago but are now rather rare. They are made principally from Pedro Ximénez and Muscat grapes that are allowed to dry in the sun in order to concentrate their sugar. The wines are aged by the same SOLERA system used in the SHERRY district some 100 miles to the west.

Malbec *(Mal'-beck)***:** Fine red wine grape, grown extensively in the BORDEAUX district where it is used in blends to soften the slow-maturing Cabernet Sauvignon. Also known as Cot or Pressac, the Malbec is the principal variety in the region of CAHORS, and is grown to a large extent in South America where it is occasionally spelled Malbeck.

Malconsorts *(Mal'-cawn-sor)***:** Excellent red wine vineyard in the commune of VOSNE-ROMANÉE, in Burgundy's CÔTE DE NUITS. Officially rated Premier Cru (First Growth), the Malconsorts vineyard consists of about 15 acres planted in Pinot Noir, which yield especially scented red wines prized for their finesse and breed.

Malmsey: The richest, darkest and sweetest kind of MADEIRA, made from the Malvasia (Malvoisie) grape. The name Malmsey originated from the English mispronunciation of Malvasia, and nowadays applies primarily to the FORTIFIED WINES of the island of Madeira, not the golden sweet wines made in the Mediterranean region from the Malvasia and known by the original name. See MALVASIA.

Malolactic Fermentation: Secondary fermentation by which malic acid is converted into lactic acid through the action of *Lactobacillus* bacteria, an important process that helps reduce much of the youthful harshness in many wines. Malic acid gives the green, unripe quality to wines in their first year, and after it is broken down into lactic acid and

170

carbon dioxide, the wines are usually much more agreeable.

Because carbon dioxide is released during malolactic fermentation, it is best that this secondary fermentation be carried out in cask some time before the wines are bottled, otherwise the wine will become cloudy and fizzy, spoiling both appearance and flavor. Bottled wines suffering from this malady have often been bottled too early, before malolactic fermentation is completed. It has recently been demonstrated that various species of *Lactobacillus* bacteria differ in many wine districts, which could determine the individual character of a region's wines to a considerable degree.

Malvasia *(Mal-va-zee'-ah)*: White grape variety, grown principally in Mediterranean climates and known under several different names. The name originated from the little Greek coastal town of Monemvasia in the Peloponnesus, where the grape was first cultivated, and it spread throughout the Aegean. Malvasia is the Italian spelling; the grape is called Malvoisie in French, Malvagia in Spanish, and MALMSEY in English, although nowadays the latter term relates specifically to the sweet FORTIFIED WINES of the island of MADEIRA.

Today, the Malvasia is still grown in its original location, and the Greek islands of Crete and Rhodes produce some interesting Malvasia wine. In Italy, Malvasia is grown in many southern wine regions, but the island of Lipari north of Sicily produces what many regard as the best example of Malvasia: Malvasia di Lipari. In France, under the name Malvoisie, the grape is grown in many sweet wine regions — most notably at BANYULS and ROUSSILLON. To a limited extent, Malvasia is also grown in the warmer climatic regions of California.

Mancha, La: One of Spain's largest wine

171

regions, located south of the city of Madrid. There are over 500,000 acres under vines; the climate is very warm, resulting in mostly ordinary wines with the possible exception of the good red wines of the VALDEPEÑAS district, which is included in the La Mancha region.

Manzanilla *(Man-than-neel'-ya)***:** An exceptionally light and dry Spanish SHERRY, produced within the Sherry district but specifically around the city of Sanlúcar de Barrameda on the Guadalquivir River, 12 miles to the northwest of the city of Jerez. Manzanilla is usually the driest and most austere of Sherries, comparable to a FINO but lighter in color and with an unusually fragrant, tangy bouquet. It is said that these characteristics derive from the salty air that blows in from the Atlantic Ocean.

Marc *(Mar)***:** French for grape pressings or POMACE, consisting of the skins, seeds and pulp remaining after fermentation. Marc can be distilled to make brandy, which is called Eau-de-Vie-de-Marc in French; the marc brandies of BURGUNDY and CHAMPAGNE are famous. In the French Champagne region, however, marc has a slightly different meaning: the capacity of one standard-sized wine press, equivalent to 8,800 pounds of grapes (4,000 kilograms).

Marche *(Mar'-kay)***:** Wine region in east-central Italy; the chief city is Ancona, on the Adriatic Sea. By all odds its best wine is the white VERDICCHIO, grown in two D.O.C. regions: Verdicchio dei Castelli di Jesi and Verdicchio di Matelica. The golden BIANCHELLO DEL METAURO, another good white wine, is also rated D.O.C. Red wines of the Marche region are not as famous, though the D.O.C. red Rosso Conero and Rosso Piceno, made from Montepulciano and Sangiovese grapes, have some repute. The

172

Marche region as a whole typically produces in excess of 24 million cases of wine each year.

Marcobrunn *(Mar'-co-brun)***:** Celebrated vineyard in the RHEINGAU district, Germany, divided equally between the adjoining wine communes of ERBACH and HATTENHEIM. Its soil and exposure are exemplary; in dry years, its scented and fruity Riesling wines are among the best in the Rheingau. Formerly, the wines were often called "Erbacher Markobrunn" on the Erbach side, and "Marcobrunner" on the Hattenheim side, but under the 1971 German Wine Law, all wines must now be sold as Erbacher Marcobrunn. The leading proprietors are the Staatsweingut, Schloss Schönborn, Langwerth von Simmern, and Schloss Reinhartshausen.

Marconnets *(Mar'-cawn-nay)***:** The name of two excellent red wine vineyards in the CÔTE DE BEAUNE, Burgundy, both rated Premier Cru (First Growth). The more famous of the two lies in the commune of BEAUNE and consists of about 25 acres planted in Pinot Noir; the vineyard plot continues into the commune of SAVIGNY-LES-BEAUNE to the north, and Savigny's Marconnets vineyard is reckoned to be one of the commune's best. There are some subtle differences between the Beaune and the Savigny wines, but they are difficult to pinpoint.

Margaux *(Mar-go')***:** Outstanding wine area in the HAUT-MÉDOC district, some 18 miles to the north of the city of BORDEAUX. The area entitled to the APPELLATION CONTRÔLÉE Margaux consists of the associated communes of Margaux, Soussans, Arsac, CANTENAC, and Labarde; the soil and exposure in each of these communes is similar. Largely because of the soil, the fine red wines of Margaux are typically among the

173

most scented and refined in the world. The leading wine estate or CHÂTEAU is Château Margaux (see MARGAUX, CHÂTEAU), which is officially ranked as a Premier Cru (First Growth) in the 1855 Médoc classification, but of all the wine communes in the Médoc, Margaux has the largest number of classified growth *(cru classe)* châteaux. *Seconds Crus* (Second Growths): Rausan-Ségla, Rauzan-Gassies, Durfort-Vivens, Lascombes, and Brane-Cantenac. *Troisièmes Crus* (Third Growths): Kirwan, d'Issan, Giscours, Malescot-St. · Exupéry, Cantenac-Brown, Boyd-Cantenac, Palmer, Ferrière, and Marquis d'Alesme-Becker. *Quatrièmes Crus* (Fourth Growths): Pouget, Prieuré- Lichine, and Marquis-de-Terme. *Cinquièmes Crus* (Fifth Growths): Dauzac and du Tertre.

Margaux, Château *(Mar-go')*: One of the finest red wine estates of BORDEAUX, located in the commune of MARGAUX in the HAUT-MÉDOC district. The estate is owned by Ginestet S.A., a Bordeaux wine shipping firm, and is officially classified as a Premier Cru (First Growth), one of only three others in the whole Médoc. In good vintages, the wines of Château Margaux are unsurpassed, characterized by a magnificent bouquet and great delicacy. The estate extends over 650 acres, but only about 160 acres are given over to producing vines; typically, about 20,000 cases of wine are made each year. (A small amount of white wine called Pavillon Blanc du Château Margaux is also made, but it is only entitled to the appellation Bordeaux, there being no Médoc appellation for white wines; production is being progressively more restricted.)

174

Markgräflerland *(Mark-gray'-flur-land)*: Wine sub-region or BEREICH in the region of BADEN, Germany, located between the cities of Freiburg and Basel. The leading grape variety is the Gutedel or Chasselas, which yields mild, pleasant white wines known locally as Markgräfler; Ruländer, Silvaner and Traminer are also grown. The name Markgräfler derives from *Markgraf,* the German word for count.

Marque *(Mark):* French for "brand." A *marque déposée* is a registered trade mark; a *vin de marque,* however, is merely a branded wine, sold without the restrictions on the use of wine place-names applicable to the laws of APPELLATION CONTRÔLÉE or V.D.Q.S.

Marsala *(Mar-sahl'-la):* The most famous FORTIFIED WINE of Italy, a D.O.C. wine produced in the north-west corner of the island of Sicily. Its center is the coastal town of Marsala, although several Marsala producers have their offices in Trapani to the north.

Marsala may only be made from three grape varieties: Grillo, Catarratto, and Inzolia. Before brandy is added to bring it up to about 18-20% alcohol, the wine is straw colored and full-flavored. Its characteristic sweetness is primarily a result of a grape concentrate made from boiled must, *mosto cotto,* which is added in proportion to the desired sweetness in the finished wine.

Marsala is customarily sold in several grades: *Fine,* the lightest and least expensive, which must attain at least 17% alcohol; *Superiore,* the most usual grade in the export trade, which must be aged in cask for at least 2 years and have at least 18% alcohol; *Vergine* (also called "solera type" because it is made by the same SOLERA system used for Spanish Sherry), which must be aged for 5 years, is light in color and very dry. The terms *Stravecchio* or *Extra* are sometimes used to indicate additional age. *Speciale* or "special" is appropriately named, as it is a Fine Marsala made with a number of different

175

flavors — eggs, strawberry, banana, coffee, etc.

Marsannay *(Mar′-san-nay)*: Little town in BURGUNDY, France, just south of the city of Dijon; its full name is Marsannay-la-Côte. Its vineyards usually produce some of the best rosé wines of Burgundy from the Pinot Noir grape, under the appellation ''Bourgogne Marsannay-la-Côte.'' Some light red and white wines are also produced in Marsannay, but the rosés are clearly the best.

Martillac *(Mar′-tee-yack)*: Wine commune in the GRAVES district, south of the city of BORDEAUX. The southernmost wine commune in Graves with officially classified *(cru classé)* wine estates or CHÂTEAUX, Martillac boasts several fine châteaux: Smith-Haut-Lafitte, La Tour-Martillac, Domaine de la Solitude, La Garde, Haut-Nouchet, etc.

Mavrodaphne *(Mav-ro-daff′-nee)*: Rich, sweet red Greek wine; a specialty of the northern Peloponnesus region, though it is also produced on the nearby island of Cephalonia.

Maximin Grünhaus *(Max′-ee-mean Grune′-house)*: Outstanding wine estate in the RUWER district, Germany. Owned by the von Schubert family, the estate consists of 52 acres of vineyard west of the little village of Mertesdorf. Formerly the property of the St. Maximin abbey, the vineyard is divided into three sites or *lagen*: Abtsberg, Herrenberg and Bruderberg, and on each bottle the specific lage will be identified. The lagen names reflect the former church hierarchy: Abtsberg was the reserve of the abbot, Herrenberg belonged to the clergy, and Bruderberg was left to the lay brethren. Of the three, Herrenberg is the largest lage.

The vineyard is renowned for its delicate

and scented Riesling wines, though like many Ruwer wines they are generally only at their best in great vintages.

May Wine: A light Rhine wine that has been sweetened and flavored with woodruff herbs *(Waldmeister,* in German). It is usually served chilled in a punch bowl, with strawberries or other fruit floating in it.

Mazis-Chambertin *(Ma-zee' Shawm'-bear-tan):* Renowned red wine vineyard in the CÔTE DE NUITS, Burgundy, located in the commune of GEVREY-CHAMBERTIN and rated Grand Cru (Great Growth). The vineyard adjoins the famous CLOS DE BÉZE vineyard to the south, and consists of about 20 acres planted in Pinot Noir; the wines are noted for their strength and finesse. Average annual production amounts to some 2,600 cases.

Mazoyères-Chambertin *(Ma-zo-yair' Shawm'-bear-tan):* Fine red wine vineyard in the CÔTE DE NUITS, Burgundy, officially rated Grand Cru (Great Growth) — among Burgundy's best. The vineyard adjoins that of CHARMES-CHAMBERTIN, and a Mazoyères-Chambertin, may legally be sold as a Charmes-Chambertin, as some growers maintain that the latter is easier to pronounce, but a Charmes-Chambertin may not be sold as a Mazoyères. Vineyard size and production statistics for the two vineyards are generally combined.

Médoc *(May'-dawk):* World-famous wine region, extending some 50 miles to the north of the city of BORDEAUX on the left bank of the GIRONDE estuary. Its southern half is the HAUT-MÉDOC district: the Bas-Médoc district forms the northern half. All of the most famous Médoc wine estates or CHÂTEAUX lie in the Haut-Médoc, and Haut-Médoc is also an APPELLATION CONTRÔLEE for regional wines that are generally superior to those labeled "Médoc," which normally come from the less distinguished Bas-Médoc district.

The total area of vineyard in the Médoc is about 17,300 acres, and wine production often exceeds 3.4 million cases a year. But the Médoc is not famous for quantity, rather for superb quality. The region's soil is alluvial, which provides ideal drainage for such noble grape varieties as Cabernet Sauvignon, Cabernet Franc, Merlot, Malbec, and Petit-Verdot. No other varieties are permitted. In most Médoc vineyards Cabernet is dominant, although it is customary for an estate to be planted in several different varieties, adding balance and complexity to the wine. Characteristically firm and tannic in their youth, fine Médoc wines normally require two years of aging in cask and often many more in bottle.

The Haut-Médoc consists of six outstanding communes, which are, from north to south: SAINT-ESTÈPHE, PAUILLAC, SAINT-JULIEN, LISTRAC, MOULIS, and MARGAUX. In 1855 the leading Médoc châteaux were classified into five groups of *crus* (growths), based on the prices their wines were fetching on the Bordeaux market. Wine estates considered not worthy of classified growth *(cru classé)* status were either rated *cru exceptionnel* (exceptional) or *cru bourgeois* (bourgeois). While any wine from a classified growth château is likely to be distinguished, the 1855 classification has several shortcomings. With only one exception, it has remained unchanged for over a century, and its rigid sequential structure implies that a fifth growth is necessarily inferior to a fourth growth, which is often not the case. Another deficiency with the classification is that it does not include outstanding châteaux from other regions in Bordeaux. For these reasons, a re-classification is a distinct possibility in the near future.

THE OFFICIAL 1855 CLASSIFICATION
OF THE MÉDOC
(1976 status)

Premiers Crus (First Growths)
Château Lafite-Rothschild
Château Margaux
Château Latour
Château Haut-Brion
Château Mouton-Rothschild (1)

Seconds Crus (Second Growths)
Château Rausan-Ségla
Château Rauzan-Gassies
Château Léoville-Las-Cases
Château Léoville-Poyferré
Château Léoville-Barton
Château Durfort-Vivens
Château Gruaud-Larose
Château Lascombes
Château Brane-Cantenac
Château Pichon-Longueville-Baron
Château Pichon-Longueville,
    Comtesse de Lalande
Château Ducru-Beaucaillou
Château Cos d'Estournel
Château Montrose

Troisièmes Crus (Third Growths)
Château Kirwan
Château d'Issan
Château Lagrange
Château Langoa-Barton
Château Giscours
Château Malescot-Saint-Exupéry
Château Cantenac-Brown
Château Boyd-Cantenac
Château Palmer
Château La Lagune
Château Desmirail (2)
Château Calon-Ségur
Château Ferrière
Château Marquis d'Alesme-Becker

179

Quatrièmes Crus (Fourth Growths)
Château Saint-Pierre-Sevaistre (3)
Château Talbot
Château Branaire (Duluc-Ducru)
Château Duhart-Milon-Rothschild
Château Pouget
Château La Tour-Carnet
Château Lafon-Rochet
Château Beychevelle
Château Prieuré-Lichine
Château Marquis-de-Terme

Cinquièmes Crus (Fifth Growths)
Château Pontet-Canet
Château Batailley
Château Haut-Batailley
Château Grand-Puy-Lacoste
Château Grand-Puy-Ducasse
Château Lynch-Bages
Château Lynch-Moussas
Château Dauzac
Château Mouton-Baron-Philippe (4)
Château du Tertre
Château Haut-Bages-Libéral
Château Pédesclaux
Château Belgrave
Château Camensac
Château Cos-Labory
Château Clerc-Milon
Château Croizet-Bages
Château Cantemerle

Crus Exceptionnels
  (Exceptional Growths)

Château Villegeorge
Château Angludet
Château Chasse-Spleen
Château Poujeaux-Theil
Château La Couronne
Château Moulin-Riche
180   Château Bel-Air-Marquis d'Aligre

(1) Declared a First Growth in 1973.
(2) This vineyard no longer exists; the name is

now used as a subsidiary brand by Château Palmer.
(3) Formerly two châteaux, Saint-Pierre-Sevaistre and Saint-Pierre-Bontemps.
(4) Before 1956, known as Mouton d'Armailhacq.

Melon *(Muh-lawn')*: White wine grape, originally grown in the BURGUNDY region but now widely cultivated in the lower LOIRE River valley, where it is now called MUSCADET and produces a good dry white wine of the same name.

Mendocino *(Men-doe-seen'-o)*: Premium wine-producing country of California, north of SONOMA county and the northernmost part of the ''North Coast Counties.'' Its chief town is Ukiah, on the Russian River. A relatively new wine region that shows considerable promise, Mendocino currently has over 8,700 acres of vineyard; there are six bonded wineries, but only three have any nationwide commercial distribution: Cresta Blanca, transplanted from its former location in the Livermore Valley and now the property of Guild Wineries; Fetzer, a fairly small, family-owned winery, and Parducci, one of the area's oldest wineries.

Mendoza *(Men-doe'-sa)*: Major wine region and province in western Argentina, producing over 75% of that country's wine. Some 519,000 acres of vineyard are in Mendoza, most of them owned by large wineries or *bodegas* geared to mass production. The Andes Mountains rise up in western Mendoza, blocking rainfall and necessitating irrigation, one factor in the large production. The leading grape variety is Malbeck (Malbec), used to make robust red wines.

Mercurey *(Mair'-coo-ray)*: Wine district in

the CHALONNAIS region, southern Burgundy, noted for its good red wines made from the Pinot Noir grape — usually the best of the Chalonnais. Some light white wine is also made from the Chardonnay, but the fruity, rather early-maturing reds are superior. Some 193,500 cases of wine are produced annually.

Merlot *(Mair-lo')*: Fine red wine grape grown extensively in the BORDEAUX region. The soft, perfumed red wines that it gives are used for blending with Cabernet Sauvignon in the MÉDOC district, or exclusively in the SAINT-ÉMILION and POMEROL districts to the east, where it is the dominant variety. The Merlot is also grown in northern Italy, particularly in the regions of TRENTINO and ALTO ADIGE; across the border in Switzerland it is no less important, particularly in the region of TICINO. In California, major new plantations of Merlot now cover more than 4,000 acres; a number of recent California Cabernet Sauvignons have been markedly improved by a slight admixture of Merlot, which tends to soften the characteristic astringency of Cabernet.

Methuselah: An oversized wine bottle with a capacity of eight ordinary bottles, used occasionally in the French CHAMPAGNE district.

Meursault *(Mere'-so)*: Outstanding wine commune in the CÔTE DE BEAUNE, Burgundy, famous for its soft, scented white wines made from the Chardonnay. A little light red wine is also produced, but the white is superior and is commercially much more important. Meursault's best vineyards are rated Premier Cru (First Growth); the most famous is PERRIÈRES, which has a central sub-plot, the Clos des Perrières, that is particularly renowned. Other distinguished vineyards include Genevrières, Charmes, La

Goutte d'Or, and Poruzots. The Meursault commune includes a small portion of the vineyards of BLAGNY to the south; notable vineyards in the Blagny section include Jennelotte, La Pièce-Sous-Le-Bois, and Dos d'Âne. The total area under vines in Meursault is 1,186 acres; the equivalent of some 150,000 cases of wine is produced annually, over 90% of it white.

Mexico: Spanish settlers introduced the vine to Mexico in the 16th century, but only recently has interest in wine been strong in that country. There are currently over 60,000 acres of vineyard in Mexico, mostly in the north center of the country and to a certain extent in the Baja California region, but not all are planted in quality wine grapes and much is used for brandy distillation. The climate is very dry, and irrigation is necessary in many vineyards. Mexican wines are presently not very significant on the U.S. market, but several well-established wineries like Bodegas de Santo Tomás, Nazario Ortiz Garza, and Bodegas de San Lorenzo (Casa Madero) show considerable promise.

Michigan: The southeastern shores of Lake Michigan have been planted in vines for nearly a century, though today table grapes are more important than wine: the state is the nation's fourth largest grape producer. A number of producers make only grape juice in Michigan, but between the cities of Benton Harbor and Kalamazoo, centered near the town of Paw Paw, several wineries have sprung up in the past few years. Wineries that specialize in wines made from HYBRID varieties — of which Tabor Hill Vineyard, Bronte Vineyard and Warner Vineyards are notable examples — have already achieved considerable success.

183

Midi (*Me'-dee*): French for "the south"; the vast sweep of land along the Mediterranean coast ranging westwards from the mouth of the Rhône River to the Spanish border. It includes the departments of Gard, HÉRAULT, AUDE, and Pyrénées-Orientales. Most of the wine of the Midi is ordinary, but in upland regions where production is restricted, some notable wines are made. See LANGUEDOC.

Mildew: Serious cryptogamic (fungal) disease of the vine, caused by the organism *Plasmospora viticola;* also called downy mildew. Native to North America, mildew was introduced in the late 19th century in the European vineyards, where it was tremendously destructive. Mildew attacks the green portions of vine and cripples, it, but it can be controlled with copper sulphate (Bordeaux mixture). See OÏDIUM.

Millésime *(Meal-lay-seem′)*: French for "vintage." A non-vintage wine is called "non-millésimé."

Minervois *(Mee-nair-vwah′)*: Wine region in the old province of LANGUEDOC, southern France, east of the city of Carcassonne. Red, white and rosé wines entitled to the V.D.Q.S. seal are produced in the Minervois region; the reds — made from Cinsault, Carignan and Grenache grapes — are usually the best, and some are among the finest inexpensive wines that France has to offer. The equivalent of some 2.7 million cases of wine is produced annually.

Mis en Bouteilles au Château: see CHÂTEAU-BOTTLED.

Mis en Bouteilles au Domaine: see ESTATE-BOTTLED.

Mission: Historic red wine grape, the first VINIFERA variety to be planted in California in the late 18th century by Spanish settlers. In other respects it is less significant: although there are still some 6,000 acres planted in Mission in California, it gives rather common wine, suitable primarily for blending purposes and for making inexpensive California "sherry" and "port."

Missouri: Wine was first produced from wild grapes in Missouri in 1823, and wine-making has been on a good basis in the state ever since. Several Missouri wineries — Stone Hill Wine Co. in Hermann, Bardenheier's Wine Cellars in St. Louis, and Mount Pleasant Vineyards in Augusta — proudly reflect on a century of wine-making experience. Today, a majority of Missouri's vineyards lie west of St. Louis along the Missouri River, and a few (Stolz Vineyards, St. James Winery) are located further south on the Ozark Plateau. Most of their wines are made from native American varieties — Concord, Niagara, Catawba, etc. — but there is considerable interest in HYBRID varieties, which adapt well to the inland climate.

Mistelle *(Mee-stell')*: French term for grape juice or must that has received an addition of brandy before fermentation takes place, allowing some residual sugar to remain. Mistelles are widely used in the manufacture of VERMOUTH and other wine apéritifs.

Mittelrhein: German for "Middle Rhine," a wine region or ANBAUGEBIET extending southwards along the banks of the Rhine River from near Bonn to Bingen. It includes two sub-regions or BEREICHE: Bacharach and Rheinburgengau. The most northerly of the German wine regions, the Mittelrhein is one of the smaller and less important; the wines are virtually unknown on the export market. Centuries ago, the region was celebrated for its fine Riesling wines — in particular, those from the villages of Bacharach, Boppard, Oberwesel and St. Goarshausen, but their production is minuscule today. There are 2,110 acres under vines, and in a typical year over 900,000 cases of wine are produced in the Mittelrhein, yet much is consumed by the tourists that visit the region for its scenery.

Monbazillac *(Mawn-ba-zee-yack')*: White wine region in southwestern France, near the city of BERGERAC. Named for the picturesque Château de Monbazillac that overlooks the region, the sweet white wines of Monbazillac have been praised for centuries. They are normally harvested in the late autumn, like the more famous wines of SAUTERNES made some 50 miles to the southwest, though Monbazillacs are slightly drier, less fine, and considerably less expensive. The region extends over some 6,600 acres; annual production averages some 915,000 cases a year.

Monferrato *(Mawn-fair-rot'-toe)*: Range of hills in northern Italy, a part of the district of PIEMONTE. Monferrato has several wine regions; one of them, Barbera del Monferrato, has D.O.C. status.

Monimpex: The Hungarian State Export Agency, which controls the wine and spirit export sales of that country.

Monopole *(Mo-no-poll')*: French for "monopoly"; when seen on a wine label, it indicates that the wine is an exclusive of that producer, signifying either a blended wine sold under a proprietary brand name, or else that the producer owns that vineyard in its entirety.

Montagne de Reims *(Mawn-tahn'-yuh duh Rans')*: The most northern portion of the French CHAMPAGNE country south of the city of REIMS, with vineyards planted primarily in black Pinot Noir grapes. Beaumont-sur-Vesle, Mailly, Puisieulx, Sillery and Verzenay are its most important towns.

Montagne-Saint-Émilion *(Mawn-tahn'-yuh Sahnt Eh-meel-lyon')*: Secondary red wine commune in the BORDEAUX district, located

3 miles to the north of the village of SAINT-ÉMILION and legally entitled to use its name. Montagne lies in hilly country overlooking Saint-Émilion, and its vineyards do not enjoy the same excellent exposure as those further south, but the wines are similar and are often outstanding value, being considerably less expensive. The leading wine estates (CHÂTEAUX) are: Calon, Montaguillon, Plaisance, Roudier, and Vieux-Château-Négrit.

Montagny *(Mawn-tan-yee')*: White wine region in southern BURGUNDY, the southernmost part of the CHALONNAIS district. Montagny is famous for its fresh, light white wines made from the Chardonnay grape, among the best of the Chalonnais. Certain outstanding Montagny vineyards have been rated Premier Cru (First Growth); the more famous include Les Charmelottes, Les Vignes du Soleil, Les Bonnevaux, Les Chanteoiseaux, and Sous-les-Roches. The vineyard area totals about 750 acres, including the communes of Buxy and Saint-Vallerin; average production is about 31,000 cases of wine annually.

Montepulciano *(Mawn-tay-pool-chon'-no)*: Town in southern TUSCANY, Italy, famous for its fine red wine, VINO NOBILE DI MONTEPULCIANO, that is rated D.O.C. Montepulciano is also the name of an unrelated red grape variety grown in the ABRUZZI region, used for making the red MONTEPULCIANO DI ABRUZZO.

Montepulciano di Abruzzo *(Mawn-tay-pool-chon'-no dee Ah-broot'-zo)*: Good red wine produced in the ABRUZZI region, southern Italy. Dry and with a fine bouquet, it is entitled to D.O.C.

187

Monterey: City and county in central California, with more than 30,000 acres of vineyard. One of California's newest and

Stockton

Esc

Ripon

Mo

San Jose

MODESTO-
RIPON-
ESCALON

Santa Cruz

Gilroy

San Juan Bautista

Hollister

Salinas

Pai

La Cienega

Monterey

Soledad

King City

So

Pacific Ocean

Monterey

central California
wine districts

See pages 36-37 for
northern California wine districts

ced

ɪco

• Madera

ɪTEREY • Fresno   Fresno–
San Joaquin

• Visalia

• Tulare

o Robles   • Delano

ɪpleton

ı Luis Obispo   Bakersfield •
• Lamont

Santa Barbara
•

most promising wine regions, Monterey enjoys a temperate climate, owing to cool breezes that blow in from the Pacific Ocean. The fertile Salinas Valley between the Gavilán and Santa Lucia mountain ranges has some of the best climatic conditions in California for vineyards. The immense new Monterey Vineyard in Gonzales is one of the nation's largest; Paul Masson, Mirassou, Wente Bros. and Almadén each have important vineyards in Monterey, although their main offices are located elsewhere. The little Chalone Vineyard near Soledad is one of California's best white wine producers.

Monthélie *(Mawn-tay-lee')*: Wine commune in the CÔTE DE BEAUNE, Burgundy, adjoining the famous commune of VOLNAY. Primarily an area for light, scented red wines made from the Pinot Noir, Monthélie is not a well-known Côte de Beaune commune, and many of its fine wines sell for much less than comparable ones from Volnay. There are several good vineyards rated Premier Cru (First Growth); the finest is generally reckoned to be the Clos des Champs-Fulliot, along with the nearby Cas Rougeot, Clos Gautey, and La Taupine. There are some 250 acres under vines; production averages about 30,000 cases a year.

Montilla *(Mon-tee'-ya)*: Sturdy wine from the Montilla-Moriles district in southern Spain, near the city of Córdoba. Montilla is about 250 miles northeast of the SHERRY district, and until recently its wines were often sold as Sherries. Montilla differs from Sherry, however, in that it does not receive any addition of brandy — a factor that preserves its unique winey character. The grapes grown in the Montilla district are the same Pedro Ximénez grapes used in the Sherry district, and the identical, special FLOR yeast develops over the wine in cask. Montillas are generally marketed in the same grades as Sherries — Fino, Oloroso, etc., and even the term ''Amontillado'' is used, although this expression originally arose in the Sherry district to describe wines that took on a Montilla-like character. Montilla is an excellent substitute for Sherry and deserves to be better-known.

Montlouis *(Mawn-lou-wee′)*: White wine region in the central LOIRE River valley, adjoining the famous region of VOUVRAY and likewise praised for its fine, scented white wines made from the Chenin Blanc grape. The area of Montlouis is smaller than Vouvray and the wines are generally less costly, being not so well-known. Prior to 1938 Montlouis were often sold as Vouvrays, but since then they have been marketed under their own appellation. There are some 1,230 acres of vineyard, which produce the equivalent of 170,000 cases of wine annually.

Montrachet *(Mon-rah-shay′)*: Magnificent white wine vineyard in the CÔTE DE BEAUNE, Burgundy, rated Grand Cru (Great growth) like a few other outstanding white Burgundy vineyards, but officially the highest ranked of them all. Its 18½ acres, planted entirely in Chardonnay, are divided equally between the adjoining communes of Puligny and Chassagne, which have assumed its name to become PULIGNY-MONTRACHET and CHASSAGNE-MONTRACHET, respectively. Neighboring vineyards have also assumed the name Montrachet to show their relationship with their noble neighbor (see CHEVALIER-MONTRACHET, BÂTARD-MONTRACHET, BIENVENUE-BÂTARD-MONTRACHET, and CRIOTS-BÂTARD-MONTRACHET), and occasionally their wines will challenge Montrachet in a good vintage, though they are almost always somewhat less expensive.

Montrachet has been proclaimed the

191

greatest dry white wine in the world. Pale-gold in color, the wine is succulent, scented and sensational. Unfortunately, total average annual production hardly ever exceeds 2,600 cases, accounting for the rarity and high cost of this exceptional wine.

Morey-Saint-Denis *(Mor'-ray San Duh-nee')*: Notable wine commune in the CÔTE DE NUITS, Burgundy, with some 325 acres of vineyard. It takes its name from the fine CLOS SAINT-DENIS vineyard, rated Grand Cru (Great Growth); the commune's other outstanding Grand Cru vineyards include the CLOS DE TART, CLOS DE LA ROCHE, and a small portion of BONNES-MARES — the bulk of the latter vineyard lies in the neighboring commune of CHAMBOLLE-MUSIGNY to the south. One excellent vineyard rated Premier Cru (First Growth) that is nearly in the same class is the CLOS DES LAMBRAYS, like the Clos de Tart owned by a single proprietor. Other good Premier Cru vineyards in Morey-Saint-Denis include the Clos de la Bussière, Les Ruchots, Clos des Ormes, and Les Fremières. One vineyard, Monts-Luisants, is unusual for these parts in that it is planted in white grapes.

The many fine red wines of Morey-Saint-Denis are not as well-known as those of several other Côte de Nuits communes, and for this reason can offer exceptional value. They typically have an underlying firmness that softens with age, and the best of them rank with the finest red wines of Burgundy.

Morgeot *(Mor-zho')*: Fine red and white wines rated Premier Cru (First Growth), produced in the commune of CHASSAGNE-MONTRACHET in the CÔTE DE BEAUNE, Burgundy. By law the name Morgeot may be substituted for a number of different vineyards in Chassagne-Montrachet. Probably the best-known is the original plot of Morgeot (10 acres); others entitled to this appellation include Guerchères, La Chapelle, Vigne Blanche, Les Petits Clos, etc. The usage is optional, but many growers prefer the name Morgeot because it is so famous.

Morgon *(Mor-gawn')*: Wine commune in the BEAUJOLAIS district, southern Burgundy, and its excellent red wine. Officially one of the nine *crus* (growths), areas that generally produce the best Beaujolais, Morgon is usually one of the fullest and most robust of the *crus:* unlike most Beaujolais, which is best consumed when quite young, Morgon improves with age and is relatively long-lived for a wine made from the Gamay grape. There are 2,026 acres of vineyard; average annual production amounts to some 350,000 cases.

Moscatel de Setúbal *(Mos-ca-tell' duh Set-too'-bahl)*: Sweet Portuguese FORTIFIED WINE produced south of the city of Lisbon. Made from the Muscat grape, it has a pronounced, characteristic Muscat flavor and aroma, a dark color, and good aging potential.

Moscato *(Mos-cot'-toe)*: Italian for "Muscat," a sweet wine grape grown in many different parts of Italy. Most Moscatos are white, though one — the Aleatico — is red. Moscato is the variety used for the famous sparkling sweet *spumante* of ASTI in the region of PIEMONTE; elsewhere in Piemonte, Moscato is grown for use in VERMOUTH manufacture, and also near the little town of Canelli to make the interesting Moscato di Canelli. The Moscato Trentino, produced in the region of TRENTINO, is somewhat fuller and sweeter, with a fine bouquet. Further south, Sicily's Moscato di Siracusa, from the town of Siracusa in southeast Sicily, is well-known. The Moscato di Cagliari on the island of Sardinia, and the Moscato di Pantelleria from the little Mediterranean island of Pantelleria, are extremely sweet and high in alcohol — usually over 15%.

Mosel *(Moz'l)*: German for *Moselle,* an important European river some 320 miles long. It draws its source in France's Vosges Mountains, continues on through the Grand Duchy of Luxembourg, and winds across Germany until it drains into the Rhine River at Koblenz. Vineyards abound on its banks throughout its eastward journey, but by far the most famous and important lie in the section in Germany — and in particular in the *Mittel-Mosel,* located between the villages of TRITTENHEIM and ERDEN.

All of the fine wines of the Mosel are white, and almost all are produced from the noble Riesling grape. The soil of the Mosel is predominantly slate, and slate and Riesling partly account for the excellence of the wines. But equally significant is the Mosel's cool climate, which allows the grapes to have optimum sugar-acid balance. The vines cling tenaciously to incredibly steep hillsides, which provide optimum drainage and exposure but necessitate herculean labor to manage the precipitous vineyards.

The Mosel has two tributaries, the SAAR and RUWER Rivers, which flow into the Mosel near the city of TRIER. Both rivers also have important vineyard areas. Under the 1971 German Wine Law, the three regions were combined into one wine region or ANBAUGEBIET: Mosel-Saar-Ruwer. The wines of each region have their own distinct properties, but the best all share a family resemblance: an unsurpassed floral bouquet, coupled with a piquant spiciness. Their delicacy is exquisite: rarely do the wines exceed 11% alcohol.

194

The 1971 German Wine Law divided up the Mosel into several sub-regions or BEREICHE: *Bernkastel,* between the villages of Longuich and Zell; *Zell/Mosel* further downstream in the direction of Koblenz, and *Obermosel,* upstream above the city of Trier. Though officially part of the Mosel Anbaugebiet, the Bereich Saar-Ruwer is a separate region, and its wines differ somewhat from those of the Mosel.

Bereich Bernkastel includes world-famous wine villages like BERNKASTEL, PIESPORT, BRAUNEBERG, GRAACH, WEHLEN, ZELTINGEN, ÜRZIG, and Erden, as well as lesser-known towns such as Klüsserath, Leiwen, Trittenheim, DHRON, NEUMAGEN, WINTRICH, KRÖV and TRABEN-TRARBACH. Bereich Zell/Mosel is much less important, including the vineyards of ZELL, Merl, Edig, Bruttig, Winningen and others. The wines are not often marketed in the U.S. under a vineyard name. Even rarer are the small wines of the Bereich Obermosel, which are even hard to find in Germany.

The best wines from the Mosel villages are sold under the name of the town where they are produced, followed by a vineyard name (EINZELLAGE). Exceptional vintages accentuate the nuances of the wines, and warm autumn weather also allows the late-harvested grapes to reach full maturity, permitting the fine SPÄTLESE and AUSLESE wines that have made the Mosel a world-renowned wine region. The total area under vines in the Mosel-Saar-Ruwer Anbaugebiet is 28,478 acres; annual production is in excess of 13.7 million cases of wine.

Moselblümchen *(Moz'l-blim'-shen):* German for "little flower of the Mosel," a trade name for a regional wine from the MOSEL district. Under the 1971 German Wine Law, a wine labeled Moselblümchen is a TAFELWEIN, most often a blend of wines from lesser vineyards that have received a large dose of sugar to increase their alcoholic strength. Various brands of Moselblümchen are common on the U.S. market, but they are hardly among the better wines that the Mosel region has to offer.

Moselle *(Mo-zell′)*: French for MOSEL, a river originating in France and flowing into Luxembourg and West Germany. Near its source some pale, light wines are produced in the old province of Lorraine; called ''Vins de Moselle,'' they are officially rated V.D.Q.S. but are rarely seen outside the region. In California, Moselle is a GENERIC name occasionally used by some producers to describe a light, semi-dry white wine.

Moulin-à-Vent *(Moo′-lan ah Vahn′)*: World-famous wine commune in the BEAUJOLAIS district, southern Burgundy, and its outstanding red wine. Named for an old windmill that nowadays no longer has its sails, Moulin-à-Vent is one of the nine Beaujolais *crus* (growths), those districts that are apt to produce superior wine. A good Moulin-a-Vent is usually the finest of the *crus* — sturdy, well-balanced, and with great character. The vineyard area of Moulin-à-Vent covers about 1,335 acres; average production is the equivalent of some 263,000 cases of wine annually.

Moulis *(Moo-lee′)*: Wine commune in the HAUT-MÉDOC district, north of the city of BORDEAUX. Although Moulis has no classified growth *(cru classé)* wine estates or CHÂTEAUX, it has a number of very good ones, two of which are rated *cru exceptionnel* (exceptional growth): Chasse-Spleen and Poujeaux-Theil. Other good Moulis châteaux rated *cru bourgeois* include Gressier-Grand-Poujeaux, Dutruch-Grand-Poujeaux, Poujeaux-Marly, Pomys, and La Closerie du Grand-Poujeaux.

196

Mousseux *(Moo-suh′)*: French for ''frothy'' or ''sparkling.'' Under French law, any sparkling wine produced outside the

CHAMPAGNE district — however made — may not be called Champagne, only *vin mousseux* (sparkling wine). Many of them, however, are quite good; some of the best produced outside the Champagne district are made in the LOIRE River valley — most notably at VOUVRAY and SAUMUR — and also in Burgundy (Bourgogne Mousseux).

Mouton-Rothschild, Château *(Moo'-tawn Rawt'-shield)*: World famous wine estate in the HAUT-MÉDOC, located in the commune of PAUILLAC north of the city of BORDEAUX. Owned by the de Rothschilds (a prominent French family of bankers) since 1853, Mouton-Rothschild was ranked as a Second Growth (Second Cru) in the 1855 Médoc classification, but largely through energetic promotion by its present owner, Baron Philippe de Rothschild — and on the merits of its great wines — it was officially promoted to a Premier Cru (First Growth) in 1973. Since 1945 every vintage of Mouton-Rothschild has featured an original work of art on the label. The estate also boasts a splendid museum filled with art treasures, each with wine as a theme.

Usually one of the fullest and most robust of the great Médocs, Mouton-Rothschild takes years and even decades to reach maturity. The vineyard consists of about 150 acres of producing vines; total production in a good year is about 13,600 cases, all CHÂTEAU-BOTTLED.

Müller-Thurgau *(Mew'-ler Tir'-gow)*: White HYBRID grape variety developed in Germany, a cross between the Riesling and the Silvaner; sometimes also designated "Riesling x Silvaner" on a wine label. It is now the most widely-planted wine grape in Germany, accounting for about one-third of the total vineyard area. The grape is hardy and productive, but its wines tend to be rather mild and soft, sometimes lacking in acidity.

Münster *(Minster)*: The name of two wine towns in the NAHE district, Germany. The more famous of the two lies in the BEREICH (sub-region) Schloss Böckelheim and is officially called Bad Münster, on account of its famous mineral spas. The leading vineyards (EINZELLAGEN) are: Rotenfelser im Winkel, Höll, Steigerdell, Gotzenfels, and Königsgarten. The other village with this name lies downstream in the Bereich Kreuznach, and is called Münster-Sarmsheim. Its leading Einzellagen are: Steinkopf, Pittersberg, Dautenpflänzer, Kappellenberg, and Königsschloss; on a label, these names will be preceded by the words "Münster-Sarmsheimer," whereas the wines of Bad Münster are simply called "Münsterers."

Muscadelle *(Moos'-cah-dell)*: White wine grape grown in the SAUTERNES and GRAVES regions of BORDEAUX. Grown in conjunction with the more important Sémillon and Sauvignon Blanc, the Muscadelle imparts an agreeable Muscat flavor to the wines, but it is normally planted only in small proportions in the vineyards.

Muscadet *(Moos'-cah-day)*: Famous dry white wine produced near the city of Nantes in the lower LOIRE River valley, France; also the name of the informing grape variety, originally called the Melon de Bourgogne, which was brought to the Loire from Burgundy several centuries ago. Muscadet is a wine that should ideally be drunk when very young — within a year or so after it is made. Some Muscadet is kept in barrel on the lees for a short while before being bottled, thus gaining in flavor: this is known as "Muscadet Sur Lie."

There are three APPELLATION CONTRÔLÉE zones for Muscadet: Muscadet, the largest region, south of Nantes; the nearby region of "Muscadet de Sèvre-et-Maine," named after two rivers that flow into the Loire at Nantes; and the "Muscadet des Coteaux de la Loire" further upstream. Each district has its differences; the Coteaux de la Loire usually makes the best wine in hot years. The total vineyard area is in excess of 22,000 acres, mostly consisting of small plots managed by local growers. The production of Muscadet is prodigious, averaging about 3.4 million cases annually.

Muscat: Multi-purpose grape, suitable for raisins, table grapes, or wine. It is one of the world's oldest cultivated varieties; some of Europe's earliest vineyards were planted in Muscat. Nowadays it is grown chiefly in warm climates to make sweet wines; good French examples include the Muscats of BEAUMES-DE-VENISE, FRONTIGNAN, and LUNEL. A related variety is also grown for dry wine in ALSACE. The Muscat is called MOSCATO in Italy, where it makes many good sweet wines; the Muscat of Samos is one of Greece's better wines. In California, a variety called Muscat of Alexandria occupies about 13,500 acres of vineyard throughout the state, but it is not a good wine grape, being cultivated chiefly for raisins and table grapes. Good sweet Muscat wines from other varieties, however, are made by a number of California producers.

Muscatel: Any wine made from the Muscat grape. In California, this term is often used for a common FORTIFIED WINE, many poor examples of which have given it a bad name.

Musigny (*Mooz'-een-yee*): Outstanding vineyard in the CÔTE DE NUITS, Burgundy, which since 1878 has attached its famous name to the nearby town of Chambolle, now called CHAMBOLLE-MUSIGNY. Celebrated for its delicacy and scent, Musigny is one of the most refined wines of the Côte de Nuits. The vineyard consists of three parcels: Les

Musigny, Les Petits Musigny, and Combe d'Orveau, planted chiefly in red Pinot Noir vines, although a little is also planted in white Chardonnay to make the rare white Musigny Blanc, equally as fine as the red. Both wines are rated Grand Cru (Great Growth), the highest rank for a Burgundy. Including the plot of Musigny Blanc, the vineyard is about 26 acres large; production in a good vintage is approximately 3,800 cases.

Must: Grape juice, either pressed or crushed, to be made into wine; called *moût* in French.

Must Weight: The number of grams by which one liter of grape juice (must) is heavier than the same quantity of distilled water. Since a solution of sugar has a higher density or specific gravity than water, must weight is a fairly accurate gauge of the sugar content of the must and the alcoholic strength of the wine to be made. A calibrated HYDROMETER is usually employed to determine must weight.

Mutage *(Mew-tahj')*: French term for the process of adding brandy to partially fermented must to stop it from fermenting, so that residual sugar is retained. Wine that has been subjected to this process is said to be *muté*.

N

Nackenheim *(Nock'-en-heim)*: Renowned wine village in the RHEINHESSEN region, Germany; with the adjoining village of NIERSTEIN, the finest Rheinhessen wine town. There are 296 acres of vineyard in Nackenheim; a tiny amount of red wine is made, but it is the excellent white wines —

made from Riesling and Silvaner — that have made the village famous. The leading vineyards (EINZELLAGEN) are: Rothenberg, Engelsberg, and Schmitts-Kappelle.

Nahe *(Nah'-uh):* River in Germany, a tributary of the Rhine; also a wine region or ANBAUGEBIET, with 10,393 acres of vineyard. Although the many fine wines of the Nahe are not well-known outside of Germany, some of them are among that country's best. The river banks provide excellent exposure for Riesling, Silvaner and Ruländer vines.

The 1971 German Wine Law divided up the Nahe into two sub-regions or BEREICHE, Kreuznach and Schloss Böckelheim; the former lies downstream, near where the Nahe flows into the Rhine at Bingen; the latter is further upstream, and produces wines that tend to be lighter than those made further downstream. Both Bereiche are named after the two best-known Nahe wine towns, KREUZNACH and SCHLOSS BÖCKELHEIM, and it is important not to confuse regional wines that bear the name of the Bereich with better wines made exclusively in those two towns. Other fine Nahe wine villages include: NIEDERHAUSEN, Münster-Sarmsheim and Bad Münster (see MÜNSTER), NORHEIM, ROXHEIM, Laubenheim, Langenlonsheim, Dorsheim and Rüdesheim (no relation to the more important town of RÜDESHEIM in the RHEINGAU). The equivalent of some 4.5 million cases of wine is made on the Nahe each year, virtually all of it white; various Anheuser family firms are famous producers.

Napa: Perhaps the most famous fine wine region in California, if not the whole United States; a fertile valley, county and city located some 50 miles north of San Francisco. Vineyards have been planted in the Napa Valley since the early 19th century; today, there are over 23,000 acres of vineyard, most of them planted in fine wine grapes. The city of Napa lies near San Pablo Bay and marks the southern limit of the region; some 25 miles to the north, the town of Calistoga marks the northern limit.

The leading fine wine grape in Napa is the Cabernet Sauvignon. Over 5,400 acres of it have been planted throughout the valley, making Napa one of America's most important Cabernet regions. Especially when planted in cool upland vineyards, Cabernet Sauvignon in Napa often makes some of the world's best Bordeaux-type wines. No less important is the Chardonnay (also called Pinot Chardonnay); 2,500 acres have been planted in the Napa Valley, and some superb white Burgundy-type wines have come from Napa vineyards. Other leading grape varieties include Pinot Noir, Johannisberg Riesling, Sauvignon Blanc, Chenin Blanc, Gamay Beaujolais, Petite Sirah, Gamay, Gewürztraminer, and Zinfandel. Some wholly remarkable Zinfandels have been produced in Napa, its cool climate revealing hidden subtleties in the grape that often do not develop in warmer wine regions of California.

The Napa Valley is divided into two sections: the Lower Valley, around Napa, and the Upper Valley, around the town of St. Helena. Because it is near the bay, the Lower Valley — though further south — is cooler, and has rather heavier soil than regions further north. Other towns within the Napa Valley include, from north to south: Calistoga, Rutherford, Oakville, and Yountville.

Among the leading Napa Valley wineries are: Beaulieu Vineyard, traditionally one of the most famous, now owned by the Heublein Corporation and especially celebrated for its "Private Reserve" Cabernet Sauvignons; Inglenook, also owned by Heublein, producing a wide variety of quality wines; Beringer Brothers, now owned by the Nestlé Corporation, which under the wine-making direction of Myron Nightingale has produced some memorable wines; Charles Krug, long the property of the Mondavi family and one of the Napa Valley's most important producers; the Robert Mondavi winery, a quality-oriented family concern related to the Mondavis of Krug that opened in 1966 and has produced many notable successes; Louis Martini, one of the most respected California producers over several generations; the Christian Brothers, managed by a monastic order originally established in France, famous for their brandies as well as their table wines; and Sterling Vineyards, a new winery opened in 1973 that has already scored some impressive achievements.

Though their distribution is less widespread nationally, some smaller Napa Valley producers are no less important — perhaps even more important in terms of quality and individuality. Donn Chappellet's impressive new winery is already producing some outstanding wines, as is Joseph Heitz Cellars, noted for Cabernet and Chardonnay. Many of the wines of Oakville Vineyards — particularly the selections bearing the name of the owner, W.E. van Loben Sels — are celebrated. Schramsberg and Hanns Kornell are among the famous producers of bottle-fermented American champagne; Freemark Abbey and the smaller Stony Hill and Mayacamas wineries have produced some fabulous wines, but they are hard to find outside California. The little Sutter Home Winery specializes in Zinfandel. Promising new Napa Valley wineries are: Cuvaison, Stag's Leap Wine Cellars, Château Montelena, Caymus Vineyards, Joseph Phelps Vineyards, Clos du Val, Burgess Cellars (formerly Souverain Cellars), Franciscan Vineyards and Spring Mountain.

The excellence of Napa Valley wines has been consistently demonstrated at impartial tastings held all over the world, where many of them have surpassed more famous wines from traditional producing areas. The Napa Valley Development Council serves to limit industrial and residential growth in order to preserve the integrity of the vineyards.

Nature *(Nah-tur')*: French for "natural." Until fairly recently, this term referred to the rare still wines of the French CHAMPAGNE district, called "Vin Nature de la Champagne" because there were no intervening processes to make them sparkling. French law discouraged the export of such wine, however, because of the conflict with this name and the famous sparkling wine of Champagne. A new appellation, Coteaux Champenois, avoids such a conflict and allows a distinctive name for these unusual and interesting red and white wines, and the first wines under this appellation were released on the U.S. market in 1975.

Néac *(Nay'-ack)*: Wine commune in the BORDEAUX district, adjoining the commune of LALANDE-DE-POMEROL. Néac's estates have been entitled to the latter appellation since 1954, and the wines will rarely be sold as Néacs.

Nebbiolo *(Neb-be-oh'-lo)*: Fine red wine grape grown in northern Italy, used to make all the best Italian red wines, particularly those from the region of PIEMONTE (see BAROLO, BARBARESCO, GATTINARA, GHEMME, etc.) and the wines of the VALTELLINA district. Some regional Piemontese wines are also made from the Nebbiolo in the region of Alba and are entitled to the D.O.C. Nebbiolo d'Alba. There are over 380 acres of Nebbiolo planted in California's Central Valley, where the grape thrives in the warm climate.

204

Nebuchadnezzar: The largest and bulkiest bottle, used rarely — if at all — in the French

CHAMPAGNE district, with a capacity of 20 ordinary bottles. Champagnes in such enormous containers have not been commercially exported to the U.S. for many years.

Négociant *(Nay-go'-see-on)*: French for "merchant" or "shipper." In the wine trade, a négociant is usually a buyer who purchases wines from a property or estate and then blends them with other wines to sell them under his own label. He may also qualify himself as a "négociant-éléveur," who purchases the wines in cask during their first year from a grower or *propriétaire,* and then "raises" them in his cellars before releasing them after aging and bottling. A négociant-éleveur may also buy the grapes and vinify the wine himself. Négociants perform a valuable service, both to the proprietors who often find it difficult to produce and sell their wines, and to the buying public who need an experienced intermediary to guide them in their purchases.

Negrar *(Nay-grar')*: Little village located in the heart of the VALPOLICELLA district, not far from Lake Garda, where many of the leading producers of Valpolicella have their cellars.

Neuchâtel *(Nuh'-shat-tel)*: City and lake in western Switzerland, also a famous wine region. Like most Swiss white wines, the light, fragrant wines of Neuchâtel are made from the Chasselas grape, and are vinified dry. A little red Pinot Noir is also grown for red Neuchâtel, and the little village of Cortaillod specializes in red wine, but the reds are very pale in color — almost rosé — and are not as well-known as the whites. Some white Neuchâtel is left on the lees *("sur lie"),* which causes a faint sparkle. Including the vineyards on Lake Bienne to the northeast, which form part of the Neuchâtel appellation, there are 1,375 acres under vines; total pro-

205

New York State

Westfield
Lake Erie
Niagara Falls
CHAUTAUQUA
Lake Ontario
Canandaigua
Conesus
Naples
Hammondsport
FINGER LAKES
Geneva
Washingtonville
New City
Albany
Hudson River
Highland
Marlboro

duction of all Neuchâtel is the equivalent of some 346,300 cases annually.

Neumagen *(Noy'-mog-en)*: Wine village on the MOSEL River, Germany, adjoining the village of Dhron to the north. The two villages have been amalgamated under the 1971 German Wine Law into one community, called Dhron-Neumagen. See DHRON.

New York State: The second most important wine region in the U.S. after California, New York State produces some 10% of all the wine annually consumed in this country — in excess of 21 million gallons, from 36,000 acres of vineyard. New York is also the largest producer of sparkling wines in America, which constitute one-fifth of the total production. After over a century of wine-making, the New York wine industry is now in a process of expansion. Many new vineyards are being planted, and techniques and grape varieties are changing to meet new public demands and trends.

Compared to other famous wine regions, the climate in New York State is one of extreme contrasts. The summers are marked with periods of searing heat; the winters are cold and forbidding. Thus native American grape varieties of the species LABRUSCA have traditionally been the mainstay of the New York wine industry because of their hardiness and productivity. Wine made from labrusca varieties (Concord, Niagara, Delaware, Catawba, Dutchess, Ives, Moore's Diamond, etc.) has a pronounced grapey flavor and aroma that is markedly different from the softer flavor of VINIFERA varieties native to Europe and California. For many years, New York producers found ready acceptance for labrusca wines. Now, faced with a changing market, many producers are turning to HYBRID varieties (Chelois, Baco Noir, Seyval Blanc, Foch, de Chaunac, etc.), made

207

from a cross between labrusca and vinifera and combining hardiness and productivity with improved taste characteristics. The products of this "second generation" are beginning to appear in force on the market, and they are continually improving. Vinifera is also grown, though on a smaller scale.

In order to mute the characteristic, forceful flavor of labrusca, New York wineries have often blended their wines with those from other regions, most notably California. Federal law allows up to 25% of other wines to be blended with New York wines if sold under this name; if more than 25% is added, the wine must be labeled "American wine." Some New York State wineries have even purchased vineyards elsewhere in the U.S. to augment their output.

Presently, New York State wineries are moving to expand their output of wines under VARIETAL labels, identifying the grape variety used. In the past, their wines were usually given GENERIC labels — rhine, chablis, sauterne, etc. — and though generic labeling is still employed, varietal labeling for premium New York wines is increasing.

When New York's wineries were first established over a century ago, the shores of the Finger Lakes — Canandaigua, Keuka, Seneca, Cayuga, Skaneateles, Owasco, Conesus and others — were a logical location for vineyards. The terrain slopes gently, aiding drainage; the soil is ideal, and the lakes provide a fine microclimate. Today, the Finger Lakes district has the largest concentration of wineries in the eastern United States. Of the lakes, Keuka has the greatest vineyard acreage, and near its southernmost tip is the little town of Hammondsport, where several important wineries have their headquarters.

The Finger Lakes wineries include: Taylor, the world's third largest sparkling wine producer and the largest winery in the area;

Pleasant Valley Wine Co., now owned by Taylor and noted for its sparkling wines sold under the Great Western brand label; Gold Seal, one of the earliest wineries in the area to achieve success with viniferas; Widmer's Wine Cellars, which has been producing fine wines since 1888; Vinifera Wine Cellars, directed by Dr. Konstantin Frank, a talented Russian-born winemaker who produces wines only from vinifera, and whose wines have fetched high praise from experts; Bully Hill Winery, managed by Walter S. Taylor, who founded the winery in 1970 and produces fine wines exclusively from hybrids; Canandaigua Industries, which features the well-known brands of Richard's, Virginia Dare, Mother Vineyard and Wild Irish Rose; and Boordy Vineyards in Penn Yan, where famous wine-maker Philip Wagner continues to perfect wines made from hybrids, under the direction of Seneca Foods Corporation.

Though they are less important commercially, other regions in New York produce good wines. The Chautauqua area near Lake Erie has over 2,600 acres of vineyards planted in wine grapes; Frederick S. Johnson Winery and Fredonia Products are leading Chautauqua producers. The Hudson River Valley, where Brotherhood, the oldest active winery in the U.S. (est. 1839) is located, is becoming a center of renewed interest in wine. Two excellent Hudson Valley wineries: High Tor, managed by Richard Voigt, and Benmarl Vineyards, directed by Mark Miller, have recently produced fine wines from both vinifera and hybrids; the Hudson Valley Wine Co. in Highland is another major producer.

Niagara: White wine grape of the species LABRUSCA, grown primarily in New York's Finger Lakes district and also in the Niagara Peninsula in Canada. Characteristically fruity, it makes pleasant sweet wines and is

209

generally vinified to retain some residual sugar.

Niederhausen *(Nee'-der-how-zen)***:** One of the finest wine villages in the NAHE River valley, Germany, with 371 acres of vineyard; most of them planted in Rieslings. Niederhausen's best wines are typically racy and full-flavored, especially those from the leading vineyards or EINZELLAGEN: Hermannshöhle, Hermannsberg, Steinwingert, Rosenheck, Klamm, Kertz, Rosenberg, and Pfingstweide.

Nierstein *(Near'-shtine)***:** Outstanding wine village in the RHEINHESSEN district, Germany; the most celebrated in the entire area. With over 2,000 acres of vineyard, Nierstein has the largest acreage under vines in Rheinhessen and some of the region's most important cellars. Under the 1971 German Wine Law, however, Nierstein has also become the name of a BEREICH (sub-region), and wines merely labeled "Niersteiner," without a vineyard name, are regionals that can come from dozens of villages within the Bereich. The 1971 Wine Law also substantially delimited Nierstein's vineyards, and three traditionally famous ones — Auflangen, Rehbach, and Spiegelberg — have become composite vineyards or GROSSLAGEN. The most frequently used Nierstein Grosslage name for inexpensive regional wines is "Gutes Domthal," relating to wines that can vary a great deal in quality. But the ten leading single vineyards or EINZELLAGEN within Nierstein — Hipping, Pettenthal, Hölle, Orbel, Kranzberg, Ölberg, Glöck, Heiligenbaum, Bildstock, and Patersberg — are deservedly famous. Both Riesling and Silvaner vines produce outstanding wines in Nierstein, especially in vineyards located near the Rhine front.

Norheim *(Nor'-heim)***:** One of the leading

210

wine towns in the NAHE River valley, Germany, with 138 acres of vineyard planted predominantly in Riesling. The best vineyards (EINZELLAGEN) include: Kafels, Dellchen, Klosterberg, Götzenfels, and Kirschheck.

Nose: An alternate term for BOUQUET.

Nuits-Saint Georges *(Nwee San Zhorzh')*: Famous wine town on the CÔTE DE NUITS, Burgundy; the medieval city of Nuits gave its name to the Côte, and since 1892 Nuits has added its name to that of its most celebrated vineyard, Les Saint Georges. Many important wine shippers have their cellars in Nuits; the town is celebrated primarily for its many good red wines, though a small amount of white is also made.

The best vineyards in Nuits-Saint Georges are rated Premier Cru (First Growth), and are located in three different areas. On the border with the neighboring town of VOSNE-ROMANÉE to the north, the most famous vineyards are: Les Boudots, Aux Cras, Aux Murgers, and Aux Thorey. Immediately south of Nuits are the notable vineyards of Les Saint Georges, Les Pruliers, Les Porets, Les Vaucrains and Les Cailles. The adjoining commune of Prémeaux to the south is included in the Nuits-Saint Georges appellation; its best vineyards are: Clos de la Maréchale, Clos des Corvées, Clos des Corvées-Paget, Aux Perdrix, and Les Didiers. There are minor differences between the Prémeaux wines and those of Nuits-Saint Georges; the former are apt to have a slight, characteristic earthy flavor *(goût de terroir)* that is quite agreeable.

Including the vineyards of Prémeaux, the area under vines in Nuits-Saint Georges is 927 acres; annual production averages about 110,000 cases of wine, virtually all of it red.

211

Oak: The most widely used type of wood for wine cooperage; employed for the best casks and, to a certain extent, fermenting tanks. Oak is an ideal material for cask aging because it allows air to enter the wine slowly and mature it; in addition, tannin and other material is imparted to the wine, improving the flavor. The oak grown in certain traditional areas, such as the Limousin and the Nevers regions in France, differs somewhat from American white oak, the best of which comes from Tennessee. Experiments conducted recently in California with casks made from different types of oak confirm that imported oak is highly important to the character and style of the best American wines, especially those made from Cabernet Sauvignon and Chardonnay.

Oberemmel *(Oh-ber-em'-mel)*: Noted wine town in the SAAR region, Germany, with some 200 acres of vineyard — most of them planted in Rieslings. Oberemmel adjoins the much more famous town of WILTINGEN, and its fine wines share many of the same noble characteristics, though they are little-known outside of Germany. The leading vineyards (EINZELLAGEN) include: Hütte, Agritiusberg, Altenberg, Karlsberg, and Rosenberg.

Öchsle *(Erks'-luh)*: A scale used to measure the sugar content of grape musts, employed in Germany and in Switzerland as a legal determinant for minimum MUST WEIGHT standards. Named for Ferdinand Öchsle, who devised it in the early 19th century, the Öchsle scale relates directly to the specific

212

gravity of the must: as measured by a calibrated HYDROMETER, grape must with a specific gravity of 1.096 would have an Öchsle reading of 96°. The Öchsle reading divided by 8 gives the approximate alcoholic content of the wine after fermentation, so theoretically must with 96° Öchsle would yield a wine of 12% alcohol. However, very high Öchsle readings will result in a wine with considerable residual sugar, because not all the sugar is converted into alcohol, and for this reason many great German wines retain both lightness and unresolved sugar.

Ockfen *(Awk'-fen)*: Outstanding wine village in the SAAR region, Germany, with 158 acres of vineyard; in warm years, often one of Germany's best wine producers. Famous for its fine, well-balanced and perfumed Riesling wines, Ockfen is particularly renowned for one great vineyard, Bockstein; the other leading vineyards (EINZELLAGEN) include: Herrenberg, Geisberg, and Heppenstein.

Oechsle: see ÖCHSLE.

Oenology: The science of winemaking, which includes the intricate chemical and technical aspects of vinification. An oenologist is a trained professional who has been certified in the practice of oenology, following his wine-making apprenticeship in an accredited program.

Oestrich *(Uhs'-trich)*: Important wine town in the RHEINGAU district, Germany; with 865 acres of vineyard, one of the largest in the area. Oestrich adjoins the more famous village of HATTENHEIM, but mostly through differences in the soil its wines are quite different, tending to be rather full in body. In good vintages, Oestrich makes some outstanding wines. The leading vineyards (EINZELLAGEN) are: Lenchen, Doosberg, and Klostergarten.

213

Ohio: In the days before the Civil War, Ohio was America's most important wine-making state. Vineyards were first planted in 1823 along the Ohio River near Cincinnati by Nicholas Longworth, the first American to successfully make good sparkling wines from the Catawba grape. Various vine diseases and prohibition dealt severe blows to Ohio's vineyards during the ensuing century, but in the 1960s there was a strong resurgence of winemaking, and it is once again a significant industry in the state.

Today, Ohio has over thirty wineries. Vineyards are still located along the Ohio River in Longworth's "American Rhineland" — and a promising newcomer there is Château Jac Jan Vineyard — but more important plantings lie in the north, on the shores of Lake Erie near the town of Sandusky. The largest producer in Ohio is Meier's Wine Cellars in Cincinnati, which owns extensive vineyards on Isle St. George in Lake Erie near Sandusky. Mantey Vineyards in Sandusky, founded nearly a century ago, is operated by Paul Mantey, whose brother Norman manages the Mon Ami Champagne Cellars division of Catawba Island Wine Co. Tarula Farms in Clarksville, and Valley Vineyard Farm in Morrow (both founded in the 1960s), are gaining in reputation. Traditionally, Ohio has grown native American grape varieties, but there are extensive new plantings of HYBRIDS throughout the state.

Oïdium *(O-ee′-dee-um)*: Serious cryptogamic (fungal) disease of the vine, caused by the organism *Uncinula spiralis;* also called "powdery mildew" to distinguish it from "downy mildew," which is of American origin (see MILDEW). Oïdium attacks the green foliage, weakens and often kills the vine, and splits the skins of the grapes. It caused severe damage in Europe in the 1850s, but it can be effectively controlled with

214

finely-ground sulfur powder, which is regularly dusted in the vineyards throughout the summer months.

Oloroso *(O-lo-ro'-so)*: A dark and full-bodied type of Spanish SHERRY, which because it does not mature through the action of the same FLOR yeast as the drier and lighter FINO Sherries, develops a style all its own: noble bouquet, combined with a characteristic "nutty" flavor. Olorosos are used in making sweet Cream Sherries, though in their natural state they are completely dry — the sweetness is added before the wines are bottled and shipped.

Oltrepò Pavese *(Awl-tray-po' Pa-vay'-see)*: Italian for "on the other side of the River Po, in the Pavia area"; a hilly vineyard region in the area of LOMBARDY, Italy, near the city of Pavia. A relatively new wine region in Lombardy, the Oltrepò Pavese area entitled to D.O.C. produces a number of good red and white wines form Barbera, Bonarda, Riesling, Moscato, and Cortese, although Barbera is the most widely-grown variety for red wines. The wines are usually identified by grape variety, as in "Bonarda dell'Oltrepò Pavese." From good vintages, some red wines from the Oltrepò Pavese region can stand among the best in Italy.

Oppenheim *(Awp'-en-heim)*: Famous town in the RHEINHESSEN district, Germany, with 833 acres of vineyard; most of them planted in Silvaner, although Riesling and Müller-Thurgau are also grown. Oppenheim's soft, scented white wines are among the Rheinhessen's best, although much "Oppenheimer" without a vineyard name that is sold in the U.S. is regional wine, not to be confused with the best vineyards or EINZELLAGEN in Oppenheim: Sackträger, Herrenberg, Kreuz, Daubhaus, Schlossberg, Gutleuthaus, Schloss, Paterhof, and Herrengarten.

Oregon: A large-scale wine industry is new to Oregon, although wine-making has been carried out in the state for over a hundred years. The climate in the western part of the state is similar to many fine wine regions in Europe. Fruit and berry wines are made in regions where grapes cannot grow, but two regions seem favorable to viticulture: the Willamette River valley south of Portland, and the Roseburg area in Douglas County some 200 miles to the south. Bjelland Vineyards, Hillcrest Vineyard, Knudsen-Erath Winery and Charles Coury Vineyards are among the leading producers.

Original-Abfüllung *(Awr-rig′-in-nal Ab′-fool-ung)*: German wine term used before 1971 to indicate a wine that had been ESTATE-BOTTLED by a single producer. Under the 1971 German Wine Law, use of this term is no longer permitted on a German wine label, and in its place the term ERZEUGER-ABFÜLLUNG, or ''producer bottling,'' has been substituted.

Ortsteil *(Orts′-tile)*: German for ''part of a community.'' Under the 1971 German Wine Law, an Ortsteil is a vineyard estate that is entitled to sell its wines under its own name, without specifying the town or the vineyard community in which it lies. The STEINBERG, Schloss Johannisberg (see JOHANNISBERG, SCHLOSS) and Schloss Vollrads (see VOLLRADS, SCHLOSS) estates in the RHEINGAU region are Ortsteils; in the SAAR region, the SCHARZHOFBERG is also an Ortsteil.

Orvieto *(Orv-yay′-toe)*: Fine white wine produced in the region of UMBRIA, central Italy, near the city of Perugia. A specialty of the Umbria region that has only recently received D.O.C. status, Orvieto is produced from several different grape varieties — Trebbiano, Verdicchio, Malvasia, Verdello, and Procanico — and is sold in two different forms. When vinified to retain some residual sugar in the traditional manner, it is called *abboccato* or semi-dry, but nowadays the taste is for drier wines, which are labeled *secco*. Orvieto used to be sold primarily in the squat, straw-covered FIASCHI flasks native to central Italy, but with recent high labor costs more and more wine is being bottled in conventional bottles. The wine tends to be fruity, pleasant, and extremely easy to drink.

Oxidation: The reaction of various components in wine (alcohol, tannins, acids, and coloring matter) with oxygen. There is always some dissolved oxygen in wine acquired during fermentation and cask aging, which initially helps to mature it. But in later stages oxidation damages the wine, causing it to turn brown and take on a flat, musty flavor. It is particularly unpleasant in white wines consumed when too old, and an oxidized wine is said to be "maderized" when in this condition. See MADERIZATION.

P

Paarl *(Parl)*: Important town and wine region in South Africa, situated some 40 miles to the northeast of Capetown. Paarl is the location of an immense wine cooperative run by the K.W.V. wine association; some of South Africa's best wines are made there, in addition to superior sherries and brandies. See SOUTH AFRICA.

Palatinate *(Pa-lat'-tin-nate)*: see RHEIN-PFALZ.

Palette *(Pah-let')*: Wine district in southern France, located in the old province of

217

PROVENCE southeast of the city of Aix-en-Provence. One of the few wine districts in Provence that is rated APPELLATION CONTRÔLÉE, Palette is celebrated for its equally good red and white wines, in addition to fine, sturdy rosés, although the region's production is limited. The principal grape varieties used are Clairette, Grenache, Mourvèdre and Cinsault. One particularly fine estate in Palette is the little Château Simone.

Palomino *(Pal-o-meen'-o)*: White grape variety grown in the Spanish SHERRY district, used for 90% of all the wine produced. Its local name is Listán. There are almost 6,000 acres of Palomino planted in California, mostly in the warm Central Valley, where it is used to make some of the best California sherries; however, it is poorly suited to the making of table wines.

Passe-Tout-Grains *(Pahss Too Gran')*: In the region of BURGUNDY, France, a light red wine produced from a blend of Pinot Noir and Gamay grapes vatted together, with a minimum of one-third Pinot Noir. By law, the wines must attain at least 9.5% alcohol. Passe-Tout-Grains are pleasant light wines, usually inexpensive, which serve an important need in an area so famous chiefly for great wines.

Passito *(Pas-see'-toe)*: Sweet Italian wine made from sun-dried or partially raisined grapes. After the harvest, grapes destined for passito wines are selected and left to dry either in the sun or on special racks, where they lose moisture. A sweet passito wine is the specialty of the little town of Caluso in the region of PIEMONTE (see CALUSO PASSITO); further south, the VINO SANTO of TUSCANY is similar.

Pasteurization: Process by which wine is heated briefly and rapidly to a temperature of about 150° F. (65° C.). Named for the great French chemist Louis Pasteur (1822-1895), who discovered its beneficial properties, pasteurization stabilizes wines by ridding them of harmful bacteria and other microorganisms. But because it tends to affect the flavor of the wine as well, it is usually performed only on ordinary wines.

Pauillac *(Poy′-yack)***:** World-famous red wine commune in the HAUT-MÉDOC district, located some 30 miles north of the city of BORDEAUX between the celebrated communes of SAINT-ESTÈPHE and SAINT-JULIEN. Pauillac has three of the world's most renowned wine estates: LAFITE-ROTHSCHILD, LATOUR, and MOUTON-ROTHSCHILD; these are rated Premier Cru (First Growth), the highest rating for a Bordeaux wine. Pauillac is also the location of one of the largest oil refineries in southwest France, and its village is the most important in the Haut-Médoc, but its great fame is based solely on its excellent red wines. Made predominantly from Cabernet Sauvignon, Pauillacs tend to be tannic and austere in their youth, but develop into noble and aristocratic Bordeaux wines with sufficient bottle age. The leading wine estates (CHÀTEAUX), as ranked in the 1855 classification of the Médoc, are as follows: *Premiers Crus* (First Growths): Lafite-Rothschild, Latour, and Mouton-Rothschild. *Seconds Crus* (Second Growths): Pichon-Longueville-Baron, Pichon-Longueville, Comtesse de Lalande. *Quatrièmes Crus* (Fourth Growths): Duhart-Milon-Rothschild. *Cinquièmes Crus* (Fifth Growths): Pontet-Canet, Batailley, Haut-Batailley, Grand-Puy-Lacoste, Grand-Puy-Ducasse, Lynch-Bages, Lynch-Moussas, Mouton-Baron-Philippe, Haut-Bages-Libéral, Pédesclaux, Clerc-Milon, and Croizet-Bages. Note that Pauillac is the only famous Haut-Médoc wine commune with no *Troi-*

Pécharmant *(Pay'-shar-mon)***:** Red wine region in southwest France, officially part of the BERGERAC district. Although not well-known outside the region, the fine red wines of Pécharmant tend to be fruity and well-balanced. They evoke the characteristics of those produced in the BORDEAUX region some 60 miles to the west, and the grape varieties used are similar. Average annual production is on the order of some 28,600 cases.

Pedro Ximénez *(Pay-dro He-may'-nays)***:** Sweet white grape grown in the SHERRY district in Spain, and to an even greater extent in the MONTILLA and MÁLAGA districts to the east, where it is the chief variety. At harvest time, selected Pedro Ximénez grapes are left to dry on mats of straw over a period of about two weeks, allowing the sun to evaporate the moisture and concentrate the sugar. The grapes are then made into a very sweet, concentrated wine used to sweeten other wines, or after an addition of brandy and some cask aging, on its own as a rare and costly wine known as a ''P.X.'' Such wines are hard to come by, but they are unquestionably among the finest and most luscious sweet FORTIFIED WINES made.

Pernand-Vergelesses *(Pair'-non Vair'-zhuh-less)***:** Little hillside town and wine commune in the CÔTE DE BEAUNE, Burgundy, with some 350 acres of vineyard. Pernand-Vergelesses adjoins the more famous commune of ALOXE-CORTON, and its best red and white wines are legally entitled to the name CORTON and CORTON-CHARLEMAGNE, respectively. The leading vineyard sold under its own name is the Ile des Vergelesses, rated Premier Cru (First Growth); other good vineyards in Pernand Vergelesses include: Les Basses-Vergeles-

220

ses, Creux de la Net, En Caradeaux, and Les Fichots. Because they are little-known, some red Pernand-Vergelesses wines are excellent value; annual production is the equivalent of some 27,600 cases of wine, about 10% of it white.

Perrière *(Pair-yair')*: French for "rock quarry" or "pebbly soil," a local term used in the BURGUNDY region in France to indicate a vineyard situated on or near chalk rubble. Such soil is ideal for white Chardonnay grapes; the Perrières vineyard in MEURSAULT, rated Premier Cru (First Growth), usually produces some of the best white wines of Burgundy. A similarly-named vineyard of comparable excellence lies in the adjoining commune of PULIGNY-MON-TRACHET; to the north in the CÔTE DE NUITS there is a rare white wine vineyard in the commune of NUITS-SAINT GEORGES with this name. Good red wines are produced from the CLOS DE LA PERRIÈRE vineyard in the commune of FIXIN.

Pessac *(Peh'-sock)*: Wine commune in the region of GRAVES, located on the southwestern outskirts of the city of BORDEAUX. Some Pessac wine estates (CHÂTEAUX) are among the most famous in the world, but several are currently threatened by housing developments. The best-known is Haut-Brion (see HAUT-BRION, CHÂTEAU), but Châteaux La Mission-Haut-Brion, Pape-Clément, and Les Carmes Haut-Brion also produce celebrated wines.

Pétillant *(Pet'-tee-yawn)*: French for "semi-sparkling," a term for a wine with residual carbon dioxide, although not to the degree of a fully sparkling wine (see MOUSSEUX). Such wines often develop a faint sparkle through early bottling, when there is some residual sugar. By French law, the amount of pressure in *pétillant* wines must not exceed two atmospheres.

Petit Chablis *(Puh-tee′ Shab-lee′)*: A light, usually inexpensive white wine made in the French CHABLIS district, produced from secondary vineyard parcels along the regional boundary. The minimum alcoholic strength must be 9.5%, and the wine must be made solely from the Chardonnay grape. Petit Chablis was formerly a little local wine that was rarely bottled or exported, but it is now becoming increasingly more important in the trade; in recent vintages, production has increased some 40% over what it was a decade ago.

Petit-Verdot *(Puh-tee′ Vair-doe′)*: Red grape variety grown in the BORDEAUX district, France, usually used in blends with Cabernet Sauvignon, especially in the MÉDOC region. It adds considerable body to red wines, but because it is succeptible to rot, it is only planted on a limited scale.

Petite Sirah *(Puh-teet′ Seer-rah′)*: Red grape variety grown extensively in California, where almost 13,000 acres of it have been planted. The Petite Sirah is named for the robust Syrah grape native to the RHÔNE River valley in France, to which it was originally thought to be related, but grape specialists (ampelographers) have recently determined that it is actually an entirely different variety known in France as the Durif (or Duriff), which is also grown in the Rhône region. Formerly used predominantly in blends to supply needed body and color to GENERIC burgundy wines, it can produce some rather spectacular, full-bodied and fruity VARIETAL wines when grown in cool coastal vineyards.

222 **Pétrus, Château** *(Pay-truce′)*: Magnificent and full-bodied red wine from the POMEROL district, usually one of the most robust of all BORDEAUX wines. Named for the fisherman apostle Saint Peter, Pétrus is unofficially ranked as the leading Pomerol, and in some vintages it is among the most expensive Bordeaux wines; the estate is only about 30 acres large, and production rarely exceeds 3,500 cases. Its rise to fame was largely the work of its late owner, Mme. Edmond Loubat, whose niece Mme. Lily Lacoste is now co-owner; the estate is managed by Jean-Pierre Moueix, an important Pomerol proprietor. The richness of the wine reflects the very high proportion of Merlot grapes used — over 95% — and it is full of scent, warmth, and finesse.

Pfarrkirche *(Far'-keer-shuh)*: German for "parish church," an ecclesiastical order owning a vineyard estate.

Phylloxera *(Fil-lox'-er-ah)*: A burrowing plant louse of the Aphididae family (full name: *Phylloxera vastatrix*) that is one of the most serious vineyard parasites. Native to the eastern U.S., phylloxera attacks the roots of the vine and eventually kills it. Introduced accidentally in Europe in the 1860s, the insect laid waste to all major vineyard areas and did millions of dollars worth of damage; various methods of combatting it failed until the technique of grafting the European vines onto American rootstocks (which are immune) was perfected. This is now standard procedure in most of the world's vineyards, for there are few areas where phylloxera has never struck, and the insect remains a constant threat unless grafted vines are planted.

Pichet *(Pee'-shay)*: French for "pitcher," a small container, sometimes made of wood or earthenware, used to serve wines at the table.

Picpoul *(Peek'-pool)*: White grape variety grown in southern France, used in making Armagnac brandy and light white wines. See FOLLE BLANCHE.

223

Piemonte *(Pee-ay-mawn'-tay)*: Italian for "Piedmont," a wine region in northwestern

Italy, at the foot of the Italian Alps. Its capital is the city of Torino (Turin), and wine is one of its foremost products: annual production often exceeds 45 million cases.

A hilly region famous for its outstanding cuisine, Piemonte has two principal centers of wine production. The largest and most important is central Piemonte, due east of Torino around the Monferrato Hills. The other region lies further north in the Novara Hills near the city of Milan, where the Alps begin to rise up to precipitous heights. Along the Swiss border in the extreme northwest is the French-speaking district of the Valle d'Aosta; although this is a separate, autonomous district, its wines share a close similarity with those of Piemonte. Fine Valle d'Aosta wines can be exquisite; unfortunately, these rare mountain wines are encountered only infrequently outside the region.

The chief grape variety in Piemonte is the Nebbiolo, said to take its name from the fog *(Nebbia)* that cloaks the Piemonte hills at harvest time. The Nebbiolo is used for all the best Italian red wines; another important grape is the Barbera, which yields substantial and robust red wine. The best of it is rated D.O.C., and is produced around the towns of Alba, Monferrato and Asti. Other red Piemontese grapes for which D.O.C. zones have been established include Freisa, Dolcetto, and Grignolino. Good but little-known red Piemonte wines include Carema, Brachetto d'Acqui, Fara, Sizzano, and Boca.

Piemonte is also a region of intense white wine production, much of it used in the manufacture of VERMOUTH, which is a Torino specialty. The sweet Moscato grape is grown for the sparkling wine of ASTI, Asti Spumante, one of the best known Italian sparkling wines. A sweet wine, CALUSO PASSITO, is the specialty of the little town of Caluso north of Torino. The Cortese is another important Piemontese white wine grape.

The noble red wines of Piemonte rank with the world's best — they are heady, robust, and aristocratic. BAROLO and BARBARESCO from central Piemonte are world-acclaimed; GATTINARA and GHEMME from the Novara Hills are less well-known but similar in quality. Even the regional Piemontese wines share many of their superior characteristics, but the best are not always easy to come by outside of Italy.

Piesport *(Peez'-port)***:** Famous wine village on the MOSEL River, Germany, with 148 acres of vineyard planted predominantly in Riesling. The piquant, scented white wines of Piesport are among the Mosel's best, especially in dry years, for the soil retains moisture. However, much regional wine of lesser quality is also produced around Piesport, and a "Piesporter" without a vineyard name is merely a regional wine, which usually cannot compare to better wines from single vineyards (EINZELLAGEN). The most famous Piesport Einzellage — and often one of the leading Mosel wines — is Goldtröpfchen; other fine vineyards include: Schubertslay, Gunterslay, Domherr, Falkenberg, Gärtchen, and Treppchen. It should be noted that the familiar Piesporter Michelsberg is not an Einzellage; under the 1971 German Wine Law, this name has become a composite vineyard (GROSSLAGE), used for regional wines from lesser vineyards around Piesport.

Pineau de la Loire *(Pee'-no duh la Lwahr')***:** The local name for the Chenin Blanc grape in the LOIRE River valley, France; also used by some California producers for their wines made from the Chenin Blanc.

Pineau des Charentes *(Pee'-no day Shar-ront')***:** A wine apéritif made in the Cognac district, southwestern France, in the departments of Charente and Charente-Maritime. Originally made by accident some 400 years ago, Pineau des Charentes is produced by adding some young Cognac brandy to a partially fermented white wine. Alcoholic strength ranges from 17% to 22%. Pineau des Charentes is pale-gold in color, has a clean, fruity freshness, and is quite popular in France; some very good examples are now being exported to the U.S.

Pinot *(Pee'-no)*: A family of noble grape varieties, widely planted in many of the world's best wine regions. Red varieties include Pinot Noir and Pinot Meunier; white varieties include Pinot Blanc and Pinot Gris. Though they are named Pinot in California, the Red Pinot (Pinot St. George) and White Pinot (Chenin Blanc) are not members of the Pinot family and should not be labeled as such.

Pinot Blanc *(Pee'-no Blawn')*: Fine quality white wine grape, originally native to the Burgundy region in France but now grown in many wine regions. Its acreage is decreasing in Burgundy and Champagne in favor of the Chardonnay; under the name Klevner, it gives good white wines in Alsace and in some parts of southern Germany. 1,300 acres of Pinot Blanc have been planted in California, where the grape makes some of America's best white wines and champagnes.

Pinot Chardonnay: see CHARDONNAY.

Pinot Gris *(Pee'-no Gree')*: Fine grape variety used to make white wines, although its skins are reddish when ripe. It is grown in Alsace, France, and across the border in Germany in the region of Baden, where it is known as Ruländer (after a merchant named Ruland, who brought it to Germany from France in 1711). Called Pinot Grigio in Italian, it is planted extensively in northern Italy; strangely enough, it is often called

226

"Tokay" or "Tocai," although it has nothing to do with Hungarian Tokay. Wines made from the Pinot Gris have a characteristic fullness and an interesting, scented bouquet.

Pinot Meunier *(Pee'-no Muhn'-yay)*: Red grape variety grown in the French CHAMPAGNE district, where (as with Pinot Noir, below) it is fermented without the skins so that a white wine is obtained. Its acreage in Champagne is generally decreasing, but it is hardy and productive and adds strength to Champagne blends. The name meunier ("miller," in French) derives from the white, powdery underside of its leaves, which appear to be dusted with flour.

Pinot Noir *(Pee'-no Nwahr')*: Outstanding red wine grape, widely grown in the region of BURGUNDY, France, and to the north in the CHAMPAGNE district. It is called "black" although its berries are deep purple when ripe. The Pinot Noir is responsible for all the great red Burgundies, in addition to some fine rosés; in the Champagne district, the grapes are pressed before fermentation to obtain white juice (see BLANC DE NOIRS), and three-fourths of all Champagne is made from Pinot Noir. The grape is grown nearly everywhere in Europe, particularly in Switzerland and the Italian Tyrol; because it is a late-ripener that was brought from Burgundy, it is called Spätburgunder in Germany and Austria, but in those regions its wines are usually very pale and light. Over 11,000 acres of Pinot Noir have been planted in California; however, most California Pinot Noirs seem to have little in common with the Burgundies of France, tending to be fruity but rather lacking in depth and complexity.

Pinot St. George: see PINOT.

Pomace: The residue of grape skins, seeds and pulp remaining in the fermenting vat after

227

the wine or juice is removed. It can be distilled to make brandy, called *Eau-de-Vie-de Marc* in French and "pomace brandy" in California.

Pomerol *(Pawm-uh-roll′)*: Outstanding red wine commune in the BORDEAUX district, France; one of the smallest wine regions in Bordeaux, with less than 1,730 acres under vines. The generous red wines of Pomerol are similar to those produced in SAINT-ÉMILION, which borders to the east, except that Pomerols are perhaps even fuller in flavor; the region was formerly a part of Saint-Émilion until 1923. The soil is rich in iron and clay, factors that contribute to the distinctive flavor of Pomerols. The equivalent of about 228,700 cases is produced annually.

The dominant vine in Pomerol is Merlot, which imparts a characteristic softness and scent; the other leading variety is Cabernet Franc, locally called the Bouchet. The vineyards are located near the city of Libourne some 20 miles east of Bordeaux; two neighboring districts, LALANDE-DE-POMEROL and NÉAC, lie just to the north and are separated by a small stream. The Pomerols are generally superior to wines from the latter districts, through somewhat better soil and exposure; Pomerol's commune wines are among the best regional wines of Bordeaux.

Pomerol is one of the few Bordeaux wine regions whose wine estates (CHÂTEAUX) have not been classified officially, yet because there are so many good châteaux, some sort of distinction between them is useful. The following unofficial classification is based on the current standing of leading Pomerol châteaux, reflected in the prices they generally fetch in the trade. The single best Pomerol is reckoned to be Pétrus (see PÉTRUS, CHÂTEAU), followed by:

Château Beauregard
Château Certan-de-May

228

Château Certan-Giraud
Château Clinet
Clos l'Église
Domaine de l'Église
Château l'Église-Clinet
Château l'Evangile
Château Feytit-Clinet
Château Gazin
Château Gombaude-Guillot
Château La Conseillante
Château La Croix-de-Gay
Château Lafleur
Château Lafleur-Pétrus
Château Lagrange
Château La Grave-Trigant-de Boisset
Château La Pointe
Château Latour-Pomerol
Château Le Gay
Château Moulinet
Château Nénin
Château Petit-Village
Clos René
Château Rouget
Château de Sales
Château Trotanoy
Vieux-Château-Certan

Pommard *(Po-mar')*: One of the most famous wine communes in the CÔTE DE BEAUNE, Burgundy, and one of the largest, with some 850 acres under vines; total production often exceeds 114,300 cases annually. Since the Middle Ages, Pommard has been celebrated for its fine red wines made from Pinot Noir, prized for their scent and finesse; a tiny amount of white wine is also made, but it is unimportant commercially. The vineyards adjoin those of BEAUNE to the north, and the wines have much in common.

Possibly because the name is easy to pronounce, Pommard is one of the best-known names in the Burgundy wine trade, but there is a big difference between *commune* wines merely labeled ''Pommard'' and the wines of

229

individual vineyards. Pommard's best vineyards have been rated Premier Cru (First Growth), and in good vintages wines from these vineyards are liable to be very fine. ÉPENOTS and RUGIENS head the list; the former is typically graceful and scented, the latter apt to be somewhat fuller. Other good vineyards include: Clos Blanc, Clos de la Commaraine, Les Arvelets, Les Argillières, Pézerolles, Chanlains, Les Chaponnières, and Les Jarollières.

Port: Famous sweet dessert wine; specifically, a product of Portugal named for the city of Oporto, produced from 61,775 acres of vineyards in a strictly delimited zone in the Alto Douro (Upper Douro) region, from approved grape varieties and by traditional methods. Since 1968 wines shipped to the U.S. from this area must bear the name ''Porto'' or ''Vinho do Porto'' to distinguish them from domestic ports produced in California and elsewhere, which are usually made by different methods.

Port is a rich, ruby-red wine made from several different grape varieties: Touriga, Mourisca, Tinta Francisca, Tinta Madeira, Bastardo, Tinta Cão, etc. A comparative newcomer, White Port, is made from Malvasia, Verdelho, Rabigato, or Gouveio. The grapes are planted in unbelievably steep, terraced vineyards along a 50-mile sweep of the Douro River; each vineyard estate is known as a *quinta,* which is customarily managed by a farmer who sells his produce to a shipper. The terraces had to be carved out of solid schist by digging and blasting, and they represent a monumental engineering feat. The delimited region of Port in the Alto Douro was first established in 1756, and it has stayed essentially the same for over two centuries.

230

The characteristic fruity sweetness of Port derives from an addition of brandy before fermentation is completed. At the harvest, grapes are taken to the *quinta* and are crushed in great stone troughs *(lagares)*, often still by treading with the feet. At a predetermined moment, the wine is drawn off into barrels containing high-proof brandy. This stops fermentation and leaves considerable unresolved sugar in the wine, with a final alcoholic strength of 20%. The wine is then left to age in oak casks.

Though the actual making of Port takes place at the *quinta* in the Alto Douro, the wine is generally not kept there for more than a few months. Soon after it is made, it is taken downstream to the city of Vila Nova de Gaia, a suburb of Oporto, to the shippers' warehouses or *lodges* for further aging, which can take as long as 50 years. Almost all Ports are the blended produce of several *quintas,* which furnish wines with the characteristics desired by the shipper.

The vintage displays its qualities soon after the wine ''falls bright'' in the spring. In an exceptional year — which occurs only a few times each decade — a shipper will ''declare a vintage'' and set aside the single product of that year as Vintage Port. The rarest and finest of Ports, Vintage Port is kept in cask only for about two years before continuing its development in bottle, often for decades. During this time it throws a heavy, crusty sediment, and before it is consumed the wine must be decanted to remove the sediment . The bottle must be stored upright well in advance of decanting to allow the sediment to settle, but the pleasures of such an exquisite wine reward those with patience.

Not all Port, naturally, is of this quality, and most of it is blended and aged further in cask to mature it. The simplest (and generally the least expensive) grade of Port is Ruby Port, a blend of many different wines whose quality depends on the standards of the shipper. A somewhat more expensive grade is Tawny Port, a blended wine of good quality that has spent many years in cask, causing it to obtain a tawny, pale-brown color and lose some of its sugar. Fine Tawny Ports are often as costly as Vintage Ports, because of the lengthy amount of time spent in cask and the loss due to evaporation. Inexpensive Tawny Ports can often be made by blending Ruby Port with White Port, but the result is never as good.

Another type of Port produced by some shippers is ''Late-Bottled Vintage Port.'' This is a Port of near vintage quality that has been kept unblended in cask for about 4-6 years prior to bottling, during which time it loses its sediment in the cask. Late-Bottled Vintage Ports mature sooner and are usually much less expensive than Vintage Ports, but they are generally lighter and never quite as fine. ''Crusted Port'' is similar, except that it is not necessarily that of a single vintage, and, as its name implies, throws off a sediment in the bottle. These fine Ports should not be confused with a ''Port of the Vintage,'' which despite its rather misleading name is not a Vintage Port but in fact a Tawny Port, containing perhaps some wine from a given vintage but blended with many different wines while in cask.

Great vintages of Port during the past few decades have been: 1975, 1970, 1967, 1966, 1963, 1960, 1958, 1955, 1950, 1948, 1947, and 1945; a fine Vintage Port is at its best when at least 15 years old. Among the leading Port shippers that export in quantity to the U.S. are: Croft, Taylor/Fladgate, Fonseca, Graham, Warre, Robertson, Sandeman, Cockburn, Silva & Cosens Ltd. (Dow), Gonzales Byass and Niepoort.

The grape varieties used in making Port have been brought to the U.S. and grow well in California's Central Valley; many American ports compare favorably with some Ports from the Alto Douro.

Portugal: The region of what is now modern Portugal was called ''Lusitania'' by the Romans, who were among the first to appreciate the local wines. Today, wine is one of Portugal's most valuable export products, and the fame of Portuguese wines is world-wide. Though Portugal is only about the size of the state of Indiana, a good deal of the arable land is given over to vineyards, and the Portuguese annually consume over three times as much table wine as is produced in California, despite the fact that the two most famous Portuguese wines — PORT and MADEIRA — are dessert wines and not table wines.

Both Port and Madeira have been subject to strict quality controls for centuries, but only recently has there been government involvement in delimiting other good vineyard areas. The government has classified eight wine regions under the *Denominação de origem* (Denomination of Origin) laws, and several more (Alcobaca, Ribatejo, Lagoa, etc.) are scheduled for approval in subsequent years. Wines entitled to *Denominação de origem* bear a special seal affixed over the neck of the bottle, the *selo de garantia,* guaranteeing their quality and authenticity. Most Portuguese wine destined for everyday enjoyment *(vinho de consumo)* is not subject to these controls, but better quality wine marked for export is, with the result that in England such wines have been called ''Europe's best-kept secret.''

Most Americans associate Portuguese wines with rosé, which presently constitutes a major portion of Portuguese wine exported to the U.S. No specific region has been delimited, however, for some of the best-known Portuguese rosés on the American market (Mateus, Lancer's, Alianca, etc.), and many excellent Portuguese wines are sold under a brand name, not a place of origin. Besides the fruity rosés, the light, refreshing VINHO

233

VERDE wines — from the Minho and Douro Littoral areas in the north, along the Spanish border — are popular. The "green wines" of the Vinho Verde region are produced from grapes grown on high pergolas, picked before they are fully ripe. High in acidity but low in alcohol (8-11%), they are at their best when consumed rather young.

Most of the best Portuguese wines are red, and they age particularly well. COLARES, produced to the northwest of the city of Lisbon, is traditionally one of Portugal's most famous red wines, but very little is exported, as the wines are becoming rare. A much larger and more promising region is DÃO, located some 150 miles to the northeast, where some outstanding reds and interesting whites are produced. Dão's better producers are becoming increasingly more export-minded, and their wines are gaining in importance. Carcavelos and Bucelas, two wine regions near Lisbon, were at one time celebrated for their red and white wines, but they are not well known outside the region today. The sweet MOSCATEL DE SETÚBAL, produced around the city of Setúbal south of Lisbon, is a fine dessert wine.

Port, produced in the upper Douro (Alto Douro) region — and Madeira, made on the island of Madeira some 530 miles to the west of Lisbon — are the best-known and historically the most famous wines of Portugal. They are of sufficient modern-day importance to warrant separate entries in this dictionary.

Portuguiser *(Por-too-geez′-er)*: Red wine grape grown in Germany, accounting for about two-fifths of all the red wine vineyards in that country. The Portuguiser is widely planted in the RHEINHESSEN and RHEIN-PFALZ regions, but its wines tend to be rather light, lacking in color and body. Despite its name, it has nothing to do with the wines of Portugal.

Pouilly-Fuissé *(Poo'-yee Fwee-say')*: Outstanding white French wine, produced in southern Burgundy in the MÂCONNAIS region. Made from the Chardonnay grape, Pouilly-Fuissé is now one of the best-known wines in America. Wines bearing this distinguished name may be produced only in four authorized communes: Fuissé, Solutré-Pouilly, Vergisson and Chaintré, and by law they must attain a minimum alcoholic strength of 11%. There are 1,482 acres under the Pouilly-Fuissé appellation, some more ideally situated than others, and usually the best wines carry some indication of a vineyard name; by law they must attain a minimum alcoholic strength of 12%. The leading vineyards include: Château Fuissé, Clos Ressier, Les Bouthières, Les Clos, Les Champs, Les Vignes-Blanches, Les Menestrières, Les Perrières, and others; however, some names appear to be associated with vineyards but are in fact brand names. The equivalent of some 411,000 cases of Pouilly-Fuissé is produced annually.

Pouilly-Fuissé is a wine to be enjoyed young, and is best when about two years old. It fades soon afterwards, and for this reason wines more than about five years old should be avoided.

Pouilly-Fumé *(Poo'-yee Foo-may')*: Fine white wine produced from the Sauvignon Blanc *(Blanc Fumé)* grape near the village of POUILLY-SUR-LOIRE on the upper LOIRE River valley, France, Despite the similar-sounding name, the wine of Pouilly-Fumé has nothing to do with the Pouilly-Fuissé from the Burgundy region (see above). The word "fumé" means "smoke" in French, and the wines are said to derive their smoky, spicy qualities from the soil on which they are

235

grown. The region adjoins SANCERRE on the other side of the Loire, and the wines have much in common, being made from the same grape variety; however, wines that bear the name ''Pouilly-sur-Loire'' are *not* made from Sauvignon but rather the Chasselas, and are lighter and fruitier. The area under vines entitled to the appellation Pouilly-Fumé is about 1,975 acres; average annual production amounts to some 180,500 cases. The Château du Nozet (which uses the brand name ''De La Doucette'') and Château de Tracy are among the leading producers.

Pouilly-Loché *(Poo'-yee Lo-shay')*: White wine region in the MÂCONNAIS district, southern Burgundy, located around the little town of Loché. The interesting white wines of Pouilly-Loché are similar to those of the famous POUILLY-FUISSÉ region to the west, but are generally not quite as fine, although they are made from the same grape variety — the Chardonnay — and Pouilly-Lochés are usually somewhat less expensive. The vineyard area is small, however, and only about 8,000 cases are produced annually.

Pouilly-sur-Loire *(Poo'-yee Sir Lwahr')*: Village in the upper LOIRE River valley, France, famous principally for its clean, dry white wine made from the Sauvignon Blanc *(Blanc Fumé)* grape, the fine POUILLY-FUMÉ. A lesser quantity of good but somewhat less distinguished wine called ''Pouilly-sur-Loire'' is made from the Chasselas, which yields rather light wines that do not always travel well, though they are popular carafe wines in the region. The production zone in Pouilly-sur-Loire includes the communes of St.-Andelin, Tracy, Garchy, St.-Laurent and Mesves; some 50,700 cases of Pouilly-sur-Loire are produced annually, excluding the more important production of Pouilly-Fumé.

Pouilly-Vinzelles *(Poo'-yee Van-zell')*: White wine region in the MÂCONNAIS district, southern Burgundy, located around the little town of Vinzelles. Made from the same, outstanding Chardonnay grape used in the famous POUILLY-FUISSÉ region just to the west, the wines of Pouilly-Vinzelles are similar but tend to be somewhat lighter and fruitier. Production is limited to about 17,100 cases annually, but because they are generally inexpensive, some good Pouilly-Vinzelles represent excellent value.

Pourriture Noble *(Poo'-ree-tur Nawbl')*: French for "noble mold," the fungus that collects on the skins of the grapes in certain wine regions, concentrating the juice and allowing the making of luscious sweet wines. See BOTRYTIS CINEREA.

Prémeaux *(Pray-mo')*: Wine village in the southern CÔTE DE NUITS, Burgundy, officially part of the commune of NUITS-SAINT GEORGES. The wines of Prémeaux are entitled to the Nuits-Saint Georges appellation and are similar; the best vineyards are: Clos des Corvées, Clos de la Maréchale, Clos des Corvées-Paget, Aux Perdrix, and Les Didiers. Production statistics are combined for the two communes and are listed under Nuits-Saint Georges.

Press Wine: Wine obtained by pressing the skins and pulp remaining in the vat following fermentation, after the FREE RUN wine is drained off. Press wine contains a great deal of tannin and coloring matter; because it tends to be harsh, many producers do not bother with it, but in some regions it is blended with free-run wine to add valuable strength and color.

237

Prosecco *(Pro-sek'-ko)*: White wine made from the Prosecco grape, grown in the province of Treviso in the region of VENETO, northern Italy. Its full name is Prosecco di Conegliano-Valdobbiadene, after the two communes for which the D.O.C. zone is specified. Prosecco may take several forms; most usually it is a pleasant, light dry wine, but it is sometimes made sparkling or semi-sparkling, and occasionally it is semi-sweet *(amabile)* as well.

Provence *(Pro-vawnss')*: Picturesque old province on the Mediterranean coast in southern France; noted for the local dialect, Provençal (which is still spoken in some regions) as well as lush scenery and delightful wines. Today, Provence consists of the departments of Var, Alpes-Maritimes, Hautes-Alpes, Vaucluse, Bouches-du-Rhône, and Alpes-de-Haute-Provence. In relation to its better wines, the most general place-name is CÔTES DE PROVENCE, defining red, white and rosé wines, produced throughout the region and entitled to the V.D.Q.S. seal. Provençal red and white wines may be quite good, but in general the rosés are superior. They are often sold in unusual amphora-shaped bottles, which helps to identify them.

There are several wine regions in Provence that have been granted APPELLATION CONTRÔLÉE status, by virtue of their interesting and original wines. Probably the most famous is BANDOL, noted for its sturdy red wines; the little village of CASSIS to the northwest is celebrated both for its seafood and the crisp white wines that complement it so well. PALETTE, further inland, produces a gamut of good red, white and rosé wines. Bellet is another appellation many miles to the east, but its wine production is limited and most of it is consumed on the spot by tourists in Nice, Cannes and Antibes.

Pucelles *(Pew-sell')*: French for "virgins"; specifically, a fine white wine vineyard in the commune of PULIGNY-MONTRACHET, in Burgundy's CÔTE DE BEAUNE. The Pucelles

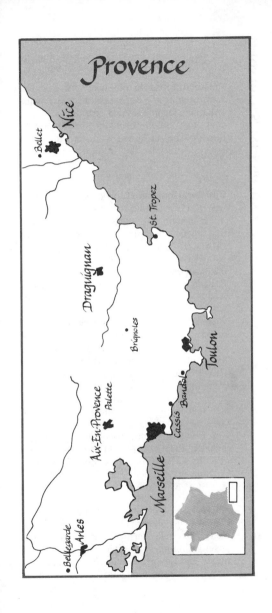

Provence

Nice
Bellet
St. Tropez
Draguignan
Brignoles
Aix-En-Provence
Palette
Toulon
Cassis
Bandol
Marseille
Bellegarde
Arles

plot consists of about 17 acres planted in Chardonnay, and annually produces exquisite white wines prized for their great delicacy.

Puisseguin-Saint-Émilion *(Pweese'-gan Sahnt Eh-meel-lyon')*: Village and wine commune located some 5 miles to the northeast of SAINT-ÉMILION in the BORDEAUX district. The sturdy red wines of Puisseguin are entitled to the Saint-Émilion appellation; they are usually well-made, which makes many of them excellent value.

Puligny-Montrachet *(Pool'-een-yee Mon-rah-shay')*: World-famous wine commune in the CÔTE DE BEAUNE, Burgundy; like the adjoining commune of CHASSAGNE-MONTRACHET to the south, named for the magnificent MONTRACHET — the most celebrated white wine vineyard in Burgundy, rated Grand Cru (Great Growth). Above it on a slight slope is the equally renowned CHEVALIER-MONTRACHET vineyard, producing white wines of similar quality, and just below Montrachet is the BÂTARD-MONTRACHET vineyard with the associated BIENVENUE-BÂTARD-MONTRACHET parcel. Each one of these Grand Cru vineyards is capable of annually producing some of the greatest white Burgundies, but there is a wealth of similarly fine vineyards surrounding them, rated Premier Cru (First Growth); the better vineyards include: COMBETTES, PUCELLES, CAILLERETS, Clavoillon, Les Folatières, Les Chalumeaux, Perrières, and Les Referts. See also BLAGNY.

Puligny's 578 acres of vineyard are planted almost exclusively in Chardonnay, although there is a tiny amount of Pinot Noir grown as well. The chalk-marl soil and excellent exposure combines to yield succulent, perfumed and flavorful white wines with a lingering aftertaste; production averages about

70,000 cases of wine annually, less than 5% of it red.

Punt: The concave indent on the bottom of a wine bottle, designed to give it added strength and also confine the sediment to a narrow area on the bottom.

Puttonyo *(Poo-tawn'-yo)*: In Hungary, a vat, about 8 to 10 gallons capacity, made of wood, like half a barrel, and carried on the back. Used in the vineyards of the Tokay region to collect overripe grapes. The number of puttonyo of overripe grapes added to the standard vat indicates the sweetness and quality of the TOKAY labeled ASZÚ: 3 puttonyos is the lightest Tokay Aszú, 4 puttonyos sweeter, and 5 puttonyos the sweetest wine, made exclusively from overripe grapes. Such outstanding wines are not made every year, and they are necessarily expensive.

Q

Qualitätswein *(Kval-ee-tates'-vine)*: German for "quality wine." Under the 1971 German Wine Law, a wine labeled Qualitätswein must be produced in one of the eleven designated German wine regions (ANBAUGEBIETE). The exact legal terminology is *Qualitätswein bestimmter Anbaugebiete,* abbreviated as Q.b.A.; the terms Qualitätswein and Q.b.A. are interchangeable.

The concept of Qualitätswein arose because of a discrepancy in the old wine laws, which prohibited an ESTATE-BOTTLED wine to be made with the addition of sugar, necessary in years when the grapes do not ripen fully. Under the 1971 Wine Law, this is al-

241

lowed — within limits — for estate-bottled wines, which are now labeled ERZEUGER-ABFÜLLUNG or "producer-bottling." After the wine is made, it is subject to approval by a professional tasting committee, and when released for sale all Qualitätswein are accompanied by an official certification number, the *Amtliche Prüfungsnummer,* which appears on the label along with the vintage year. The certification number identifies the region, the winery, the particular lot of wine, and the date the wine was certified; it is an official guarantee that the wine has met applicable quality standards.

Qualitätswein Mit Prädikat *(Kval-ee-tates'-vine Mit Pray'-dee-kat):* German for "Quality Wine with Special Attributes." Under the 1971 German Wine Law, a wine labeled Qualitätswein Mit Prädikat must be made from sound, ripe grapes in one of the eleven designated wine regions (ANBAUGEBIETE). It is a quality wine or QUALITÄTSWEIN (see above), except that no addition of sugar is allowed. In ascending order of excellence, the quality categories prescribed for Qualitätswein Mit Prädikat are as follows: KABINETT, SPÄTLESE, AUSLESE, BEERENAUSLESE, and TROCKENBEERENAUSLESE; in addition, there is the rare EISWEIN, produced from partially frozen grapes, which can be made in all *Prädikat* categories.

A wine in any of the *Prädikat* categories will usually be superior to one labeled Qualitätswein, because the requirements for manufacture — in accordance with the legal minimum MUST WEIGHT standards for each category — are more stringent. (For a chart showing these standards, see GERMANY.).

Quarts de Chaume *(Kahr Duh Shome'):* Small but outstanding white wine region in the lower LOIRE River valley, France, located near the village of Rochefort-sur-Loire in the old province of ANJOU. The region is named for an estate originally divided into four parts *(quarts)* near the little hamlet of Chaume; there are some 125 acres of vineyard planted in Chenin Blanc grapes, and in late autumn the grapes are picked when overripe, yielding luscious, naturally sweet wines that are exceptionally long lived; average production is about 6,000 cases a year. The leading vineyard estates are: Château de Belle-Rive, Château de Suronde, Château de Beaumard, and L'Écharderie. See also BONNEZEAUX.

Quincy *(Can'-see)*: White wine region in the upper LOIRE River valley, France, situated along a tributary, the River Cher, near the city of Bourges. Quincy has some 495 acres of vineyard planted chiefly in Sauvignon Blanc grapes, and is renowned for its light, clean and fruity white wines; average production is about 35,000 cases annually.

Quinta *(Keen'-ta)*: Portuguese for "vineyard estate." In the making of PORT, the wines are made at the quinta, aged briefly, and then are shipped down to the city of Vila Nova de Gaia for further blending and aging.

R

Racking: The process of transferring new wine from one container to another, with the purpose of separating the wine from the lees and gross sediment. Racking usually results in a slight loss of wine, but it is essential if the wine is to be clear and bright before bottling. The French term for racking is *soutirage;* in German it is *Abstich*. See also FILTRATION and FINING.

243

Rainwater: A dry or medium-dry MADEIRA,

with a golden color and a fragrant bouquet. Originally the proprietary brand of a shipper named Habisham in Savannah, Georgia (who received the nickname "Rainwater Habisham"), Rainwater is now a general term for a type of Madeira, and several Madeira shippers use this name, not always for the same kind of wine. It is said to have originated from a special technique of clarification devised by Habisham, which made the wines clear and brilliant, like rainwater.

Randersacker *(Rahn'-der-sock-er)*: Village in the region of FRANKEN (Franconia), Germany, located just to the south of WÜRZBURG. Randersacker has 568 acres of vineyard: the best sites are planted in white grape varieties (Silvaner, Riesling, Müller-Thurgau), although a little red is also grown. In good years Randersacker makes some of Franken's best wine; the leading vineyards (EINZELLAGEN) include: Marsberg, Pfülben, Teufelskeller, Sonnenstuhl, and Dabug.

Rauenthal *(Rau'-en-tahl)*: One of the most famous wine villages in the RHEINGAU district, Germany, with 252 acres of vineyard. Rauenthal's vineyards are set back in the hills away from the Rhine, giving finely-scented Riesling wines with a characteristic spiciness. The best-known (and most valuable) Rauenthal vineyard or EINZELLAGE is Baiken, which often makes one of the Rheingau's best wines; other good Einzellagen include: Gehrn, Wülfen, Rothenberg, Langenstück, and Nonnenberg. It should be noted that Rauenthaler Steinmächer, however, is not an Einzellage but a composite vineyard or GROSSLAGE some 1134 acres large; its wines are generally inferior to those from the Einzellagen. The choicest Rauenthal holdings belong to the Staatsweingut, Schloss Eltz, and Langwerth von Simmern.

Ravello *(Ra-vell'-lo)*: Little village south of Naples in the region of CAMPANIA, Italy, noted for its wines of the same name. Red, white and rosé wines are produced in Ravello; though not rated D.O.C., the wines are good and are well-known in the U.S. The leading producer in Ravello is Ditta P. Caruso.

Récemment Dégorgé *(Ray'-sem-mawn Day-gor-zhay')*: French for "recently disgorged." In the French CHAMPAGNE district, some producers occasionally set aside a few select bottles of a particularly fine vintage Champagne, and leave them for an additonal period of time in the cellars to mature, without disgorging them (see DÉGORGEMENT). These wines, which carry a premium, are usually finer and fuller in flavor than regular vintage Champagnes; they may also be abbreviated as "R.D." The wines are normally disgorged and released for sale about ten years after the vintage, when most of their contemporaries are well past their prime, and they are ready to enjoy immediately.

Recioto *(Ray-chaw'-toe)*: A special wine produced in the region of VENETO, northern Italy. Recioto wines are made from the uppermost portions of the grape bunches, which have received a maximum amount of sunshine and are extra high in sugar; the term is derived from the word *recia* (which means "ears," in the local dialect), and thus the wines are made from the "ears" of the bunches. After picking, the grapes are then dried on special wicker racks prior to being pressed. Recioto wines are usually sweet and full-bodied, although dry reciotos are also made (see AMARONE). The most famous reciotos come from the VALPOLICELLA district and are red, called Recioto della Valpolicella, although there is some white recioto from SOAVE as well. Because of their

245

high sugar content, recioto wines are sometimes also made sparkling.

Récolte *(Ray′-cawlt)*: French for "harvest" or "vintage."

Regional: A wine made in a region or district, as opposed to a specific town or vineyard. Regional wines are usually inexpensive blended wines; though they are rarely outstanding, they fill an important need in the trade. Well-known examples include MÉDOC, CÔTES-DU-RHÔNE, and LIEBFRAUMILCH.

Rehoboam: An oversized bottle used occasionally in the French CHAMPAGNE district, with the capacity of six ordinary bottles.

Reims *(Ranss)*: City in northern France with a population of some 160,000; occasionally spelled *Rheims,* the old medieval name. Reims is the largest city in the French CHAMPAGNE district, where many of the leading Champagne producers have their offices and cellars. The semicircular sweep of vineyards immediately south of the city, the MONTAGNE DE REIMS, is planted predominantly in black Pinot Noir grapes, and the wines tend to be rich and full-bodied. G.H. Mumm, Veuve Clicquot-Ponsardin, Taittinger, Piper-Heidsieck, Charles Heidsieck, Louis Roederer, Ruinart Père et Fils, Pommery & Greno, Krug and Lanson are among the important Champagne firms with offices in Reims.

Remuage *(Ray-moo-ahj′)*: French for "shaking" or "riddling"; specifically, a process employed in the French CHAMPAGNE district for removing the sediment in the bottle, following the secondary fermentation. Remuage was first devised in the 19th century by Madame Veuve Clicquot née Ponsardin (1777-1866), and it is now standard procedure in the Champagne process. The bottles are placed in adjustable, angled racks or *pupitres,* which can be tilted, and skilled workmen twist the bottles regularly over a period of about 90 days, tilting the *pupitres* until the bottles are upside down and all the sediment has collected on the cork. The bottles are then taken to be disgorged (see DÉGORGEMENT).

Reserva *(Ray-sair′-va)*: Spanish for "reserve," a selected lot of wine that has been set aside for further aging in cask or in bottle. This term is used most frequently in the RIOJA district.

Retsina *(Ret-seen′-ah)*: Greek wine to which pine sap or resin has been added, giving it a woody, pitch flavor. The practice of resinating wines is said to have originated in Ancient Greece when wines were stored in pitched amphorae; such wines are very popular in Greece, though to most Americans they are an acquired taste.

Rheingau *(Rhine′-gow)*: Possibly the most famous wine district in Germany, located west of the city of Frankfurt between the villages of Assmannshausen and HOCH-HEIM, where the Rhine River takes a nearly straight 20-mile course southwest. From the river, the land rises up to the Taunus Mountains in the north, protecting the region from cold north winds; nearly all the vineyards have an incomparable southerly exposure, resulting in one grand array of well-known wine towns.

Yet the Rheingau is neither the largest vineyard area in Germany nor the most productive, and it is hard to believe that for all their fame, only 7,460 acres are under vines. But the Rheingau is renowned primarily for select bottlings, produced by centuries-old vineyard estates. The nobility still figures heavily among Rheingau producers, and family coats-of-arms appear often on finely-ornamented labels. Four-fifths of the land is planted in Riesling, and from the fine loess-loam soil of the Rheingau, scented and flavorful white wines are the result; a small amount of red wine of purely local fame is the specialty of Assmannshausen.

The Rhine River also contributes to the excellence of the wines: it reflects the sun's rays during the day, and tends to hold the heat at night; in addition, it produces the autumn mists that encourage the formation of what the Germans call *Edelfäule* or "noble mold" (see BOTRYTIS CINEREA), which, although it does not appear every autumn, allows the making of some of the world's finest naturally sweet wines.

The Rheingau begins upstream at Hochheim, near where the Main River flows into the Rhine, and continues westward past the well-known wine towns of WALLUF, RAUENTHAL, ELTVILLE, ERBACH, KIEDRICH, HATTENHEIM, HALLGARTEN, OESTRICH, Mittelheim, WINKEL, JOHANNISBERG, GEISENHEIM, and RÜDESHEIM; at Assmannshausen, just west of Rüdesheim, the Rhine abruptly shifts north, marking the westernmost boundary of the region.

In general, the wines of the Rheingau take the name of the town where they are made, with the exception of some from select estates that are famous enough to be sold under their own name; examples include the STEINBERG and Schloss Vollrads (see VOLLRADS, SCHLOSS). The village of Johannisberg is dominated by one great estate, Schloss Johannisberg (see JOHANNISBERG, SCHLOSS), one of the Rheingau's oldest and most famous, and under the 1971 German Wine Law the entire Rheingau was classified under a single sub-region or BEREICH, Johannisberg. Total annual production averages close to 2.8 million cases.

Rheinhessen *(Rhine'-hess-en):* Rhinehessen, or Hessia, is the second largest wine region or ANBAUGEBIET in Germany, with nearly 49,000 acres under vines, exceeded only by the RHEINPFALZ region (see below). The region lies on the left bank of the Rhine River to the north of the Rheinpfalz, and the vineyards form a vast area beginning south near the city of WORMS, continuing due north along the Rhine as far as Mainz, and then paralleling the RHEINGAU district on the other side of the river, on a southwest course to BINGEN.

Most of the Rheinhessen region produces blended wine, but although they tend to be rarer, the fine white wines from the Rheinhessen's better producers can stand with the best in Germany — especially the luxurious and fruity wines made from late-harvested grapes. Rheinhessen wines have a characteristic softness — some call them "feminine" — which is a function of the soil and the temperate climate in which they are grown. They are made mostly from the Müller-Thurgau grape, which now accounts for nearly 40% of the vineyards in Rheinhessen; a wine for which the grape variety is not specified will probably be made from Müller-Thurgau. The Silvaner, which used to be the dominant variety, is now less widely planted. Riesling is relatively rare in the Rheinhessen, although in top vineyards it makes some of the region's finest wines. The Scheurebe, a Riesling/Silvaner cross, is gaining rapidly in certain vineyards. Some interesting red wine from the Spätburgunder or Portuguiser is also a Rheinhessen specialty, but most of it is consumed in Germany.

The Rheinhessen is most famous for LIEBFRAUMILCH, quite possibly the best known wine name in Germany, although not many would suggest that it is Germany's best wine. The name allegedly derives from the Liebfrauenstift church near the city of Worms, and in the past all sorts of German

249

wines were openly sold as Liebfraumilch, but under the 1971 German Wine Law the usage of this name is now restricted to a QUALITÄTSWEIN (quality wine) that must attain certain legal minimum standards.

The 1971 Wine Law delimited the Rheinhessen region into three sub-regions or BEREICHE. The most important is NIERSTEIN, named for its most famous wine town and better known for its regional wines — usually sold under the name Niersteiner Gutes Domthal — than those of its best vineyards (EINZELLAGEN). Bereich Nierstein also includes the celebrated wine villages of NACKENHEIM, OPPENHEIM, BODENHEIM and DIENHEIM, which form a chain of well-exposed vineyards on the left bank of the Rhine; Alsheim, Harxheim and Guntersblum are other prominent towns in the Bereich. Further south, Bereich Wonnegau includes the towns of Worms, Alzey, Bechtheim and Osthofen; most of the wine is used for blending, and few of these names will appear on a wine sold in the U.S. The remaining Bereich is Bingen, named after the most western city in the Rheinhessen. Included in Bereich Bingen are the villages of INGELHEIM (famous for its good red wine, a rarity in Germany), Gau-Algesheim, Ockenheim, Bornheim, and Dromersheim. Bereich Bingen extends up to the NAHE River to the west, but the Nahe valley is an independent wine region and its vineyards are discussed separately.

Wine production in the Rheinhessen district is prodigious. Over 24 million cases are typically produced annually, white wine accounting for about 90% of the total.

250 **Rheinpfalz** *(Rhine'-fahlts):* The Rheinpfalz area, or Palatinate, is the largest wine region (ANBAUGEBIET) in Germany, with nearly 50,000 acres of vineyard. Located on the left bank of the Rhine River north of the border with France, the Rheinpfalz region is one of the warmest and driest agricultural areas in Germany. Orchards and vineyards abound in the rolling countryside, and the mild climate assures optimum ripening conditions. The region produces over 26 million cases of wine annually.

The world Pfalz derives from the Latin *Palatium,* for the region was noted for its wine during the Roman Empire, and it was named for the Palatine Hills in Rome, the first residence of the Roman emperors. The Rheinpfalz vineyards presently extend along the gentle slopes of the Haardt Mountains.

The Haardt is divided into three districts. In the south is the Ober-Haardt (Upper Haardt), which begins at the town of Schweigen on the French border and extends up to the village of Neustadt. The Mittel-Haardt (Middle Haardt) continues up about as far as Bad Dürkheim (see DÜRKHEIM), and North of Bad Dürkheim the Unter-Haardt (Lower Haardt) extends northwards up to the RHEINHESSEN region.

Over four-fifths of Rheinpfalz wine is white; the light red wine, made mostly from the Portuguiser, is primarily consumed locally and is less important commercially. Only a small area in the Rheinpfalz is planted in superior vines. A decade ago 40% of the vineyards were given over to the productive Silvaner, which primarily supplied the ordinary carafe wine known as *Schoppenwein* in German, but now the Silvaner has been supplanted by the even more productive Müller-Thurgau. Some fine, full-bodied white wine is made from the Gewürztraminer and the Scheurebe. The noble Riesling, which figures so heavily in the RHEINGAU and MOSEL districts, only accounts for about 15% of the Rheinpfalz vineyards. But in the Mittelhaardt the percentage of Riesling suddenly

251

climbs to 70%, and there some of the finest white wines in Germany are made.

The 1971 German Wine Law divided the Rheinpfalz into two sub-regions or BEREICHE: Südliche Weinstrasse, and Mittelhaardt-Deutsche Weinstrasse. The primary access road through the Haardt is the ''Weinstrasse,'' or wine road, which has been officially designated as such since 1932. The Weinstrasse commences at Schweigen at the immense Weintor (wine gate), and then leads past fields and orchards through the Mittelhaardt, passing by the famous wine towns of FORST, DEIDESHEIM, WACHENHEIM, RUPPERTSBERG, KÖNIGSBACH, Dürkheim, UNGSTEIN, and KALLSTADT. The first four towns are generally considered the most valuable in the entire Rheinpfalz, and their wines fetch appropriate prices in the trade. The three most famous Rheinpfalz wine producers — Bürklin-Wolf, Bassermann-Jordan, and Reichsrat von Buhl — are known colloquially as ''the three B's,'' through their initials; they own some of the finest vineyard holdings in Ruppertsberg, Forst, Deidesheim and Wachenheim. Other leading Rheinpfalz producers include: Dr. Deinhard, Stumpf-Fitz, and several important wine cooperatives *(Winzervereine)*.

Rhine Wine: Strictly defined, a wine from the Rhine region in Germany, comprising the present-day regions of the RHEINGAU, RHEINHESSEN, RHEINPFALZ, and MITTELRHEIN. As generally used in the U.S. wine trade, a ''Rhine wine'' has no specific definition other than a light, semi-dry white wine, and this GENERIC term is used by some producers to identify wines of this type.

252 **Rhône** *(Rone)***:** European river some 504 miles long, drawing its source in Switzerland, flowing through Lake Geneva, and then continuing its journey due south through France to its mouth near the city of Marseilles.

Navigable for much of its length, the Rhône is a principal waterway; it is also one of France's leading vineyard areas. The most general term for Rhône wines is CÔTES-DU-RHÔNE, applying to red, white or rosé wines produced from 96,370 acres of vineyards in about 120 different communes.

Most of the Rhône's southern journey takes it through hot and dry country, and because the grapes receive a maximum amount of sun, vintages vary less in the Rhône than in other fine French wine regions. The wines tend to be full-flavored — reds are robust and need a long period of time to mature; whites are powerful and long-lived. The lively, stylish rosés are among the best in France.

It is common practice in the Rhône to blend wines of various grape varieties, depending on the district where they are grown. The principal red Rhône grape is the Syrah, a variety used on its own only in a few northern districts; it is normally blended with some white grapes to add finesse. This is standard practice in the famous red wine regions of CÔTE ROTIE, HERMITAGE and CROZES-HERMITAGE to the north; one white grape, the Viognier, is used for the brilliant white wines of CONDRIEU. Sturdy red and white wines are made in the nearby areas of CORNAS and SAINT-JOSEPH. Further south near the city of Avignon, the famous red wine of CHÂTEAUNEUF-DU-PAPE is made from as many as 13 different grape varieties, of which the Mourvèdre, Syrah, Cinsault, and Grenache are most important. The Grenache is also used for the fine rosés of TAVEL and LIRAC. See also GIGONDAS.

In addition, the Hermitage and Crozes-Hermitage regions also make some excellent white wines from Marsanne and Roussanne grapes, and some interesting sparkling and semi-sparkling wines are made in SAINT-PÉRAY and in the village of Die (see CLAIRETTE). The sweet Muscat wine of the

253

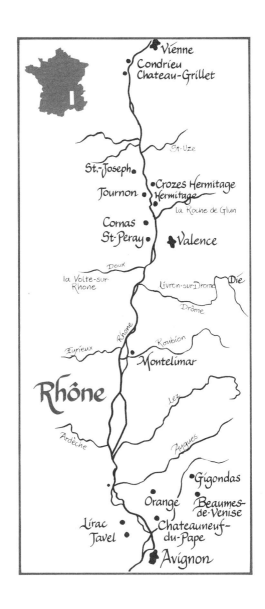

BEAUMES-DE-VENISE region is also acclaimed, but it is rare in the U.S.

Richebourg *(Reesh'-boorg)*: World-famous red wine vineyard in the CÔTE DE NUITS, Burgundy, rated Grand Cru (Great Growth). Located in the celebrated commune of VOSNE-ROMANÉE, the vineyard consists of 19 acres planted in Pinot Noir, and is one of the largest in Vosne-Romanée. Richebourg is usually one of the most full-bodied of the Côte de Nuits Grand Crus; about 3,100 cases are produced annually. The vineyard is shared by several owners, of which Louis Gros, the Domaine de la Romanée-Conti, and Charles Noëllat are the most important.

Riesling *(Reese'-ling)*: One of the finest white wine grapes, used for the great wines of the Rhine and the MOSEL in Germany, and some of the best white wines of ALSACE in France. Its yield is small and it ripens later than other varieties, but its wines are nobly scented and have great suavity. Because it is grown for the famous wines of Schloss Johannisberg (see JOHANNISBERG, SCHLOSS) on the Rhine, it is named Johannisberg Riesling in California; over 8,000 acres have been planted throughout the state. The Riesling is also grown in northern Italy, Switzerland, and in many eastern European countries as well. It is one of the few grape varieties susceptible to the "noble mold" (see BOTRYTIS CINEREA), and thus is ideal for superb, lusciously sweet wines made from late-harvested grapes.

There are a number of grape varieties unrelated to the Riesling that have assumed its famous name, and for this reason the true Riesling is called "White Riesling" or "Rhine Riesling" to distinguish it from others such as Wälschriesling, Grey Riesling, Main Riesling, and Emerald Riesling. In California and Australia, a wine may be labeled "Riesling" even if it is made from the more productive Sylvaner or Sémillon. Wines made from these varieties — though they may be similar in style — are generally not quite as fine.

Rioja *(Ree-o'-ha)***:** Outstanding wine region in north-central Spain near the French border, named for the Rio Oja River, a tributary of the Ebro, which flows through it. A dry, mountainous region, the Rioja has climatic conditions similar to those in BORDEAUX, France, and shares many of the same wine-making traditions, for in the late 19th century winemakers from Bordeaux came to the Rioja region to escape the PHYLLOXERA, which was then ravaging their vineyards. They brought the same time-honored techniques with them to the Rioja, and many are still in use today.

The Rioja region is divided into three different parts. The upper district, Rioja Alta, has the coolest climate and usually makes the lightest and most refined wines. The wines become more intense in the middle part, Rioja Alavesa, and decidedly coarser in the lower portion, Rioja Baja. The headquarters of the Rioja wine trade is the little town of Haro in Rioja Alta, where many of the leading producers have their cellars or BODEGAS.

Red Rioja is a blend of several different grape varieties: Garnacha (identical to the Grenache grown in France), Tempranillo, Graciano, and Mazuelo. White Rioja is produced from Malvasia, Viura, and Calagraño. However, more important to Rioja's character than the grape varieties is the amount of time the wine ages in cask. Traditionally, Rioja spends many years in the wood before it is bottled. This is beneficial to the sturdy red wine, making it soft and palatable, but many of the white Riojas suffer from being in cask too long and often tend to turn prematurely brown and flat. New methods of vinification, however, are improving the white wines.

Part of the reason Rioja wines are superior

is that the vineyard area of 123,500 acres has been delimited under the *Denominación de Orígén* wine laws, one of the few regions in Spain where this has been authorized. No Rioja is bottled and sold if it does not meet minimum standards, and a small stamp of authenticity on the label, the Certificate of Origin, identifies the wine as genuine Rioja.

Many Rioja producers identify the "style" of their wines by the shape of the bottle: lighter, drier wines are put in Bordeaux-shaped bottles, while fuller, richer wines are put in Burgundy-shaped bottles. The terms *Reserva* or *Reserva Especial* indicate particularly fine wines from great vintages that have spent many years in cask; lighter wines with little cask aging are sold as "clarete." Vintages do vary in the Rioja, but in general a vintage date indicates a good wine, for wine unworthy of a vintage date is not bottled but sold instead as ordinary table wine in the district.

Among the better producers of Rioja are: Bodegas Bilbainas, Marqués de Riscal, Federico Paternina, Marqués de Murrieta, Compañia Vinicola del Notre de España (which uses the brand name C.U.N.E.), R. López de Heredia (Viña Tondonia), Bodegas Muerza, Bodegas Unidas (Siglo), and many wine cooperatives.

Riserva *(Ree-sairv'-ah)*: Italian for "reserve," a special lot of wine that has received additional aging, either in cask or in bottle. In certain famous Italian wine regions, usage of the word riserva is legally restricted only to those wines which have been aged at least three or four years before being sold. Such wines are of superior quality, and the prices they command are usually higher than others in their class.

257

Romanée, La *(Ro'-man-nay)*: Tiny but highly-acclaimed red wine vineyard in the

CÔTE DE NUITS, Burgundy, located in the famous commune of VOSNE-ROMANÉE and rated Grand Cru (Great Growth). Owned by a single proprietor, the vineyard consists of two acres planted in Pinot Noir, adjoining the great ROMANÉE-CONTI vineyard which lies below it. Average production is a scant 300 cases a year.

Romanée-Conti (*Ro'-man-nay Cawn'-tee*): Perhaps the rarest and most expensive wine of the CÔTE DE NUITS, Burgundy, named for the Prince de Conti, who purchased the vineyard in 1760. Through its fame, the township of Vosne in which it lies is now called VOSNE-ROMANÉE. Officially rated Grand Cru (Great Growth), the vineyard is a mere 4½ acres large, and production averages less than 500 cases a year of intense, satiny and perfumed red wine, all of it ESTATE-BOTTLED. Romanée-Conti is managed by a sole owner, the Société Civile du Domaine de la Romanée-Conti, which has other holdings in some of the best Vosne-Romanée vineyards: La TÂCHE in its entirety, RICHEBOURG, GRANDS-ÉCHEZEAUX, ROMANÉE-SAINT-VIVANT, and a choice section of the great MONTRACHET as well.

Romanée-Saint-Vivant (*Ro'-man-nay San Vee-vahn'*): Famous red wine vineyard in the CÔTE DE NUITS, Burgundy, located in the celebrated commune of VOSNE-ROMANÉE. One of the largest Grand Cru (Great Growth) vineyards in Vosne-Romanée, Romanée-Saint-Vivant extends over some 23 acres of Pinot Noir vines and produces fine, scented red wines with a typically lingering aftertaste; production averages some 3,000 cases a year. The vineyard belongs to several proprietors, the most important being the Domaine de la Romanée-Conti (administrators of the Marey-Monge estate), Louis Latour, and Charles Noëllat.

Romania: The agricultural heartland of Romania is one of the most fertile in Europe, and the climate is ideal for grape growing. Known as Dacia in ancient times, the slopes of the Carpathian Mountains have been a prominent vineyard area for centuries, and it is interesting to note that Romania presently is the sixth largest wine-producing country in Europe, with more than 735,500 acres of vineyard.

Like most other key industries, wine-making in Romania was nationalized following World War II, and a governmental export agency called Vinexport was set up to handle the export of Romanian quality wines. Located in the capital city of Bucharest, Vinexport now ships Romanian wines to all corners of the world. France and Germany (two great wine-producing countries in their own right) are among the best customers, and the rest of Europe is an active market for Romanian wines. Romania's wine exports to the U.S. have increased substantially during the past few years, although many of the wines are as yet not well-known.

Traditionally the most famous Romanian wine is COTNARI, a fine sweet white dessert wine produced in the northeast of the country, in the province of Moldavia. Cotnari has a rival in Murfatlar, another good sweet wine grown along the shores of the Black Sea several hundred miles to the south. The Tîrnave vineyard, named for the River Tîrnave that flows westward in the center of Romania, is an important wine area noted for its scented white wines made from Feteasca, Romania's indigenous grape variety. Other good wines are made from Muscat, Cadarca (Kadarka), Cabernet, Pinot Noir, Riesling, and Aligoté. An important wine region east of the Carpathian Mountains is Focşani, the largest new plantation of vineyard in the country, and the Romanian State Government has created a spectacular experimental vineyard just to the

259

south, at Dealul Mare.

Rosato *(Ro-sot′-toe)*: Italian for "rosé," or any light pink wine.

Rosé *(Ro-zay′)*: French for "pink." A *vin rosé* is a light pink wine, normally produced by crushing red grapes and allowing the juice to remain in contact with the skins only for a very short time — usually 24 to 48 hours — so that the wine obtains a rose-colored tinge. Some well-known and excellent examples of rosé wines are made from the Grenache grape in TAVEL and LIRAC, France; the Grenache is also used for some of the best California rosés. Other good French rosés are made in Burgundy (see MARSANNAY) and in PROVENCE. Rosé wines can also be produced by blending red and white wines, or by pressing red and white grapes together in the same vat, but the wines are rather different and generally less good than those made by the traditional method.

Rosso *(Ross′-so)*: Italian for "red." This term, describing a red wine, should not be confused with *rosato,* which applies to a rosé wine.

Roussanne *(Roo-sahn′)*: White grape variety grown in the RHÔNE River valley, France, used in conjunction with the Marsanne vine to make the fine white wines of HERMITAGE.

Roussette *(Roo-set′)*: White grape variety grown in northeastern France, particularly in the old province of Savoie (Savoy), where it is used for the fine white wine of SEYSSEL. In addition to Seyssel, the Roussette is grown in other parts of Savoie, and the good white regional wine, Roussette de Savoie, is rated APPELLATION CONTRÔLÉE.

Roussillon *(Roo′-see-yawn)*: Wine region in southern France near the Spanish border, in the hilly area around the major city of Perpignan. Noted for its wines since Roman times, the Roussillon area is famous principally for sweet FORTIFIED WINES, some of which are among the best in France. Grand Roussillon is the general name for several associated regions specializing in sweet fortified wines, each of which has been rated APPELLATION CONTRÔLÉE: Côtes du Haut-Roussillon in the south, Rivesaltes in the immediate vicinity of Perpignan, and Côtes d'Agly and Maury to the north. BANYULS, located further south near the city of Port-Vendres, is the most highly acclaimed wine region in the entire Roussillon area.

Roxheim *(Rawks'-heim)*: Notable wine village in the NAHE River valley, Germany, with 244 acres of vineyard, most of them planted in Riesling. The elegant white wines of Roxheim are among the Nahe's best and share many of the same characteristics as those from nearby KREUZNACH, but they are not well-known outside Germany. The vineyards (EINZELLAGEN) include: Höllenpfad, Birkenberg, Mühlenberg, Berg, Hüttenberg, and Sonnenberg.

Ruby Cabernet: Red HYBRID grape variety, developed in 1946 by Dr. Harold Olmo at the University of California at Davis. A cross between the Carignane and the Cabernet Sauvignon, the Ruby Cabernet was developed to produce quality wines in warm climatic regions; over 18,000 acres have been planted throughout the state, with highest concentrations in the warm Central Valley.

Previously, some wineries produced a VARIETAL wine from Ruby Cabernet and labeled it "Cabernet"; as a result, many people confuse it with Cabernet Sauvignon, which is normally a superior variety in most cooler climatic regions. The B.A.T.F. ruled in 1975 that this practice is no longer permitted, and the abbreviation "Cabernet" now applies only to Cabernet Sauvignon.

261

Ruchottes *(Roo-shot')*: Excellent white wine vineyard in the CÔTE DE BEAUNE, Burgundy, located in the commune of CHASSAGNE-MONTRACHET and rated Premier Cru (First Growth). Barely 7½ acres large, the vineyard consists of two parcels, Grands-Ruchottes and Ruchottes, which usually produce some outstanding white Burgundies. The name Ruchottes is said to derive from the French word *ruche,* meaning "apiary" or "beehive," and it is suggestive of the honey-like quality of the wines from this vineyard.

Ruchottes-Chambertin *(Roo-shot' Shawm'-bear-tan)*: Fine red wine vineyard in the northern CÔTE DE NUITS, Burgundy, located in the commune of GEVREY-CHAMBERTIN and rated Grand Cru (Great Growth). Ruchottes-Chambertin is named for the great CHAMBERTIN that lies nearby, though wines from the latter vineyard are usually superior. However, Ruchottes-Chambertin is one of the finest Burgundy vineyards; there are about 8 acres planted in Pinot Noir, and production averages some 1,000 cases annually.

Rüdesheim *(Roo'-dess-heim)*: One of the most famous wine towns in the RHEINGAU district, Germany. The most western village of consequence in that notable stretch of vines, Rüdesheim is located at a sharp bend in the river, where the Rhine commences a northerly direction. The Rüdesheim vineyards or EINZELLAGEN are planted on extremely steep, terraced hillsides; the most famous of these — on the steepest terraces — are named "Berg" in acknowledgement of the degree of slope: Berg Rottland, Berg Roseneck, and Berg Schlossberg. The other fine Rüdesheim Einzellagen: Bischofsberg, Drachenstein, Klosterlay, Klosterberg, Kirchenpfad, and Magdelenenkreuz, are located behind the town on less precipitous slopes.

262

Combined, the vineyards extend over 736 acres, most of them planted in Riesling.

Because of Rüdesheim's exemplary soil and location, its wines are usually the most reliable of the whole Rheingau in rainy or mediocre vintages, although the vineyards are apt to lack moisture in dry years. At their best, the Rüdesheimers are superb — typically powerful and authoritative, with a great deal of scent and finesse. Incidentally, it is important to note that there is another wine town called Rüdesheim in the NAHE River valley to the south, but its wines are much less important than the fine Rheingau Rüdesheimers and they are not often sold in the U.S.

Rugiens *(Roo-zhan')***:** Notable red wine vineyard in the commune of POMMARD, in Burgundy's CÔTE DE BEAUNE. Officially rated Premier Cru (First Growth), the Rugiens vineyard consists of two associated parcels, Rugiens-Haut and Rugiens-Bas, which extend over about 33 acres; the fine red wines that it gives are characteristically fruity and full-bodied red Burgundies.

Ruländer *(Roo'-lender)***:** The local name for the Pinot Gris grape in the region of BADEN, Germany, where over 4,000 acres have been planted. See PINOT GRIS.

Rully *(Roo'-yee)***:** Wine region in the CHALONNAIS district, Burgundy, located to the northwest of the city of Chalon-sur-Saône. Rully is famous chiefly for its good white wines made from the Chardonnay grape; in addition, some red wine of lesser quality is also produced, and the area has an important sparkling Burgundy *(Bourgogne mousseux)* industry as well. There are some 17,000 cases of Rully produced each year.

Ruppertsberg *(Roo'-perts-bairg)***:** Famous wine town in the RHEINPFALZ (Palatinate) region, Germany, with 939 acres of vineyard. One of the most highly-acclaimed villages in the Rheinpfalz, Ruppertsberg adjoins DEIDESHEIM just to the north, and its fine, scented Riesling wines share many of the same noble characteristics. The vineyards (EINZELLAGEN) include: Reiterpfad, Hoheburg, Nussbien, Linsenbusch, Spiess and Gaisböhl; the latter is owned exclusively by the estate of Dr. Bürklin-Wolf, a top Rheinpfalz producer.

Rust *(Roost)*: Renowned wine village on the western shores of the Neusiedler See (Lake Neusiedl), Austria, in the district of Burgenland. Along with the village of Apetlon on the opposite shore, Rust is the most famous of the Lake Neusiedl vineyards, particularly for sweet wines made from late-harvested grapes — known as *Ausbruch* in Austria. Recent legislation officially delimited the entire wine region *(Weinbaugebiet)* as Rust-Neusiedlersee, in acknowledgement of its traditional importance.

Ruwer *(Roo'-ver)*: Little river in Germany, a tributary of the MOSEL, into which it flows near the city of TRIER. Many famous vineyards are planted along its slate banks; the Ruwer district is considered part of the Mosel area, and the official wine region (ANBAUGEBIET) is Mosel-Saar-Ruwer (see SAAR). Ruwer wines are typically light and refined, though they are generally only at their best in great vintages; in rainy years they are often too acid. The region has over 500 acres of vineyard; the best are planted in Riesling, yielding wines with great class. The two most famous Ruwer wine estates, MAXIMIN GRÜNHAUS in Mertesdorf and the Karthäuserhofberg in EITELSBACH, have been praised for centuries; similarly fine wines are often made in KASEL, AVELSBACH, and WALDRACH.

S

Saar *(Sahr)***:** Important river in western Germany, a tributary of the MOSEL; also a world-famous wine region. Saar wines are considered as Mosels, although they tend to be more austere than wines from the Mittel-Mosel. Over 3,800 acres in the Saar River valley are given over to vineyards, where they mingle with orchards and pastures.

Though the Saar's climate varies considerably from year to year, some of Germany's very greatest white wines are produced there. Fine autumn weather brings out delectable subtleties in the Riesling grapes, and certain Saar wines are among the most exquisite and complex white wines in the world. But in many years the weather barely permits any good wines at all, and many have to be made with the addition of sugar.

The most famous Saar vineyard is the SCHARZHOFBERG, producing some of the most prized of all German wines. The Scharzhofberg lies adjacent to the town of WILTINGEN, which also makes fine wines; other famous Saar villages include OCKFEN (especially celebrated for one particular wine, Ockfener Bockstein), AYL, KANZEM, OBEREMMEL, SERRIG, and Wawern. Incidentally, the Scharzhofberg, a specific vineyard or EINZELLAGE, should not be confused with Scharzberg, which under the 1971 German Wine Law has become a composite vineyard or GROSSLAGE that includes all of the vineyards in the Saar region.

Saint Amour *(Sahnt Ah-moor')***:** Famous wine village in the BEAUJOLAIS district, southern Burgundy, with 457 acres of vineyard. Officially one of the nine Beaujolais

265

crus (growths), those areas that are particularly noted for their wine, Saint Amour is one of the most popular Beaujolais *crus,* possibly because of its charming name. Most of the vineyards are planted in Gamay, yielding zesty, quick-maturing red wines prized for their fine bouquet, but there are also a few vineyards planted in Chardonnay that produce an equally good white wine, sold under the appellation ''Beaujolais Blanc.'' Total production of both types is some 100,000 cases annually.

Saint-Aubin *(Sahnt Oh-Ban')*: Wine village of secondary importance in the CÔTE DE BEAUNE, Burgundy, located near the famous commune of PULIGNY-MONTRACHET. There are some 345 acres of vineyard in Saint-Aubin, which produce few great wines but a generous quantity of good red and white wines; total production averages some 20,000 cases a year. The wines are sold either under the name Saint-Aubin or as CÔTE DE BEAUNE-VILLAGES.

Saint-Émilion *(Sahnt Eh-meel-lyon')*: Picturesque little wine village in the BORDEAUX country, France, located some 25 miles to the east of the city of Bordeaux near the DORDOGNE River. Wine has been made in Saint-Émilion for over 2,000 years; along with POMEROL to the west, Saint-Émilions are usually the most sturdy and full-bodied of the great Bordeaux wines. They are made predominantly from the Merlot grape, with which some Cabernet Franc (locally called Bouchet) is normally blended, and the best Saint-Émilions have a great deal of scent, fruit and complexity.

266   There are almost 20,000 acres of vineyard that produce wines under the APPELLATION CONTRÔLÉE Saint-Émilion. The central region around the town itself is divided unofficially into two districts, based on differences in the soil: the "Côtes" (slopes) Saint-Émilion section is immediately adjacent to the town on mostly chalky slopes, while the "Graves" (gravel) Saint-Émilion section is further west, on more gravelly soil. Outside of Saint-Émilion proper, there are six neighboring communes that are legally allowed to use the name Saint-Émilion: MONTAGNE-SAINT-ÉMILION, LUSSAC-SAINT-ÉMILION, PUISSEGUIN-SAINT-ÉMILION, SAINT-GEORGES-SAINT-ÉMILION, Parsac-Saint-Émilion, and Sables-Saint-Émilion (the latter two are less important). Finally, there are several communes within the central Saint-Émilion district that are not called Saint-Émilion although their wines have legal right to this name; the most important are: St. Sulpice-de-Faleyrans, St. Christophe-des-Bardes, St. Laurent-des-Combes, and St. Hippolyte. These names are included here because they may occasionally be encountered on a wine label.

Saint-Émilion is primarily a region of fine wines, and it has a great number of select estates or CHÂTEAUX. As a result, there is a rather complicated classification of Saint-Émilion wines, which was officially established in 1955. The best estates are rated Premier Grand Cru Classé (First Great Classified Growth) and Grand Cru Classé; other châteaux are either rated "Saint-Émilion Grand Cru" or, for the lowest-ranked châteaux, simply "Saint-Émilion." To qualify for the appellation, all Saint-Émilion wines are annually subjected to an impartial tasting by a professional committee before they are allowed to be sold.

The following is the official list of classified growth Saint-Émilions published by the Syndicat Viticole et Agricole de Saint-Émilion. The two most famous Premier Grand Cru Classé Saint-Émilions are

267

AUSONE and CHEVAL-BLANC, which generally fetch some of the highest prices in the Bordeaux wine trade.

LISTE DES CRUS CLASSES DE SAINT-EMILION

PREMIERS GRANDS CRUS CLASSES

A) *Châteaux*

AUSONE
CHEVAL-BLANC

B) BEAUSEJOUR (Duffau Lagarrosse)
BEAUSEJOUR (Société)
BELAIR
CANON
CLOS FOURTET
FIGEAC
LA GAFFELIERE
MAGDELAINE
PAVIE
TROTTEVIEILLE

GRANDS CRUS CLASSES

L'ANGELUS
L'ARROSEE
BALEAU
BALESTARD-LA-TONNELLE
BELLEVUE
BERGAT
CADET-BON
CADET-PIOLA
CANON-LA GAFFELIERE
CAP DE MOURLIN (R. Capdemourlin)
CAP DE MOURLIN (J. Capdemourlin)
CHAPELLE-MADELEINE
CHAUVIN
CORBIN (Giraud)
CORBIN-MICHOTTE
COUTET
COUVENT-DES-JACOBINS

CROQUE-MICHOTTE
CURE-BON
DASSAULT
FAURIE-DE-SOUCHARD
FONPLEGADE
FONROQUE
FRANC-MAYNE
GRAND-BARRAIL-
   LAMARZELLE-FIGEAC
GRAND-CORBIN-DESPAGNE
GRANDE-CORBIN
GRAND-MAYNE
GRAND-PONTET
GRANDES-MURAILLES
GUADET-SAINT-JULIEN
HAUT-CORBIN
HAUT-SARPE
JEAN-FAURE
CLOS DES JACOBINS
CLOS LA MADELEINE
CLOS SAINT-MARTIN
LA CARTE
LA CLOTTE
LA CLUSIERE
LA COUSPAUDE
LA DOMINIQUE
LANIOTE
LARCIS-DUCASSE
LAMARZELLE
LARMANDE
LAROZE
LASSERRE
LA TOUR-DU-PIN-FIGEAC (Bélivier)
LA TOUR-DU-PIN-FIGEAC (Moueix)
LA TOUR-FIGEAC
LE CHATELET
LE COUVENT
LE PRIEURE
MATRAS
MAUVEZIN
MOULIN-DU-CADET
L'ORATOIRE
PAVIE-DECESSE
PAVIE-MACQUIN

269

PAVILLON-CADET
PETIT-FAURIE-DE-SOUTARD
RIPEAU
SANSONNET
SAINT-GEORGES-COTE-PAVIE
SOUTARD
TERTRE-DAUGAY
TRIMOULET
TROIS-MOULINS
TROPLONG-MONDOT
VILLEMAURINE
YON-FIGEAC

Saint-Estèphe *(Sahnt Es-teff')*: Notable wine commune in the BORDEAUX district, France; the most northern of the important MÉDOC wine communes. Located on soil rich in clay, Saint-Estèphe's vineyards give especially robust and full-bodied red wines, perhaps a bit less scented and complex than some other Médocs but possessing a great deal of authority; they age well and are long-lived.

Saint-Estèphe's best wine estates or CHÂTEAUX are traditionally famous and were included in the 1855 classification of the Médoc. *Seconds Crus* (Second Growths): Cos d'Estournel and Montrose. *Troisième Cru* (Third Growth): Calon-Ségur. *Quatrième Cru* (Fourth Growth): Lafon-Rochet. *Cinquième Cru* (Fifth Growth): Cos-Labory. In addition, there are several outstanding châteaux that were not classified in 1855 but which now produce wine worthy of classified growth status, of which perhaps the most notable are: de Pez, Phélan-Ségur, Meyney, Les Ormes-de-Pez, Tronquoy-Lalande, and Haut-Marbuzet.

Saint-Georges-Saint-Émilion *(San Zhorzh' Sahnt Eh-meel-lyon')*: Wine commune near the SAINT-ÉMILION region east of BORDEAUX, named for its most famous wine estate, Château Saint-Georges. The wines may be sold either under the name Saint-Georges-Saint-Émilion or MON-

Saint-Joseph *(San Yo-seff')*: Wine region in the northern RHÔNE River valley, France, noted for its sturdy, full-bodied red wines made from the Syrah grape; there is also some white wine made in Saint-Joseph, but it is less important. The Saint-Joseph vineyards lie on the right bank of the Rhône opposite the famous vineyards of HERMITAGE; total production averages some 28,000 cases annually.

Saint-Julien *(San Jule'-yan)*: One of the most famous wine communes in the HAUT-MÉDOC district, located some 20 miles north of the city of BORDEAUX. Celebrated for its fine red wines, Saint-Julien has the largest number of wine estates (CHÂTEAUX) per square mile of any Haut-Médoc wine commune, although it is the smallest; the equivalent of some 228,000 cases is produced in an average year.

An adjoining commune, Saint-Laurent, lies just to the west of Saint-Julien but its wines may only be sold under the name "Haut-Médoc." In the following list of Saint-Julien châteaux as ranked in the 1855 classification of the Médoc, the Saint-Laurent estates have been marked with an asterisk. *Seconds Crus* (Second Growths): Léoville Las-Cases, Léoville-Poyferré, Léoville-Barton, Gruaud-Larose, Ducru-Beaucaillou. *Troisièmes Crus* (Third Growths): Lagrange, Langoa-Barton. *Quatrièmes Crus* (Fourth Growths): Saint-Pierre-Sevaistre, Talbot, Branaire (Duluc-Ducru), La Tour-Carnet*, Beychevelle. *Cinquièmes Crus* (Fifth Growths): Belgrave* and Camensac*. In addition, there are several outstanding châteaux that were not officially classified in 1855 but now produce wine equal to that of many classified growths; the most renowned is Gloria, followed by du Glana, Peymartin, Larose-Trintaudon*, and Moulin-Riche.

271

Saint-Laurent: see SAINT-JULIEN.

Saint-Péray *(San Pay-ray')*: Wine region in the RHÔNE River valley, noted for its white wines made from Roussanne and Marsanne grapes. The most famous Saint-Pérays are sparkling wines *(vin mousseux),* bottle-fermented by the traditional CHAMPAGNE process; there are also good still white wines and some sweet white wines as well. Saint-Pérays are well-known in France but are not widely exported to the U.S.; average production of all types amounts to some 11,400 cases a year.

Saint-Romain *(San Ro-man')*: Secondary wine commune in the CÔTE DE BEAUNE, Burgundy, located in the hilly country near MEURSAULT. Although Saint-Romain is not a well-known wine name, the vineyards are well-exposed and produce good red and white wines from Pinot Noir and Chardonnay, sold either under the name Saint-Romain or as CÔTE DE BEAUNE-VILLAGES. Total production averages some 16,000 cases annually.

Saint-Saphorin *(San Saf'-aw-ran)*: Vineyard area in the district of LAVAUX, Switzerland, located on the north shore of Lake Geneva near the city of Montreux. Along with the vineyards of DÉZALEY just to the west, Saint-Saphorin makes some of the best white wines of Switzerland, produced from the Dorin (Chasselas) grape.

Saint-Véran *(San Vay-rawn')*: White wine district in the MÂCONNAIS region, southern Burgundy; a new place-name created in 1971 by the French government. The vineyard area entitled to the APPELLATION CONTRÔLÉE Saint-Véran includes the wine communes of Chasselas, Leynes and Chânes near the southern border of the famous district of POUILLY-FUISSÉ, as well as Davayé and Prissé to the north; before the name Saint-Véran was adopted, these communes

272

could only sell their wines as ''Beaujolais Blanc'' or ''Mâcon Blanc.'' Made from the same Chardonnay grape as Pouilly-Fuissé, Saint-Véran has become immensely popular throughout France and the U.S.; it is similar to Pouilly-Fuissé and considerably less expensive. Some 90,600 cases are produced annually.

Sainte-Croix-du-Mont *(Sahnt Crwa dew Mawn')*: White wine region in BORDEAUX located on the GARONNE River near the famous vineyards of SAUTERNES. Sainte-Croix-du-Mont specializes in sweet white wines made from late-harvested Sémillon, Sauvignon Blanc and Muscadelle grapes; they are similar to Sauternes but are generally less sweet and not well-known outside the region. Total production averages some 166,500 cases annually.

Salmanazar: The largest commercially available wine bottle, with a capacity of twelve ordinary bottles; used by some producers in the French CHAMPAGNE district.

San Benito: County and wine district in central California, located east of the city of Salinas along the Coast Range mountains. San Benito was not an important wine region until the 1960s, when urban expansion forced many California wineries to look for new areas for their vineyards. Over 4,600 acres of premium wine grapes have been planted in San Benito; the largest single vineyard, at Paicines, is owned and managed by Almadén Vineyards.

Sancerre *(Sahn'-sair)*: Famous white wine region in the upper LOIRE River valley, France, located in the department of Nièvre near the village of POUILLY-SUR-LOIRE. Made from the same Sauvignon Blanc *(Blanc Fumé)* grape as the celebrated POUILLY-FUMÉ produced nearby, Sancerre is similar and matures perhaps even sooner;

273

very dry and with a clean, crisp quality, it is often consumed during its first year. The hilltop village of Sancerre is the region's center, but 14 different communes produce wine under the APPELLATION CONTRÔLÉE Sancerre; possibly the most famous are CHAVIGNOL, Bué, Verdigny, Sury-en-Vaux, Champtin, and Ménétréol. Combined, there are some 2,000 acres planted in Sauvignon; total production often exceeds 400,000 cases annually. In addition, an interesting rosé wine made from Pinot Noir is also produced in Sancerre, which has recently proven to be just as popular as the white wine: production of Sancerre rosé has now increased to over 86,000 cases annually.

Sangiovese *(San-gee-oh-vay'-say)***:** Fine quality red wine grape grown in central Italy, used in the region of TUSCANY for some of Italy's most famous red wines. In blends it is the principal variety used for CHIANTI and for the VINO NOBILE DI MONTEPULCIANO; a related variety is used for BRUNELLO DI MONTALCINO. In Tuscany this grape is sometimes called "San Gioveto," but Sangiovese is the preferred spelling outside Tuscany. Some experimental plantings have been made in California.

Sangria *(San-gree'-ah)***:** Wine and fruit punch, originally native to Spain but now very popular in the U.S. The traditional recipe for Sangria calls for the juice of fresh Valencia oranges blended with a light red wine, which is mixed with a little sugar, lemon juice and soda water and served in a punch bowl garnished with fresh fruit.

San Severo *(San Say-vair'-ro)***:** Good red, white and rosé wines produced in the region of APULIA (Puglia), Italy, near the town of Foggia. San Severo was originally famous for its white wines, but in recent years the reds and rosés have greatly improved. Made primarily from Bombino and Trebbiano grapes, the white is pale-gold in color and has a clean, fresh taste; the red, made from Montepulciano, is sturdy and ages well.

Santa Clara: County south of San Francisco Bay, California, with about 2,200 acres of vineyards. Historically one of the state's most important wine regions, Santa Clara now has some of California's best wineries. Major firms headquartered in Santa Clara are Almadén, Paul Masson, Mirassou, San Martin, and the Novitiate of Los Gatos; some small, family-owned wineries (Pedrizetti, Rapazzini, Guglielmo, etc.) are located near Gilroy off U.S. Highway 101. Ridge Vineyards in Cupertino makes some of America's best Zinfandels; David Bruce Winery in Los Gatos is noted for Chardonnay, and Gemello Winery for sturdy reds. Mt. Eden Vineyards continues the famous winery at Saratoga founded by the late Martin Ray.

Santa Maddalena *(Santa Mad-lay'-nah)*: Light, attractive red wine from the region of ALTO ADIGE, northern Italy. Produced from the Schiava grape grown near the town of Bolzano, Santa Maddalena is considered one of the best Alto Adige red wines; unlike many northern Italian reds, it is best when consumed rather young — usually before it is three years old. It was rated D.O.C. in 1971.

Santenay *(Sahnt'-nay)*: Wine commune in the CÔTE DE BEAUNE, Burgundy, with some 950 acres of vineyard; the most southern of the many important communes along that famous hillside. Both red and white wines are produced in Santenay; the reds are superior and are much more important commercially. Made from the Pinot Noir, red Santenays are generally rather light and should be drunk young; being not as well-known as some other Burgundies, many of them are excellent value. Certain fine Santenay vineyards have been rated Premier Cru (First Growth); the

275

most famous is Gravières, but Beauregard, La Comme, Clos Rousseau and La Maladière also produce good wines. Average production is about 93,000 cases annually, virtually all of it red.

Sardinia (Italian, **Sardegna**): Mountainous island in the Tyrrhenian Sea, located about 125 miles off the west coast of Italy. Politically a part of Italy, Sardinia has over 150,000 acres of vineyards and grows many of the same fine grape varieties as the Italian mainland. Several of Sardinia's better wines have recently been granted a D.O.C. rating; among the more notable white wines is the firm, dry Vernaccia di Oristano; Nuragus di Cagliari, another good white, is lighter. The seaport town of Cagliari produces an interesting sweet wine, Moscato di Cagliari; the reds — Cannonau and Oliena — tend to be rather heavy and full-bodied. Sardinian wines are not widely-exported, even to Italy, but as a result of the recent D.O.C. approval exports of quality wines are sure to increase.

Sassella *(Sas-sell'-ah)*: Fine red wine from the region of LOMBARDY, Italy; one of the better wines of the VALTELLINA district. Its center of production is near the town of Sondrio, not far from Lake Como. Made from the Nebbiolo grape, which in the Valtellina is called Chiavennasca, Sassella is a sturdy, scented red wine that ages particularly well.

Saumur *(So-mur')*: City of some 33,000 in the lower LOIRE River valley, France; one of the leading wine towns in that area. Dominated by a fine old château that overlooks the Loire, the Saumur vineyards are planted in several different wine grapes. Wines are sold under two APPELLATION CONTRÔLÉES, Saumur and Coteaux de Saumur, of which the former is much more important.

The white Saumurs made from the Chenin Blanc are perhaps the best; they usually have

276

an agreeable trace of sweetness, and are long-lived. Many white Saumur wines are converted into sparkling wines *(vins mousseux)*, bottle-fermented by the traditional CHAMPAGNE process, and some are among the best sparkling wines produced outside of the Champagne district. A large quantity of rosé wine made from Cabernet Franc is also produced in Saumur, raising the total of all Saumur wines to more than 650,000 cases annually.

Just to the west of Saumur is the little village of CHAMPIGNY, where primarily red Cabernet Franc grapes are grown; some of the better red wines of the Loire valley are made there. These sturdy red wines are usually sold as "Champigny" or "Saumur-Champigny," as very little red wine is exported under the name Saumur. About 185,000 cases of Saumur- Champigny are produced each year.

Sauternes (French, *So-tairn′*): Well-known trade name for sweet white wine; specifically, the unique and special product of the vineyards of Sauternes in the BORDEAUX region, France, produced from successive late picking of overripe grapes. The name "Haut-Sauternes" has no legal significance, although some shippers use it to designate a superior wine.

The vineyards of Sauternes are located some 25 miles southeast of the city of Bordeaux, and extend over about 4,700 acres planted in Sémillon, Sauvignon Blanc and Muscadelle grapes. There are several associated wine communes in the Sauternes district: from north to south, these communes include: BARSAC, Preignac, Bommes, Sauternes, and Fargues. Wine from each of these communes is legally entitled to the name Sauternes; however, wine from Barsac is usually sold under the name Barsac. Sweet white Barsacs are generally a shade drier than other Sauternes.

The luscious sweetness of a good Sauternes

277

is a result of the grapes being harvested late, when they are overripe. As the grapes ripen, a mold known as BOTRYTIS CINEREA gradually forms on the skins. This mold is normally destructive in most wine regions, as it causes the grapes to rot. But in the Sauternes district the mold is welcomed, for under the right conditions it does not induce rot but instead causes the grape skins to shrink and the juice to be concentrated. The French acknowledge the beneficial action of Botrytis by calling it ''pourriture noble'' or ''noble mold.''

But there are risks in waiting for Botrytis to develop. The mold is easily washed off by heavy rain, and in many vintages it does not develop to the required degree; hence the risk of a failed vintage in Sauternes is very high. The mold also does not mature evenly in the vineyards, and several pickings have to be performed so as to gather all the grapes that have rotted nobly. Only certain estates or CHÂTEAUX have the necessary resources to do this, and often as many as a dozen pickings are required. The grapes are pressed immediately after picking, and after the harvest the wines from each picking are blended and aged before being sold. In the trade, Sauternes can be made commercially by arresting the fermentation before all the sugar is converted into alcohol, either by filtration or by adding sulfur. But the result never equals that of the methodical, successive pickings that only the best châteaux can afford to employ.

The most famous Sauternes châteaux were classified in 1855 into two groups or CRUS (growths), based on the prices their wines were fetching in the trade. The leading château is YQUEM, ranked as a Grand Premier Cru (Great First Growth), which usually produces some of the fullest, sweetest and most expensive of all Sauternes. (In the following group of classified Sauternes châteaux, the Barsac estates have been identified with an asterisk). *Premiers Crus* (First Growths): La Tour-Blanche, Lafaurie-Peyraguey, Clos Haut-Peyraguey, Rayne-Vigneau, Suduiraut, Coutet*, Climens*, Guiraud, Rieussec, Rabaud-Promis, and Sigalas-Rabaud. *Deuxiemes Crus* (Second Growths): de Myrat*, Doisy-Daëne*, Doisy-Védrines*, d'Arche, Filhot, Broustet*, Nairac*, Caillou*, Suau*, de Malle, Romer, and Lamothe.

Outside of France, the name Sauternes has become a GENERIC term describing any sweet or semi-sweet white wine. U.S. labeling law allows American wines to be called "sauterne," but the true place of origin must be specified (e.g., California sauterne) and the name is usually spelled without the final "s."

Sauvignon Blanc *(So'-veen-yawn Blawn')*: Excellent white wine grape, grown in many regions in France and in other countries as well. In BORDEAUX it is used along with the Sémillon for the fine dry white GRAVES and ENTRE-DEUX-MERS; the Sauvignon Blanc is also grown for the famous sweet wines of SAUTERNES, BARSAC, CÉRONS and SAINTE-CROIX-DU-MONT. Further inland, in the upper LOIRE River valley, it gives the dry white wines of POUILLY-FUMÉ and SANCERRE. In the Loire region wines made from Sauvignon Blanc are sometimes called "Blanc Fumé" in the acknowledgement of their faint, "smoky" qualities.

Over 3,500 acres of Sauvignon Blanc have been planted in California, and the grape gives outstanding dry white wines — particularly in cool coastal districts. Good wines from Sauvignon Blanc have been made in other states as well, most successfully from gravelly soil.

Savennières *(Sav-ven-yair')*: Outstanding white wine region in the lower LOIRE River

279

valley, France, near the village of Roche-fort-sur-Loire. The vineyards of Savennières produce some of the finest dry white wines of the Loire made from the Chenin Blanc grape; they are similar to VOUV-RAYS but are generally drier and perhaps even more scented.

The APPELLATION CONTRÔLÉE Saven-nières includes three notable vineyards that generally produce wines under their own names: the diminutive Coulée de Serrant, at 10 acres large one of the smallest vineyards in France; the Roche Aux Moines (60 acres), and the Clos du Papillon. The total area under vines in Savennières is about 450 acres; pro-duction averages some 6,500 cases annually.

Savigny-Les-Beaune *(Sav'-een-yee Lay Bone')*: Little wine village in the northern CÔTE DE BEAUNE, Burgundy, located along a quaint river valley just to the northwest of the city of BEAUNE. Savigny's vineyards ad-join those of Beaune and share many of the same outstanding characteristics; most are planted in Pinot Noir and produce especially light, fruity red wines, but a little white wine is also made from Chardonnay. The wines typically develop very quickly but age well.

Certain famous vineyards in Savigny have been rated Premier Cru (First Growth); the most celebrated is Les Vergelesses, which extends into the neighboring commune of PERNAND-VERGELESSES, but Marconnets (shared by Beaune), Lavières, Jarrons, Clos des Guettes, Aux Gravains and Dominode can also produce exceptional wines. Because the wines are not well-known outside the re-gion, many Savignys from good producers are often excellent value. The area under vines is about 945 acres, and total production often exceeds some 113,000 cases annually.

280

Scharzhofberg *(Shartz'-hawf-bairg)*: Out-standing vineyard in the SAAR River valley,

Germany, located near the famous wine town of WILTINGEN. The vineyard faces south on a steep, slate hillside and has some 30 acres planted in Riesling; in great vintages the finely-scented and complex white wines it produces are without peer. The most famous Scharzhofberg producer is Egon Müller (proprietor of the Scharzhof, an ancient manor house at the foot of the vineyard), but excellent examples of Scharzhofberger are also made by the Vereinigte Hospitien, the Hohe Domkirche of Trier (which sells the wine under the name "Dom Scharzhofberger"), the von Kesselstatt estate, and Van Volxem.

Schaumwein *(Showm'-vine):* German for "sparkling wine." Some years ago, Germany signed a treaty with France and agreed not to call her sparkling wines "champagnes"; as a result they must either be called Schaumwein or *Sekt.* A Schaumwein may be fermented in the bottle by the traditional Champagne process or by the CHARMAT (Bulk) process, but by law it must have a minimum pressure of at least 4 atmospheres.

Scheurebe *(Shoy'-ray-buh):* Promising new HYBRID white grape variety developed in Germany. A cross between the Riesling and the Silvaner, the Scheurebe is planted primarily in the RHEINGAU and RHEINHESSEN districts and gives characteristically full-bodied white wines with a pronounced bouquet.

Schiava *(Ski-ah'-va):* Red wine grape grown in the TRENTINO and ALTO ADIGE regions, northern Italy, where it is used for the light and fruity red wines of CALDARO and SANTA MADDALENA.

Schillerwein *(Shil'-ler-vine):* Light red wine produced from red and white grapes pressed together, made in the WÜRTTEMBERG region in Germany. The name derives not from the

281

poet Schiller but from the verb *schillern,* which means "shimmer"; the wine is undistinguished and is rarely seen outside the Württemberg region.

Schloss *(Shlawss)*: German for "castle"; in relation to wine, a vineyard estate — roughly equivalent to the French CHÂTEAU.

Schloss Böckelheim *(Shlawss Berk'-el-heim)*: Renowned wine town on the NAHE River, Germany; among the best of that district. Its 136 acres of vineyard are mostly planted in Riesling and face south near an old copper mine — identified in the name of one of the leading vineyards or EINZELLAGEN, Kupfergrube, which means "copper mine." Other fine Schloss Böckelheim Einzellagen include: Königsfels, Felsenberg, Heimberg, In den Felsen, and Mühlberg.

Because of the town's great fame, the 1971 German Wine Law authorized Schloss Böckelheim to also be the name of a BEREICH (sub-region) including several other wine towns; wines from the best vineyards, therefore, are not sold merely as "Schloss Böckelheimer" but Schloss Böckelheimer followed by the name of the Einzellage in question. A "Schloss Böckelheimer" without this qualification may be assumed to be a blended regional wine, produced from dozens of villages within the Schloss Böckelheim Bereich.

Schloss Johannisberg: see JOHANNISBERG, SCHLOSS.

Schloss Vollrads: see VOLLRADS, SCHLOSS.

Scuppernong: Native American white grape variety of the Muscadine family, belonging to the sub-genus *Rotundifolia.* It is widely grown in the Carolinas and in Georgia to make rather full-bodied sweet wine, although sugar is generally added to give the required sweetness.

Sec *(Seck)*: French for "dry." Officially, this

term does not mean what it implies: in the French CHAMPAGNE region, a wine labeled Sec is not dry but in fact semi-dry; it may legally contain up to 4% residual sugar resulting from the final shipping dosage (LIQUEUR D'EXPÉDITION). Those who prefer drier Champagnes should select wines labeled BRUT or EXTRA DRY, which contain less than 1% and 3% residual sugar, respectively.

Elsewhere in France, still white wines labeled sec will usually be dry, as their name implies.

Secco *(Say'-co)*: Italian for "dry." Wines labeled *secco* will be less sweet than those labeled *abboccato* (semi-dry) or *amabile* (sweet).

Sediment: The lees or deposit thrown off by a wine as it ages. Many people think that the presence of sediment signifies a spoiled wine, when it is in fact a part of the normal aging process. The amount of sediment in a wine can be reduced by successive RACKINGS in barrel before bottling, but virtually all fine wines display it after a while.

Chemically, sediment in wine is brought about by the slow reaction and eventual precipitation of fruit acids, tannins, tartrates and other compounds as the wine ages in bottle. Full-bodied red wines usually contain a high degree of tannin, which is gradually shed as a brownish deposit during the aging process. Fine white wines produced in cool climatic regions sometimes throw off tartrate crystals, which look like little chunks of glass — even though they are both tasteless and harmless. Most sediment, however, is generally unpleasant to the taste and should be separated from the wine before serving. See DECANT.

283

Seibel *(Sigh'-bel)*: A group of HYBRID grape varieties perfected by a French grape hybridizer, Louis Seibel; the result of crossing a vine of the species LABRUSCA with a VINIFERA vine.

Sekt: German for "sparkling wine." As is the case with SCHAUMWEIN, German sparkling wines are not called champagne in Germany as a result of an international agreement with France. Wines labeled Sekt are usually produced under less stringent controls than Schaumwein, because while the latter must by law be the product of natural fermentation, Sekt wines may be produced by artificial carbonation.

Sémillon *(Say′-me-yawn)*: Fine white grape variety grown in the BORDEAUX region, France, and in many other parts of the world. It is one of the few varieties susceptible to the "noble mold" (see BOTRYTIS CINEREA), and is thus ideally suited to the making of luscious sweet wines in SAUTERNES, BARSAC, and CÉRONS. In conjunction with the Sauvignon Blanc it is also used to make dry white GRAVES and ENTRE-DEUX-MERS. Further inland, it is grown for the wines of MONBAZILLAC. In Australia, where it is successful, wines made from Sémillon are often labeled "Riesling," supposedly because they are similar in style. Over 3,000 acres of Sémillon have been planted in California, and a wide variety of good dry and semi-dry Sémillon wines are produced there; fine Sémillons have also been made in Washington State.

Sercial *(Sair′-see-al)*: The palest and driest kind of MADEIRA, produced from Sercial grapes grown on the uppermost slopes of the island of Madeira.

Serrig *(Sair′-rig)*: Little-known but outstanding wine village in the SAAR region, Germany. Its 163 acres of vineyard are planted almost entirely in Riesling and in great vintages its fine white wines are among the Saar's best; in rainy years, however, Serrigers can be rather

284

acidic. The leading vineyard (EINZELLAGE) is Vogelsang, or "bird's song"; other fine Serrig Einzellagen include: Schloss Saarfelser Schlossberg, Antoniusberg, Heiligenborn, Hoeppslei, Herrenberg, and Würtzberg.

Sèvre-et-Maine *(Sevr Eh Main')*: One of the delimited production zones for the MUS-CADET region in the lower LOIRE River valley, France; named for two rivers that flow into the Loire near Nantes. Wines from the region are entitled to the APPELLATION CON-TRÔLÉE "Muscadet de Sèvre-et-Maine"; the wines differ somewhat from those of the associated "Coteaux de la Loire" region to the east, tending to be somewhat earlier to mature in most vintages.

Seyssel *(Say-sell')*: Light, fresh dry white wine produced in the region of Savoie (Savoy) in northeastern France, near Lake Geneva. Made from the Roussette grape, Seyssel may be either a good still wine or a perhaps even better sparkling wine *(vin mousseux),* bottle-fermented by the traditional CHAMPAGNE process. Some Seyssel *mousseux* are among the finest sparkling wines produced outside the Champagne region. The equivalent of some 26,000 cases is produced annually.

Seyve-Villard *(Save Vee-yard')*: A group of HYBRID grape varieties, named for the grape hybridizer who perfected them. As there are many different types of Seyve-Villard vines, a specific vine is identified by number: among the most successful and popular is Seyve-Villard 5276, or Seyval Blanc, grown for a good white wine in many parts of the U.S.

Sherry: Internationally famous FORTIFIED WINE; specifically, the product of the seaport city of Jerez de la Frontera in southern Andalusia, Spain, produced from 20,000 acres of vineyard planted on soil unique to the area. The name Sherry is derived from Jerez and

285

hence is a place-name of geographic origin; wines called sherry are made all over the world — notably in Australia, South Africa, and the U.S. — but few are quite like the authentic product of southwestern Spain.

Like several other fine Spanish wines, Sherry is strictly controlled by the laws of *Denominación de Origen,* an official government guarantee of the wine's quality. On most Sherries the *Denominación de Origen* seal is affixed to the bottle, identifying the wine as genuine Sherry. The laws have also delimited the classic production zone according to the soil. The best soils for Sherry are known as *albarizas,* which contain a high chalk content vital to the wine's finesse; certain *pagos* (districts) of albarizas — Carrascal, Macharnudo, Añina, Balbaina, and Miraflores — are famous, but these names rarely appear on wine labels. Soils richer in clay are known as *barros,* which produce a heavier wine; the sandier soils, *arenas,* are the most productive but are on the whole less good than the other two.

Two principal grape varieties are grown in the Sherry country. The most important is the Palomino, also known by its local name Listán, which thrives on the chalky albarizas and produces the best dry Sherries. The other leading variety is the Pedro Ximénez, which is normally set aside after picking to dry on straw mats: the concentrated juice is used for making sweet Sherries.

Like other fortified wines, the alcoholic content of Sherry is largely the result of an addition of high-proof brandy, but several other factors give the wines their unique characteristics. At the time of the grape harvest, the grapes are crushed in large troughs or *lagares* — sometimes still by treading with the feet — and then the expressed must is allowed to ferment. During the winter the wines are stored in *criaderas* or "nurseries," where they are watched carefully; each cask is individually graded by means of chalk marks, or *rayas.* For reasons that are still only partly understood, some Sherries when in cask develop a white, frothy yeast known as FLOR. Occurring spontaneously and only in certain casks, the flor yeast will produce fine, light pale wines; casks of Sherry that do not develop flor will be used for making dark, full-bodied wines. This yeast is only native to a few wine regions, and many other areas that produce sherries from flor must import the yeast.

Another technique used in making Sherry is the long process of blending known as the SOLERA system. Every fall in the Sherry country, the new wines are brought to great warehouses or BODEGAS, where they are set aside to age. But via the solera method the casks are stacked in tiers so that their contents are gradually blended with the wines of many different vintages. The solera system assures that each grade of Sherry will be constant and unchanging year after year. Thus there is no such thing as "vintage Sherry" because through the solera system the casks are constantly being replenished by younger wines as they age. (The year that the solera was established is sometimes specified for a Sherry, but this is of course not the same thing as a vintage year.)

There are five basic types of Sherry. The palest and driest wine is usually MANZANILLA, produced around the associated city of Sanlúcar de Barrameda to the northwest of Jerez. Similar — but generally not quite as auterely dry — is FINO, produced from casks displaying the flor yeast. Fino and Manzanilla are among the few wines whose alcoholic strength actually increases slightly as they age in cask, owing to evaporation, and because they only receive a very small addition of brandy they are especially fragrant and delicate.

Slightly darker and less dry than a Fino is AMONTILLADO, prized for its unique "nutty" qualities; the best Amontillados are Finos that

287

have taken on a darker color and richer flavor. Fuller still is OLOROSO, which comes from casks that did not develop the flor yeast. Olorosos are sweeter than Finos, but in their natural state they are dry; the sweetness is added later. The sweetest Sherries are "Cream" Sherries, which are fine old Olorosos that have been sweetened by a grape concentrate called *dulce,* produced by adding partially fermented grape must into casks containing brandy. Sometimes brandy is added to the juice of selected Pedro Ximénez grapes to make a very sweet wine called "P.X." These special wines are occasionally set aside and sold on their own, rather than being used for Cream Sherries, but unfortunately they are very rare in the trade.

Leading producers of Sherry that export their wines in quantity to the U.S. include: Gonzalez Byass, Williams & Humbert (makers of Dry Sack), Sandeman, Pedro Domecq, Bodegas Osborne (Duff Gordon), Wisdom & Warter, Valdespino, Pemartin, Bodegas Sanchez, and Ferenando de Terry.

Other countries — including the U.S. — make similar kinds of sherry, and California actually produces over four times as much sherry as is made in the Spanish Sherry district. But only a little American sherry is made with flor yeast and aged by the solera system; inexpensive sherries are produced from table or raisin grapes, and the wine is "baked" artificially at high temperature so as to take on a caramel color and a sherry-like flavor. However, quality sherries are produced by many firms, and a new technique called "submerged-culture flor process" is simultaneously reducing the time needed to make a good sherry and improving the flavor. The yeast is introduced into the wine and blended by agitation, rather than being allowed to settle on the surface.

288

Sicily (Italian, **Sicilia,** pronounced

Si-chee'-lee-ah): The largest island in the Mediterranean Sea, some 9,680 square miles in size; also a major wine region. There are over 416,000 acres of wine grapes planted in Sicily, and the warm climate is favorable to vineyards, making wine Sicily's second most valuable export, after citrus fruits.

Sicily has only been exporting significant quantities of wines to the U.S. in recent years, but many of her better wines have received D.O.C. listings lately, and exports are sure to increase as a result. Three Sicilian wines are prominent in the wine trade: MARSALA, the most famous FORTIFIED WINE of Italy, produced in the northwest of Sicily around the town of the same name; ETNA, good red, white and rosé wines made on the slopes of Mt. Etna, an active volcano; and CORVO, especially the select bottlings from the estate of the Dukes of Salaparuta. Besides Marsala, Sicily also makes some excellent dessert wines that deserve to be better known. The Malvasia di Lipari, produced on the little Isles of Lipari off the north coast, and the Moscato di Siracusa, grown near the ancient city of Siracusa along Sicily's east coast, have been famous for centuries but were only recently granted D.O.C. status.

Silvaner: The German spelling of SYLVANER.

Soave *(So-ah'-vay)*: Perhaps the most famous white wine of Italy, and deservedly so; produced in the region of VENETO to the east of the city of Verona. A wine best consumed during its first or second year, Soave has a pale gold color and a fresh, clean taste; the chief grape variety is Garganega, although a little Trebbiano is customarily added. The region has over 15,000 acres of vineyard.

Soave is traditionally bottled in a green, fluted bottle. If the wine was produced in the central and best part of the D.O.C. region — including the towns of Soave, Monteforte and

289

Costalunga — it is allowed the distinction of "Soave Classico." Soave with an alcoholic strength in excess of 10.5% may also be labeled "Soave Superiore." A major part of the production is controlled by the Cantina Sociale di Soave, one of the largest wine cooperatives in Europe.

Solera *(So-lair′-ah)***:** A system used in the Spanish SHERRY region for blending the wines of different vintages, so as to insure a uniform output year after year. After various Sherries have been selected according to their quality and characteristics, they are set aside in a three-tiered row of casks: older wines on the bottom, so that the young wines in the uppermost row can be brought down to blend with the older wines. By the nature of the solera system there can thus be no such thing as "vintage sherry," at least commercially, because the wines of different vintages are constantly being mixed together.

Although it originated in the Sherry district, the solera system is now standard in several other Spanish regions and in many parts of the world. It improves the wines of MÁLAGA and MONTILLA, as well as those of the island of MADEIRA; the better wines of MARSALA also go through a solera, as do some of the best American sherries.

Sonoma: One of California's many fine wine districts; a county and city located just to the north of San Francisco, with much of its western boundary bordering the Pacific Ocean. Shaped roughly like a wedge, Sonoma County has many different climates — allowing a wide variety of wines to be produced. Vineyards were first planted in Sonoma in the early 19th century, and the county now has over 25,000 acres of vineyard — an increase of 200% over a decade ago. Thus, along with NAPA county, which borders to the east, Sonoma can be ranked in the

290

forefront of California's premium wine production.

Sonoma's climatic diversity results from its proximity to the coast and also the Coast Range Mountains, which border Napa. Named for Russian fur hunters who combed the area in the 19th century, the Russian River flows through most of Sonoma and follows several climatic changes. Cool breezes from the Pacific are blocked in the north, and it is actually hotter in the Alexander Valley between the cities of Cloverdale and Healdsburg than it is further south, near the city of Sonoma. South of Healdsburg, the Russian River flows west and is once again in a cool Pacific climate.

Sonoma's rise to fame as a wine-producing county was largely the work of Agoston Haraszthy, "the father of American viticulture," who in 1856 bought land near the city of Sonoma at what is now Buena Vista Vineyards. Neglected for almost a century after Haraszthy's death, Buena Vista was restored by a former journalist, Frank Bartholomew, and is now one of Sonoma's most important wineries; certain select Buena Vista bottlings are identified as "cask" offerings. Bartholomew later founded a new winery, Hacienda Cellars, near Buena Vista.

Many of Sonoma's most famous wineries were founded by Italian immigrants, who brought wine-making techniques from their home country and successfully maintained them through hard times and prohibition. A notable example is the Sebastiani Winery, in Sonoma city. Located on the former site of the capital of the republic of California, Sebastiani produces a wide variety of superior wines. Further north near the appropriately-named village of Asti is the former Italian Swiss Colony Winery, founded in 1881 and now managed by United Vintners, which specializes in bulk wines. Martini & Prati

291

Wines, Inc. near Santa Rosa is another immense operation, best known for their vermouths. Three smaller, quality-oriented concerns of Italian origin are Simi Winery and Foppiano Winery near Healdsburg, and the J. Pedroncelli Winery near Geyserville; the last two are still family-owned.

Though their origins are more diverse, other Sonoma wineries are no less famous. The F. Korbel & Bros. Winery at Guerneville, along the picturesque Russian River, makes some of America's best dry champagnes. Near Healdsburg, Sonoma (formerly Windsor) Vineyards is presently under new management and the wines are better than ever. Z.D. Winery and Kenwood are smaller but are equally celebrated. The beautiful new Souverain of Alexander Valley Winery near Geyserville is one of the showpieces of the area; near Sonoma city at the other end of the county is the tiny Hanzell Winery, built by the late James D. Zellerbach, former ambassador to Italy, which makes only premium wines from Pinot Noir and Chardonnay.

South Africa: Dutch settlers introduced the vine to South Africa in 1654, and in a short while South African vintners scored some impressive achievements. One particularly famous vineyard was planted at Constantia south of Capetown, and in the 19th century the sweet Muscat wine of Constantia was regarded as one of the world's very greatest wines. This famous property unfortunately makes no wine today, but in its absence the South African wine industry continues to grow.

Only recently has South Africa been a major table wine producer. Most of the grapes used to be grown for brandy distillation; some South African brandy can be excellent, but in the past it tended to be of poor quality. South African vintners learned how to duplicate the

SHERRY process, and South African sherries are now among the best to be found outside of Spain; the latitude of most vineyards is the same as in the Spanish Sherry district. Today the trend is turning to table wines. A new law establishing place-names for wines, the Wines of Origin Law, was passed in 1973, and a government quality seal now appears on bottles of superior South African wines that conform with the provisions of the new law.

There are over 256,000 acres of vineyards in South Africa, and over 6,000 wine growers. Production is largely in the hands of giant wine cooperatives. The South African Wine-Growers' Association (known by its initials, K.W.V.) was founded in 1918 and now controls much of the marketing of South African wines. The K.W.V. owns five important wineries across the country, and one at Paarl 40 miles to the northeast of Capetown is among the largest in South Africa. Eleven miles to the south another cooperative, the Stellenbosch Farmers' Winery Ltd., produces some excellent wines under the "Oude Libertas" label. Further inland in the Little Karoo area, grapes used for brandy and sherry are produced from irrigated vineyards.

South African table wines are usually named after the grape variety from which they are made: leading red wine grapes are Cabernet Sauvignon, Shiraz, Cinsault, and a local specialty called Pinotage, made from a cross between the Pinot Noir and the Shiraz. Good South African white wines are made from Riesling, Colombard, Clairette, and the country's own "Steen" — similar to Riesling but with a style all its own. Occasionally wines made from Steen will be sold as a "Late Harvest," indicating that the grapes were extra ripe at picking, allowing a sweeter and richer wine to be made.

293

Soutirage *(Soo-tee-rahj')***:** French for RACKING, the process of transferring new wines from one container to another in order to remove the sediment.

Soviet Union: In efforts to attract Russians to the pleasures of wine-drinking and draw them away from hard liquor, the Soviet Union authorized an enormous vineyard expansion during the 1950s by which millions of new acres were planted. These immense new plantings made the Soviet Union the third largest wine-producing nation in the world, after Italy and France, and to augment this already prodigious production the Soviet Union imports huge quantities of wine from the west.

Russia is not generally thought of as a great wine producer, though in the beginning the "noble" VINIFERA vines originated in what is now part of the Soviet Union. Grape specialists (ampelographers) have identified the original source of vinifera in modern-day Transcausasia, from where the wine grape was taken throughout the civilized world. Today, vineyards still abound in Transcausasia — the republic of Georgia is one of Russia's foremost producers — and other important wine regions are Armenia, the Crimean peninsula, Moldavia (formerly part of Romania), and the Ukraine.

Grapes do not grow easily in the icy Russian climate. The vines often have to be covered with earth to survive killing winter frosts, and many wineries tend to have primitive equipment. In response to public tastes, over three-fourths of Russian wine is sweet and high in alcohol. But some interesting sparkling wine called "Shampanskoe" or champagne is also made, and there is new interest in table wines. On the whole, Russian wines are improving, and as exports to the U.S. continue to increase, more and more Americans will eventually discover them.

Spain: The vineyards of Spain are among the world's oldest and most important. In the ancient world, Spanish wines were praised long before the wines of other countries became famous, and they are just as fine today. Largely because of the dry climate, however, total wine production in Spain is considerably less than in neighboring countries, even though some 4 million acres are presently under vines.

By far the most famous Spanish wine is SHERRY, the celebrated product of the port city of Jerez de la Frontera in southern Andalusia; yet many Spaniards never drink Sherry but prefer the local wine *(vino corriente),* very little of which is exported. With only a few exceptions, Spain's best known wines are produced primarily for the export market, and in other parts of the country the wines are not so well-known.

Laws relating to wine-making practices in Spain date back to the Middle Ages, but official legislation has only come about recently. The best wine districts in Spain are now subject to the *Denominación de Origen* laws, which authorize place-names and set quality standards for the wines. Not all quality wine in Spain is produced under the laws, nor is all wine entitled to *Denominación de Origen* superior, but the very existence of the laws shows how interested the government is in maintaining the high reputation of Spanish wines.

Spain's climatic regions vary, as do the wines. In general, those made in the cooler districts of northern Spain are light in color and alcohol, while wines produced further south are fuller in body and flavor. Prime examples of the light northern wines are those from the Ribeiro district in northwestern Spain, in the province of Galicia. The pale, fresh Ribeiro wines are produced just to the north of the VINHO VERDE district in Portugal and are quite similar. To the east, the Basque provinces make Chacoli, an even lighter wine.

295

El Ferrol
Asturias
Galicia
Leon
duero
vinho verde
UPPER DOURO
Oporto
Atlantic Ocean
Extremadura
Cintra
Colares
Bucelas
Lisbon
ESTREMADURA
Portugal
Andalucía
Jerez de la
Frontera
Sanlúcar de Barrameda
Cadíz
Puerto de St. María
Portugal

Bilbao
FRANCE
Rioja Wines
Haro
Burgos
Cataluña
Alella
Barcelona
Aragón
Tarragon
Madrid
Castilla
Nueva
Valencia
eñas
Murcia
SPAIN
Mediterranean
Sea
Spain

But just to the south of these cool coastal regions, some of Spain's best wines are made. The RIOJA district near the Sierra Cantabrica mountains is one of the leading red wine districts of Spain, although some good white Riojas are also made; Rioja is probably the best known Spanish table wine that is exported. To the southwest, near the city of Valladolid on the Duero River, another excellent but extremely rare red wine is VEGA SICILIA, made from grape varieties native to France. Select Riojas and Vega Sicilias rank with the world's finest red wines, although the latter is not a wine of *Denominación de Origen*. Two other notable wines from this part of Spain are the sturdy whites of Rueda and, further to the east in Aragón, the full-bodied reds of Cariñena.

Surrounding the city of Barcelona is the region of CATALONIA, which also produces some good wines. Catalonia is noted for Tarragona, a full-bodied sweet red wine, but today the city of Villafranca de Penedés is probably most famous for Codornieu, Spain's most celebrated sparkling wine, bottle-fermented by the traditional CHAMPAGNE process. Alella, produced near the suburbs of Barcelona, is one of Spain's best white wines. Red wine from the Penedés region tends to be sturdy and robust.

Central Spain produces mostly ordinary wine for blending. With over 500,000 acres of vineyard, the La MANCHA district produces most of the country's bulk wine, although the fruity red wines of the VALDEPEÑAS region in La Mancha are popular and exports to the U.S. are increasing. Good white wines are also made in the Valdepeñas district.

The province of Andalusia in southern Spain is best known for FORTIFIED WINES, of which Sherry is a notable example. Andalusia is also the home of MANZANILLA, one of the world's driest wines — technically a Sherry but with a character all its own. MÁLAGA, the sweet "Mountain" of the Middle Ages, was at one time as famous as Sherry but is not well-known today. Another wine stripped of its former fame is Alicante, produced on the southeast coast, which used to be known under the curious name of "Tent."

The wines of the Sherry district are famous enough to warrant a detailed separate entry in this dictionary. The wines of MONTILLA, produced 250 miles to the northeast, are similar to Sherries except that they are usually shipped unfortified; they are rapidly becoming popular as less expensive substitutes for Sherry.

Spanna *(Spahn'-na)*: The local name for the Nebbiolo grape in the region of PIEMONTE, Italy. At least one producer in the GATTINARA district also uses the name Spanna for wines produced outside the D.O.C. limits of Gattinara that do not have right to this famous name; the wines are similar and, in certain cases, even superior to some Gattinaras.

Sparkling Burgundy: In the region of BURGUNDY, France, red, white or rosé wine that has been made sparkling; called *Bourgogne mousseux* in French. Most ordinary sparkling Burgundy is made by the CHARMAT (Bulk) process, but there is a significant production of wine that is bottle-fermented by the traditional CHAMPAGNE process, identified by the words 'méthode champenoise" on the label, and some of the better wines are excellent substitutes for Champagne. Sparkling Burgundy is also produced in the U.S., although very little is fermented in the bottle.

299

Spätburgunder *(Shpäte'-boor-gunder)*: The German name for the Pinot Noir grape, grown in the AHR River valley and also in the region of BADEN and Austria. See PINOT NOIR.

Spätlese *(Shpate'-lay-zeh)*: German for "late picking." Under the 1971 German Wine Law, a wine labeled Spätlese is a QUALITÄTSWEIN MIT PRÄDIKAT, produced from grapes picked later than usual during the harvest that have received extra maturity and are thus riper and richer in sugar. The minimum MUST WEIGHT must be about 80 (varies by area), and the wines may not be made with any sugar added. Wines labeled Spätlese will usually be sweeter and more expensive than those labeled KABINETT, because the requirements for production are more stringent.

The U.S. Bureau of Alcohol, Tobacco and Firearms recently prohibited the use of the word "Spätlese" on American wines, after considerable misuse of this term by several producers for wines that bore no similarity to a true German Spätlese. As a result, wines made from grapes left on the vine longer than usual must be called "Late Harvest" or "Late Picking" to conform with B.A.T.F. laws.

Spumante *(Spoo-mawn'-tay)*: Italian for "sparkling" or "frothy." Wines labeled spumante may be produced either by fermenting in large tanks via the CHARMAT (Bulk) process, or in the bottle by the traditional CHAMPAGNE process. The most famous is Asti Spumante, a fruity, semi-sweet sparkling wine from the village of ASTI in the district of PIEMONTE.

Staatsweingut *(Shtots-vine'-goot)*: German for "state wine domain." In the 19th century the Prussian government sponsored a general promotion of German viticulture and wine estates were purchased in the MOSEL, NAHE, RHEINGAU and RHEINHESSEN districts. The Mosel estate is located in the city of TRIER;

the Nahe estate is in NIEDERHAUSEN. The Staatsweingut in the Rheingau is located in the city of ELTVILLE and is the exclusive owner of the great STEINBERG vineyard; the Rheinhessen estate is in the city of Mainz. Though officially the property of the German state governments, each estate operates independently and has its own high standards for the wines. All except the Rheinhessen estate display the same state eagle crest on their labels.

Steinberg *(Shtine'-bairg)*: One of the most famous vineyards in Germany, a 79-acre expanse of Riesling vines within the commune of HATTENHEIM in the RHEINGAU district. Founded during the 12th century by Cistercian monks, the Steinberg is adjacent to the historic KLOSTER EBERBACH monastery; the vineyard lies at the edge of a forest and sometimes does not dry out in rainy years, but in great vintages the wines are among the finest in all of Germany: they are typically powerful and fruity, with a great deal of class. Like the Kloster Eberbach, the Steinberg is administered by the Staatsweingut in ELTVILLE and select bottles are regularly sold at auctions held at Kloster Eberbach. All Steinbergers are ESTATE-BOTTLED and are produced in all categories of QUALITÄTS-WEIN, priced according to their quality.

Sulfur: Non-metallic element widely employed in many stages of wine production. In its powdered or elemental form (called "flowers of sulfur") it is dusted on the vines during the summer to prevent disease such as MILDEW and OÏDIUM; by combustion it combines readily with oxygen to form sulfur dioxide, an indispensable compound used to sterilize casks and prevent re-fermentation so as to retain residual sugar in the wine. Sulfur dioxide is used by the vintner either as anhydrous compressed gas or as metabisulfite

301

(Campden tablets) to kill harmful yeast and bacteria. Hydrogen sulfide, which gives off an unpleasant "rotten egg" odor, is both poisonous and objectionable; a few wines display it after they have been in contact with sulfur, either in elemental or in compound form.

Sur Lie *(Sir Lee')***:** French for "on the lees." In certain wine districts, most notably in the MUSCADET region in France and the NEUCHÂTEL area in Switzerland, some white wines are allowed to remain in contact with the yeast and sediment without RACKING; this often imparts a faint, agreeable sparkle to the wine that adds freshness, and occasionally produces a wine that is fuller in fruit and flavor than ones not receiving this treatment.

Switzerland: The Swiss are great wine lovers. There are few regions in Switzerland suitable for grape-growing that have no vineyards: the country is divided into 22 *cantons* or districts, and only three produce no wine. The Swiss import immense quantities of wine from other countries, most notably France and Italy, but in recent years they have set aside some of their own good wines for export. Few are as yet well-known in the U.S., but many are excellent.

There are some 30,000 acres of vineyard in Switzerland; the largest concentration follows the Rhône River from its source in the Alps and continues along the north shore of Lake Geneva. Two cantons in this area, VAUD and VALAIS, produce three-fourths of all Swiss wine — often the best of the entire country. The lake tends to moderate rapid fluctuations in temperature; protected by high mountains, the Rhône Valley is warm and sunny, allowing the grapes to ripen fully.

The canton of Vaud is divided into two smaller districts: La Côte, to the west of the city of Lausanne, and LAVAUX to the east.

302

Along the shores of Lake Geneva the Chasselas grape, known by its local name Dorin, is grown for a light, fresh white wine. This variety is normally used only for table grapes in most of Europe, but in Switzerland it gives good results and is well-suited to the climate. In La Côte its wines are especially light; one of the best wine towns in this district is Mont-sur-Rolle. East of Lausanne the wines tend to be fuller. Lavaux has two important wine villages: DÉZALEY, just on the outskirts of Lausanne, and SAINT-SAPHORIN, further east. The district of Chablais, part of the Vaud but away from the lake to the southeast, boasts two particularly renowned wine towns: Aigle and Yvorne.

The canton of Valais follows the Rhône along a southern slope of vines, and is one of the warmest and driest regions in Switzerland. The Chasselas is called Fendant in the Valais, where it grows well. Some other white grape varieties are grown here that are planted nowhere else in Europe: Amigne, grown near the town of Sion, and Arvine, planted on the unusual salt soil of Fully. The Valais grows several varieties indigenous to France but known by local names: Pinot Gris is called Malvoisie, a strong, scented white variety sometimes used for sweet wines; Marsanne is known as Ermitage in the Valais, where it makes full-flavored white wine with an interesting spicy bouquet. Sylvaner is called Johannisberg in the Valais, and its wines are substantial and flavorful. The best red wine of the Valais is DÔLE, made from the Gamay grape with a little Pinot Noir added; sometimes Petit Dôle, made only from Pinot Noir, is also produced.

Though they are less important commercially, three other regions in Switzerland produce wine. The districts of TICINO (Tessin) in Italian Switzerland grows the red Merlot variety native to BORDEAUX and specializes in a soft, fruity red wine. NEUCHÂTEL to

303

the north along the lakes of Neuchâtel and Bienne makes both red and white wine, though the white is most likely to be seen abroad. The little Herrschaft region in northeast Switzerland near Lichtenstein makes light red wines from the Blauburgunder grape, but few are exported.

Sylvaner *(Sil-von′-ner)*: Good white wine grape, widely grown in many parts of Europe. Usually spelled ''Silvaner'' in Germany, it is planted principally in the RHEINHESSEN and RHEINPFALZ districts, in conjunction with the Riesling; though Sylvaner is generally more productive than the Riesling, it can nevertheless match it in certain areas where the grape is best suited: in the region of FRANKEN (Franconia) it is usually a superior variety. The Sylvaner is also grown in ALSACE, France, but there its wines are on the whole less good than the Riesling and it is not classified officially as a *cépage noble* (''noble variety''). Over 1,600 acres of Sylvaner have been planted in California, where its wines are legally allowed to be called ''Riesling.'' California Sylvaners can be quite similar to Rieslings, but those interested in the true Riesling style should look for California wines labeled ''Johannisberg Riesling'' or ''White Riesling.''

Syrah *(Sir-rah′)*: Excellent red wine grape native to the RHÔNE River valley, France. It gives robust wines with a great deal of color and tannin, and for this reason is normally blended with other varieties to round it out: in CHÂTEAUNEUF-DU-PAPE it is blended with up to 13 different varieties. The wines of HERMITAGE usually have a little white Marsanne added for finesse; in CÔTE ROTIE, a little white Viognier is added. Only at CORNAS and SAINT-JOSEPH is Syrah used almost exclusively. In Australia the Syrah is called ''Shiraz'' after the area in Persia from where it is said to have been brought during

304

the Crusades; there its wines are similar, among that country's best. The Petite Sirah of California was originally thought to be a related variety, but is not in fact the same grape, although it often produces similarly fine wines.

Szamorodni *(Sam-aw-rawd'-nee)*: Hungarian for "as it comes" or "such as it was grown." In the Hungarian TOKAY district, Furmint grapes not harvested in an overripe condition are made into dry or semi-dry white wine labeled "Tokay Szamorodni," which are normally much less sweet and concentrated than those labeled ASZÚ.

Szekszárd *(Sek'-sard)*: Wine village in southern Hungary near the Duna (Danube) River, noted for its red wine, *Szekszárdi Vörös*.

T

Table Wine: By definition, wine with an alcoholic content below 15%, suitable for serving with meals at the table. Wines stronger than 15% alcohol (but not over 24%) must be called DESSERT WINES under U.S. labeling and taxation laws.

Tâche, La *(Tash)*: Outstanding red wine vineyard in the CÔTE DE NUITS, Burgundy, rated Grand Cru (Great Growth). Owned entirely by the Société Civile du Domaine de la Romanée-Conti (see ROMANÉE CONTI), the La Tâche vineyard extends over 17½ acres in the famous wine commune of VOSNE-ROMANÉE; its magnificent and scented red wine is one of Burgundy's very greatest — in some vintages, even superior to Romanée-Conti, though La Tâche is always some-

305

what less expensive. About 2,500 cases are produced annually.

Tafelwein *(Tof´-fel-vine)*: German for "table wine." Under the 1971 German Wine Law, Tafelwein is the simplest quality category for a German wine. Generally light, inexpensive and suitable for daily consumption, a *Deutscher Tafelwein* must be a product of Germany, originating from the five designated Tafelwein regions: Mosel, Rhein, Oberrhein, Neckar, and Main. Almost always made with sugar added, Tafelweins are usually bottled in large containers and are rarely exported to the U.S.

Tannin: A group of organic substances present in grape skins and seeds, responsible for the astringent, puckery quality in a young wine. Chemically related to phenols, tannin is present in practically all wines but is more pronounced in red wines because it is extracted from the skins as the wine ferments. Tannin is also introduced into the wine from the oak casks in which the wine ages. The amount of tannin often relates to a wine's aging potential; it is deposited as sediment — along with other substances — as the wine ages in bottle.

Tastevin *(Tat´-van)*: A small metal cup used for tasting wines in the BURGUNDY region of France. In its usual form it is silver, with circular rows of indents along the bottom to catch the light. Its name has been adopted by Burgundy's wine fraternity, the *Confrérie des Chevaliers du Tastevin*.

The term "tastevinage" relates to a special, ornate label used by the Confrérie des Chevaliers du Tastevin for their wine selections. The shipper or producer whose wine is selected pays a small fee to the Confrérie for the privilege of being "tasteviné." Wines sold under the *tastevinage* label are usually superior, though the label implies no quality guarantee.

Taurasi *(Tau-rah′-see):* Sturdy red wine from the region of CAMPANIA, Italy. Grown in the province of Avellino near the city of Naples, Taurasi is made primarily from the Aglianico grape, usually with some Barbera or Sangiovese added. The wine ages slowly and must be at least three years old before it is sold; it is one of the most flavorful red Campania wines, and is rated D.O.C.

Tavel *(Tah′-vel):* One of the best rosé wines of France, produced in the lower RHÔNE River valley near the city of Avignon. Pale orange in color, dry, fresh and scented, Tavel is made from Grenache and Cinsault grapes; by law it must attain at least 11% alcohol. The wine is one of the world's most popular rosés, and is at its best when quite young — usually before it is three years old. There are some 2,000 acres of vineyard in Tavel; about 228,800 cases are produced annually.

Tenuta *(Tay-noo′-ta):* Italian for "estate." A "tenuta vinicola" is a wine estate.

Terlano *(Tair-lahn′-no):* Light, dry white wine produced near the village of Terlano in the ALTO ADIGE district, northern Italy. Terlano is usually made from the Pinot Bianco (Pinot Blanc) grape, but several other grape varieties — Riesling, Sauvignon, and Sylvaner — are also grown in the area for Terlano: if one of these varieties is predominant, it will be mentioned on the label.

Teroldego *(Tair-rawl′-de-go):* Fruity red wine from the TRENTINO region, northern Italy, produced in the lower part of the Adige River valley. Made from the Teroldego grape variety native to the Trentino region, the wine is full-flavored and ages quite well; it is rated D.O.C.

Tete de Cuvée *(Tet duh Kew-vay′)*: French for "great growth" or "the best barrel," derived from the word *cuve,* or vat (see CUVÉE). Formerly this term was used for the very finest Burgundies from the most famous vineyards, which fetched the highest prices, but since 1935 — when the French laws of APPELLATION CONTRÔLÉE were promulgated — tête de cuvée has been largely replaced by the term Grand Cru (Great Growth). Though tête de cuvée is still roughly interchangeable with Grand Cru, it is more correct to use the latter term, since *cru* relates both to the vineyard and its wine, whereas *cuvée* refers only to the wine. See CRU.

Thompson Seedless: White grape variety; the single most important grape variety in California, where over 232,000 acres have been planted. Named for William Thompson, an Englishman who first planted the grape in the Sacramento Valley in 1872, the Thompson Seedless is known as a "three-way" variety: it can be used for raisins, table grapes, or — less successfully — for wine. Being seedless, the grape is ideal for raisins and for eating, but its wine is usually very neutral, lacking extracts and acidity. In the warm Central Valley of California, the Thompson Seedless often supplies large quantities of bland white wine to be sold as "chablis," or even to "stretch" VARIETAL wines, since Federal law allows a varietally-labeled wine to contain up to 49% of wine made from other varieties.

Ticino *(Tee-chee′-no)*: Name given to the region in southern Switzerland near Lake Lugano and Lake Maggiore, where Italian is spoken; also called *Tessin.* With some 2,750 acres of vineyard, the Ticino area produces an interesting, light red wine from Merlot grapes, called "Merlot di Ticino"; it is one of Switzerland's better reds, with an attractive bouquet. The wine was formerly known only in Switzerland, but some very good Merlots di Ticino are now sold in the U.S.

Tinta *(Teen'-ta)***:** A family of red wine grapes native to Portugal, used for the wines of PORT and DÃO. The most important Tinta varieties include: Tinta Francisca, Tinta Madeira, Tinta Cão, Tinta Alvarelhão, and Tinta Carvalha. The Tinta Madeira is also grown in California; over 1,200 acres have been planted, mostly in the warm Central Valley, where the grape is used for California port. Some superior domestic ports are called "Tinta port" to show that they have been made from this fine grape variety.

Tinto *(Teen'-toe)***:** Spanish for "red"; a *vino tinto* is a red wine.

Tokay *(Toe'-kie)***:** Celebrated sweet white wine; specifically, the special product of the Tokay district in northeastern Hungary. The famous wines of Tokay have been produced for nearly a thousand years, and the best has always been rare and expensive. While the name Tokay has been used elsewhere for sweet wines, they are generally quite different than the authentic product of Hungary.

The Tokay vineyards cover some 15,320 acres along the southern slopes of the Carpathian Mountains, on unusually volcanic soil. The chief grape variety is the Furmint, although a little Hárslevelü is also grown. Twenty-nine villages are included in the Tokay district; the most important are Tállya, Sárospatak, Tarcal and Erdöbenye. At the foot of the vineyards flows the meandering Bodrog River, which strongly influences the region's climate. It moderates wide temperature variations and its mists encourage a special mold, BOTRYTIS CINEREA, to form on the grapes in a fine vintage, causing the skins to shrink and the grapes to become overripe. This mold is the same as that in other sweet wine districts — most notably the SAUTERNES region in France — though Hungarian Tokay is made by a somewhat different process.

At the time of the harvest in Tokay, over-ripe and dried-out grapes known as *Aszú* are placed in tubs called *puttonyos*. The grapes are then crushed to a pulp and allowed to ferment slowly before being added to a barrel of regular must. Thus the sweetness of a Tokay Aszú relates to the number of put-tonyos of overripe grapes in a given vat of wine: 3 puttonyos is the driest Aszú, 4 put-tonyos sweeter, and 5 puttonyos the sweetest — made entirely from overripe Aszú grapes. On wines sold as Aszú, the number of put-tonyos used will be indicated by a neck band on the bottle.

The wines then age slowly in the cellars for as long as seven years before they are sold. During this time a faint oxidation takes place, causing the wine to turn slightly brown. Be-fore bottling, the wine is pasteurized, adding an imperceptible caramel flavor which is characteristic of a good Tokay.

Only exceptional vintages bring the right weather for Aszú wines; in most years, Bo-trytis does not form and the very sweetest wines cannot be made. But good dry wine can still be produced; wines not considered up to Aszú standard are labeled *Szamorodni* — Hungarian for ''such as it was grown'' — which are either dry or semi-dry, depending on the vintage.

Formerly, an extremely rare and exquisite wine called Tokay *Essencia* was made solely from the luscious juice that the grapes exude while waiting to be crushed, but today in Tokay the custom is to blend this nectar into wines labeled Aszú, thereby increasing their overall quality. Tokay Aszú and Szamorodni is sold only by the Hungarian State Export Monopoly, Monimpex, and the wines are al-ways bottled in clear half-liter bottles that are smaller than regular wine bottles.

Tokay is probably the world's most long-lived wine. Essencia has kept perfectly for more than 200 years, and even older wines are not uncommon. Its fame has lead to many imitations, and a form of Tokay is produced in California in the Central Valley around Lodi, though not by the same process. One popular California table grape is even called "Flame Tokay," but it is not related to the Furmint and has nothing to do with Hungarian Tokay. In the region of ALSACE, France, Tokay is the local name for the Pinot Gris grape, the wines of which are called Tokay d'Alsace. The wines are not at all like Tokay but can be excellent, and the French government in 1975 classified Tokay d'Alsace as a *cépage noble* ("noble variety") entitled to the rank of Grand Cru (Great Growth).

Tonneau *(Tawn-no′)*: In the BORDEAUX region, France, a quantity of wine equivalent to 900 liters or 238 U.S. gallons, the traditional measure of output in the Bordeaux district. Actually, there is no cask of this size; the standard Bordeaux cask is the *barrique* of 225 liters, equivalent to about 24 cases each: four *barriques* comprise one *tonneau*.

Torre Quarto *(Taw′-ray Kwar′-toe)*: Fine red wine from the region of APULIA (Puglia), Italy, produced south of the town of Foggia. Though not officially rated D.O.C., Torre Quarto is one of the finest Apulian wines — it is rich and full-bodied, and has a good bouquet. Torre Quarto is made from a number of different grape varieties, some of which are native to France, and the wines are produced exclusively by the Cirillo-Farrusi estate.

Touraine *(Too-rain′)*: Picturesque old French province, located in the central LOIRE River valley. The district includes the present-day departments of Indre-et-Loire and Loir-et-Cher, surrounding the major city of Tours. The Touraine is one of France's most scenic districts, noted for its splendid châteaux; Touraine is also an APPELLATION CONTRÔLÉE for ordinary red, white or rosé wines produced in the district. The region has some 15,000 acres of vineyard; the most important grape varieties are Chenin Blanc and Sauvignon Blanc for white wines, and Cabernet Franc and Gamay for reds and rosés. There is also a large production of sparkling wines in the region.

The best Touraine wines, however, are usually not sold as Touraine (or under the other appellation, Coteaux de Touraine) but under their own names. Perhaps the most famous is VOUVRAY, a scented white wine produced just to the east of Tours; MONTLOUIS, which adjoins Vouvray, is similar. Two outstanding red wines produced further downstream are CHINON and BOURGUEIL. A little regional wine, the best of which is white, is sold under local appellations: Touraine Azay-le-Rideau, Touraine Amboise, Touraine Mesland, etc., but it is rarely seen outside the district.

Traben-Trarbach *(Trah′-ben Trahr′-bock)*: The names of two associated wine towns on the MOSEL River, Germany, linked together by a picturesque old bridge. The 800 acres of vineyard, mostly Rieslings, lie immediately to the north and south of the towns; those in the Kautenbach valley to the south are superior. Under the 1971 German Wine Law, vineyards in the neighboring towns of Enkirch and Wolf were added to the Traben-Trarbach community. The most famous vineyards (EINZELLAGEN) include: Kräuterhaus, Taubenhaus, Würzgarten, Burgweg, Schlossberg, Königsberg, Hühnerberg, Ungsberg, and Zollturm.

Traminer (German, *Tram-me′-ner*; French, *Tram-me-nair′*)**:** Excellent white wine grape grown in many parts of France, Germany and northern Italy. Its berries are reddish when ripe, and it yields characteristically full-flavored white wine with a remarkable bouquet. The name Traminer derives from the little village of Termeno (Tramin) in the Italian Tyrol, where it was first cultivated; it is still an important grape in the Tyrol, but it produces more famous wines in the region of ALSACE in France and in Germany's Rhine Valley. A selected strain or CLONE of Traminer is called Gewürztraminer, because its wines have an especially pronounced "spicy" quality; in Alsace, where the name Gewürztraminer arose, it was recently decreed that the name Traminer shall no longer be used for Alsatian wines, the name Gewürztraminer being preferable. Elsewhere, Gewürztraminer and Traminer are roughly interchangeable; the shorter spelling is often employed, though technically the Gewürztraminer is a superior strain. Over 2,600 acres have been planted in California.

Trebbiano *(Treb-yahn'-no)*: The Italian name for a white wine grape known as Ugni Blanc or "Saint-Émilion" in France. The Trebbiano is important in many Italian wine districts; in the north, it is used in conjunction with the Garganega for SOAVE and on its own for LUGANA; further south, it is one of the varieties used for ORVIETO and EST! EST! EST!

Trentino *(Tren-tee'-no)*: Region in northeastern Italy, forming Trento province around the city of Trento. Although a separate district from the ALTO ADIGE region to the north, the two regions are known collectively as Trentino-Alto Adige, and produce similar wines: one-half of the wine exported from Italy comes from this region. The Alto Adige region ranges over more mountainous country near the Austrian border and acknowledges Austrian influence in its German labels; Trentino is more Italian in outlook.

313

Trentino is noted for its many excellent red wines. A representative example is TEROLDEGO, a dry, full-bodied red wine made from the Teroldego grape; the superior Cabernet, Pinot Noir and Merlot grapes native to France are also grown in the Trentino region, and are called Cabernet Trentino, Pinot Nero Trentino and Merlot Trentino, respectively. The light reds Marzemino, Valdadige and Vallagarina are also good, but they are rarely exported. Fine Trentino rosé wines are produced from Lagarino (Lagrein) and Schiava, as in Alto Adige. White Trentino wines are made from Riesling, Traminer Aromatico, Moscato, and Sylvaner; some excellent sparkling wine is made from Pinot Trentino.

Many of the better Trentino wines have recently received D.O.C. listings. Wines produced in the Alto Adige region are listed under Alto Adige in this book.

Trier *(Tree'-er)*: Famous city on the MOSEL River, Germany. Founded in Roman times, Trier is the headquarters of the Mosel wine trade and is the largest city in the area. Though Trier has only a few vineyards of its own, the 1971 German Wine Law included vineyards from many neighboring villages in the Trier wine community, and as a result two of the best wine towns in the RUWER district — AVELSBACH and EITELSBACH — are now officially part of Trier. Many famous wine producers have their headquarters in Trier, most notably the Vereinigte Hospitien, Bischöfliches Konvikt, Hohe Domkirche, Bischofliches Priesterseminar, Friedrich-Wilhelm Gymnasium, and Von Kesselstatt estates.

Trittenheim *(Trit'-ten-heim)*: Picturesque little wine town on the MOSEL River, Germany, with 741 acres of vineyard. Trittenheim lies at a sharp bend in the river; the vineyards are steep and the wines are generally only at their best in great vintages. The light, stylish Riesling wines of Trittenheim tend to be little known, and many are excellent value. The two most famous vineyards (EINZELLAGEN) are Apotheke and Altärchen; other good Einzellagen are Leiterchen and Felsenkopf.

Trockenbeerenauslese *(Trock'-en-bearen-ouse'-lay-zeh)***:** German for "dried berry selection," the highest achievement of German viticulture — among the rarest and most expensive wines in the world. During the harvest, a few grapes become overripe as a result of the action of the "noble mold" (see BOTRYTIS CINEREA). If weather permits them to be left even longer on the vine, the skins shrink and the water evaporates so that the grapes appear to be raisins. These are picked individually, berry by berry, and it often takes a picker an entire day to gather enough grapes to make a single bottle.

Under the 1971 German Wine Law, only wines with a MUST WEIGHT of at least 150 qualify for the rating Trockenbeerenauslese. The wines are extremely sweet and flavorful, but because of their scarcity they are fabulously expensive; the wines can only be made a few times a decade in most regions.

Tuscany (Italian, **Toscana,** pronounced *Tos-cahn'-na*)**:** Region in central Italy, surrounding the city of Florence (Firenze); also one of Italy's most important wine areas, with over 560,000 acres of vineyard. A scenic region of rolling hills, Tuscany is most famous for CHIANTI, probably the most widely exported Italian wine. Produced in a large area between the cities of Florence and Siena, Chianti used to be symbolized by the wickered FIASCO flask in which it was traditionally bottled, but now the fiasco is becoming rare. The central and best part of the Chianti region is called *Chianti Classico*.

315

Yet Tuscany has several other wines that rival Chianti in quality, although they are not as well-known in the export trade. One of the most celebrated red wines in Italy is BRUNELLO DI MONTALCINO, produced to the south of the Chianti district around the town of Montalcino, which is made from the Brunello grape — actually a variety of Sangiovese. Further to the east, the celebrated red VINO NOBILE DI MONTEPULCIANO is similar; all three of these robust wines are long-lived, and well-made examples are among Italy's very finest wines.

Tuscany produces less white wine than red, and little of it is seen abroad. The renowned VINO SANTO of the Chianti district is a fine dessert wine made from dried grapes; another good white is the Vernaccia di San Gimignano, produced near the Chianti district. The island of Elba is part of Tuscany; Elba makes a good white wine, Procanico, but not much of it reaches the mainland. The remaining Tuscan whites are Montecarlo, produced north of Florence, and Pitigliano, one of the first white Tuscan wines to receive a D.O.C. listing.

U

Ugni Blanc *(Oon'-yee Blawn')*: White wine grape, widely grown in southern France. Known by its local name ''Saint-Émilion,'' it is the chief variety used for making Cognac brandy; in the Cognac region its pale, acidic wines are ideal for distilling, less so for table wine. However, it gives the fresh, crisp white wines of CASSIS on the Mediterranean coast, and it is grown in many parts of PROVENCE for good white wines. In Italy the Ugni Blanc is called Trebbiano, and is the most widely planted white wine grape in that country (see TREBBIANO). Over 1,400 acres of Ugni Blanc have been planted in California, mostly in the warm Central Valley, where the grape's inherently high acidity is an advantage.

Ullage *(Oo-lahj')*: French term for the air space in a cask or bottle of wine, caused by slow evaporation. Too much ullage is harmful and could promote OXIDATION or ACESCENCE, and so the casks are regularly "topped up" with wine at intervals, a process known as *ouillage* in French. Once the wine is bottled, a pronounced ullage in a very old wine may be a sign that it is no longer fit to drink.

Umbria *(Oom'-bree-ah)*: Wine region in central Italy between the cities of Florence and Rome, with some 179,000 acres of vineyard. Land-locked Umbria has only a few well-known wines; by far the most famous is ORVIETO, a fresh white wine that is either dry or semi-sweet; further to the east, the red and white wines of Torgiano, produced south of the city of Perugia, are also celebrated. The local Umbria wine, Colli del Trasimeno, comes from around Lake Trasimeno and was rated D.O.C. in 1972.

Ungstein *(Oong'-shtine)*: Wine village in the RHEINPFALZ (Palatinate) region, Germany, with 791 acres of vineyard. Ungstein lies just to the north of Bad Dürkheim (see DURKHEIM), and its fine wines are similar; one-fourth of the vineyards are planted in Riesling, and there is considerable red wine production. The best-known wine name is Ungsteiner Honigsäckel, but under the 1971 German Wine Law this has become a composite vineyard or GROSSLAGE; the individual vineyards or EINZELLAGEN include: Herrenberg, Nussriegel, Bettelhaus, Osterberg, and Weilberg; Michelsberg is shared by Bad Dürkheim.

Ürzig *(Ertz'-ig)***:** Famous wine town on the MOSEL River, Germany, with 885 acres of vineyard planted entirely in Riesling. The steep sloped vineyards produce some of the Mosel's very best wines in hot years; the most famous Ürzig vineyard (EINZELLAGE) is Würzgarten ("spice garden," in German, referring to the wine's characteristics), shared by many proprietors and located on unusual red soil. Under the 1971 German Wine Law this is the only Einzellage in Ürzig; Ürziger Schwarzlay has become a composite vineyard or GROSSLAGE that includes Einzellagen from several neighboring villages, most of them considerably below Ürzig in quality.

V

Valais *(Val'-lay)***:** Wine region in southern Switzerland with some 10,900 acres of vineyard, the largest and most important vineyard area in that country. The canton (district) of Valais extends along the Rhône River valley in an east-west direction, and between the towns of Martigny and Brig there is an almost continual wall of vineyard. Being sheltered by high mountains, the Valais is the warmest and driest wine region in Switzerland; the chief grape variety is Fendant (Chasselas), which gives scented white wines. One of the best Swiss red wines is DÔLE, produced from a blend of Gamay and Pinot Noir grapes; some interesting but rather rare Valais wines are produced by grapes grown nowhere else: Arvine, a scented, full-bodied white wine, and Amigne, prized for its fine bouquet. Pinot Gris is called Malvoisie in the Valais, where it is sometimes used for sweet wines. Sylvaner is known as Johannisberg in the Valais;

the Marsanne from France is called Ermitage, another exclusive of the Valais.

Valdepeñas *(Val-de-pain′-yas)*: Wine region in central Spain, officially part of the La MANCHA district. There are some 51,900 acres of vineyard in Valdepeñas; both red and white wines of good quality are produced, though the light, attractive reds made from Cencibel are superior. Normally a little white wine is blended with the red to make it lighter and earlier to mature; the wines are generally inexpensive and good values.

A grape called Valdepeñas is grown in California, and some 2,600 acres have been planted, mostly in the warm Central Valley; however, it is not the same as the Cencibel grape of the Valdepeñas district in Spain, nor are its wines similar.

Valgella *(Val-jel′-la)*: Red wine from the VALTELLINA district in the region of LOMBARDY, northern Italy. Made from the Nebbiolo grape, which is known as Chiavennasca in the Valtellina district, Valgella is a sturdy red wine that matures slowly; it can be quite good but is generally a little lighter than some other Valtellina wines.

Valpantena *(Val-pon-tay′-na)*: Wine district east of Lake Garda in the region of VENETO, Italy. The Valpantena district adjoins the VALPOLICELLA region, and superior Valpantena wines meeting the standards for Valpolicella are allowed the geographical designation "Valpolicella Valpantena."

Valpolicella *(Val-po-lee-chel′-la)*: Excellent and famous red wine from the region of VENETO, northern Italy, produced north of the city of Verona near Lake Garda. Valpolicella is made primarily from three grape varieties — Corvina, Rondinella, and Molinara — grown in eighteen communes in the province of Verona. The central portion of

319

the Valpolicella district is called Valpolicella *Classico,* which usually produces superior wines; if the wines reach 12% alcohol they may be called "Valpolicella Superiore." A specialty of the district is Recioto della Valpolicella (see RECIOTO), made from dried grapes, which is fuller-bodied than regular Valpolicella.

Valpolicella is a light, fruity red wine that is most enjoyable when quite young — usually before it is five years old — except for the Recioto wines, which are quite long-lived.

Valtellina *(Val-tel-lee′-na)***:** Mountainous wine district in the region of LOMBARDY, northern Italy, extending along the Adda River valley east of Lake Como. Though little known, the Valtellina district produces some of Italy's very finest red wines from the Nebbiolo grape — the same outstanding variety grown in other parts of northern Italy — except that here the grape is called Chiavennasca. The grapes are grown on steep Alpine slopes that receive a great deal of sunshine; the wines tend to be hard in their youth but mature magnificently. There are several famous wine regions in the Valtellina district; usually the most celebrated wine is INFERNO, followed by SASSELLA, GRUMELLO, and FRACIA; VALGELLA tends to be a little lighter than the others. Castel Chiuro, equally good red and white Valtellina wines, are produced exclusively by Nino Negri, an important grower; Sfursat (Sforzato), a rich, full-bodied red wine made from dried grapes, is quite high in alcohol (over 14%) and is made by a number of different Valtellina growers.

Varietal: Term used in the U.S. wine trade for wines labeled according to the grape variety from which they were made, as opposed to a region or district. A varietal wine is the opposite of a GENERIC wine, which is labeled according to a district or "type," Federal

320

regulations stipulate that a varietally-labeled wine must be made from at least 51% of the grape variety specified on the label; better producers usually exceed this figure by a considerable margin, though some blending is almost always helpful in giving proper balance to a wine.

European wines are not normally named after the grape variety used because in most wine regions, approved grape varieties are planted according to wine laws issued by the government: only those varieties that produce superior wines may be planted in most fine wine regions, and the authenticity of these wines is protected by law.

Vaud *(Vo)***:** Wine region in Switzerland with some 8,000 acres of vineyard, located along the north shore of Lake Geneva. The canton (district) of Vaud includes three smaller regions: La Côte, west of the city of Lausanne; LAVAUX, to the east of Lausanne; and Chablais, away from the lake along the Rhône River valley. The Vaud is noted for its white wines made from the Dorin (Chasselas) grape, among the best in Switzerland; excellent examples are those of DÉZALEY, SAINT-SAPHORIN, Mont-sur-Rolle, Aigle, and Yvorne.

V.D.P.V. (Verband Deutscher Prädikatswein Versteigerer): An association of German vintners that serves to promote the quality and the sale of German *Prädikat* wines — the natural, unsugared wines that are true to their district and to their type. A *Versteigerer* is an auctioneer, referring to the previous importance of wine auctions in Germany before modern methods of marketing were introduced. The *Verband* includes many of Germany's top producers, and identifies its members by a square black eagle seal, with grapes on its breast. Formerly it was called V.D.N.V. (Verband Deutscher

321

Naturwein Versteigerer), but the association adopted the new title with the enactment of the 1971 German Wine Law, which prohibits the word *natur* to appear on a wine label.

V.D.Q.S. (Vins Délimités de Qualité Supérieur): French for ''delimited wines of superior quality.'' Certain districts in France produce good wines that are nevertheless not considered up to the standards of APPELLATION CONTRÔLÉE, and for these wines the government has established an intermediate quality classification: V.D.Q.S. The laws of V.D.Q.S. resemble those of appellation contrôlée: the wines are produced in officially delimited regions from approved grape varieties that have a restricted yield per hectare. All V.D.Q.S. wines are subject to official approval before being released for sale, and a government seal guaranteeing their quality appears on the label. The law also provides that certain outstanding V.D.Q.S. wines may someday achieve appellation contrôlée status, after they have shown continued improvement in quality. V.D.Q.S. wines are almost always well-made and sound, and because they are usually inexpensive, many are excellent value. Each of the more famous V.D.Q.S. wines is listed in this dictionary.

Vega Sicilia *(Vay'-ga- Si-see'-lee-ah)***:** One of the very greatest red wines of Spain, produced near the city of Valladolid on the banks of the Duero River. Made from a number of grape varieties originally native to France, Vega Sicilia is produced only by one winery, Bodegas Vega Sicilia S.A. Wines labeled Vega Sicilia always bear a vintage date and receive at least 5 years of cask aging prior to their release; the wines then improve for years in bottle. The *bodega* also sells a lesser, non-vintage wine called Tinto Valbuena, which receives less cask aging. Both wines are ex-

322

tremely rare and expensive, but they are among the finest produced in Spain.

Veltliner *(Velt'-leen-er)*: A group of grape varieties planted mostly in Austria and other parts of central Europe. The most common variety is the Grüner (Green) Veltliner, grown in lower Austria for a lively, fruity white wine; another important variety is the Frühroter (Red) Veltliner, named for its red berries; this grape is also planted to a limited extent in California.

Vendange *(Von-dahnj')*: French for "grape harvest." This term is used in connection with the process of picking and fermentation, not the wine of a particular vintage; a vintage-dated wine is termed "millésimé."

Vendemmia *(Ven-day'-me-ah)*: Italian for "grape harvest." Like *vendange* (see above), this term relates to the harvest, not to the wine of a particular vintage. In Spanish, the word is spelled *vendemia*.

Venegazzù *(Vain-nay-got-tsoo')*: Fine red and white wines from the region of VENETO, Italy, produced near the town of Venegazzù del Montello in the Treviso area. The red is made from Cabernet Sauvignon, Merlot and Malbec grapes, and is similar to a good Bordeaux; if the wine has received extra age, it is called "Riserva di Casa." White Venegazzù is made from Riesling and Pinot, and also ages well. Although not rated D.O.C., Venegazzù is among the Veneto region's finest wines; it is produced exclusively by the Conte Piero Loredan estate.

Veneto *(Vain'-nay-toe)*: Region in northeastern Italy, including the major cities of Venice, Verona, Vicenza and Padua (Padova). Veneto's western boundary is near Lake Garda, and from there the region extends eastwards to the Adriatic; there are over

323

525,000 acres of vineyard in Veneto, and many fine wines.

The Veneto region divides up into three smaller districts. The most western of these surrounds the city of Verona east of Lake Garda, and boasts the famous red wines of VALPOLICELLA and BARDOLINO and the noted white SOAVE. Middle Veneto, with its gently rolling hills and plains, extends from the city of Vicenza eastwards past Padua; the most celebrated wines of this district are GAMBELLARA, Colli Euganei, Breganze, and Colli Berici. Middle Veneto white wines are generally superior to the reds, and many have received D.O.C. listings. Finally, eastern Veneto (Venetia) includes the suburbs of Venice and the city of Treviso, northwards towards the Italian Tyrol. Near Treviso the River Piave flows down from the Tyrol to the Adriatic, and defines an important wine region; in recognition of their excellence, Vini del Piave (Piave wines) were awarded D.O.C. status in 1971. Piave wines are designated by VARIETAL labels; better red varieties include Merlot, Cabernet, Pinot Nero, Rubino, and Raboso; superior white wines are made from Riesling, Tocai, Verduzzo and Pinot Grigio.

Other celebrated Venetian wines are PROSECCO, produced near the town of Conigliano, and Verdiso, a Treviso wine. The Veneto region as a whole produces in excess of 97 million cases of wine a year, ranking it as one of Italy's most important wine regions.

Ventoux *(Von-too′)*: Dramatic mountain peak some 6,270 ft. high, located to the east of the city of Orange in the southern RHÔNE River valley, France. Its slopes are dotted with vineyards, and the Ventoux region produces a number of good red, white and rosé wines known under the name "Côtes du Ventoux" and officially rated APPELLATION CONTRÔLÉE.

Véraison *(Vay-ray-zawn')*: French term for the point during the grape maturation process, when unripe grapes change color from green to purple or translucent green, and their sugar content begins to increase. In many regions the actual time of the harvest can be determined in relation to when véraison occurs.

Verdelho *(Vair-dayl'-yo)*: A dark, medium sweet MADEIRA, made from Verdelho grapes grown on the island of Madeira. Verdelho is usually a little softer and sweeter than SERCIAL, but drier than BUAL. This grape is also grown in Portugal to make white Port.

Verdicchio *(Vair-deek'-ee-o)*: Famous white wine from the MARCHE region in Italy; made from the Verdicchio grape grown to the west of the city of Ancona. The two D.O.C. regions for this wine are called Verdicchio dei Castelli di Jesi and Verdicchio di Matelica; the former includes the communes of Cupramontana, Monterobero and Castelbellino, and is better known. Verdicchio is either dry or semi-dry, and has a clean freshness; it is one of Italy's finest white wines.

Verdiso *(Vair-dee'-zo)*: Light, dry white wine made from the Verdiso grape, grown near the city of Treviso in the VENETO region, Italy.

Verdot: see PETIT-VERDOT.

Verduzzo *(Vair-doot'-so)*: Italian white wine grape, widely grown in the VENETO and FRIULI-VENEZIA GIULIA regions of northeastern Italy. It gives dry, scented and rather full-bodied white wines called Verduzzo; some excellent examples are made in the River Piave area in Veneto.

325

Vermentino *(Vair-men-teen'-o)*: White wine grape grown in the region of LIGURIA, Italy for a light, fresh white wine of the same name. The Vermentino is also planted extensively in Corsica and in Sardinia, where it gives similarly fine wines; one particularly good Sardinian wine, Vermentino di Gallura, was awarded a D.O.C. rating in 1975.

Vermouth: A flavored or aromatized wine to which plant extracts and other flavorings have been added. The principal ingredient is wormwood, and both vermouth and wormwood derive from the German word *Wermut,* meaning the shrub *Artemisia absinthium.* Wormwood leaves are used in making French absinthe, but for vermouth the less toxic flowers are substituted.

There are two basic types of vermouth: the dry "French" type, and the "Italian" type, which is sweeter. Both forms of vermouth are named for the places where they were originally developed — Torino, Italy and Lyon, France — but today, dry vermouths are made in Italy and sweet vermouths are produced in France; the most famous producers make both types.

Vermouth production begins with a neutral, dry white wine base, such as is produced in the MIDI region in France or in APULIA, Italy. The wines are aged for at least one year before they are blended with a *mistelle* — unfermented must to which brandy is added, thus preserving the sugar and natural flavors. Then plant flavorings are added; the most common are worm-wood, quinine, camomile, coriander, cinnamon, orange peel, cloves and hyssop, though each producer naturally guards his own special formula. The flavorings are allowed to mix or infuse with the wine, then the mixture is pasteurized, refrigerated and filtered to remove sediment and impurities. After a final aging period, the wine is ready for sale as vermouth and contains about 19-20% alcohol.

Though vermouth manufacture originated in France and Italy, America is also an important producer; better American vermouths are quite similar to those of Europe. Fine vermouths are also produced in Spain, Portugal, South Africa, and many parts of South America.

Vernaccia *(Vair-natch′-ah)*: Historic white wine grape; famous during the Renaissance and now grown in many parts of Italy. Both dry and sweet Vernaccias are made; all tend to have a characteristic gold color and full body, and the best are quite sweet and high in alcohol. Better wines that have received official D.O.C. listings include the Vernaccia di San Gimignano of TUSCANY, the Vernaccia di Serrapetrona from the region of MARCHE, and the Vernaccia di Oristano from Sardinia.

Verona *(Vair-ro′-na)*: Important city in northeastern Italy, situated a few miles east of Lake Garda. The Verona district forms the western part of the VENETO region; well-known Veronese wines include BARDOLINO, VALPOLICELLA, and SOAVE.

Vigne *(Veen′-yuh)*: French for "vine," an individual vine in its entirety. Its components include the root-stock, or *cep,* and canes, or *sarments.* Also, a small vineyard holding.

Vignoble *(Veen-yawb′-l)*: French for "vineyard" or "vineyard area."

Villány *(Veel-lahn′-yee)*: Town in southern Hungary near the Yugoslavian border, famous for its red wine, *Villányi Burgundi.*

Vin *(Vanh)*: French for "wine," legally defined as a beverage produced by the partial or complete fermentation of the juice of fresh grapes.

Viña *(Veen′-ya)*: Spanish for "vineyard."

Vin de Paille *(Van duh Pie′)*: French for "straw wine," a wine made from grapes that have been left to dry in the sun on mats of straw, or indoors on racks. Since this process causes the grapes to lose water by evaporation, the wines obtained are very sweet and high in alcohol. In France this process is used for the rare wines of the JURA district; in Italy, such wines are called *passito*.

Vin de Pays *(Van duh Pay')*: French for "country wine," the local wines produced in the less famous French wine regions that are not always bottled or exported. Many of these wines can be quite pleasant, however, and in 1974 the French government authorized 44 regions from which *vins de pays* could legally originate; most of them are in the MIDI. The wines are labeled according to their place of origin and the department (administrative region) where they were produced. Few *vins de pays* have been exported to the U.S., but the wines are worth looking for when visiting the regions in which they are made.

Vinho Verde *(Veen'-yo Vair'-day)*: Portuguese for "green wine"; specifically, an especially light wine produced in a delimited zone in northern Portugal, in an area bounded on the north by the Minho River and on the south by the Douro. A Portuguese wine region that has been granted *Denominação de origem* (Denomination of Origin) status, the Vinho Verde area has about 61,775 acres of vineyard, and produces red, white and rosé wines.

The Vinho Verdes are not named "green" for their color but rather for the time when the grapes are harvested — before they are fully ripe. The wines have a pronounced but refreshing acidity and are very low in alcohol — rarely above 10%. Because they are made to be consumed young, Vinho Verdes rarely improve with age and should not be stored too long. The whites are superior, and often have a faint, agreeable sparkle; the red and rosé Vinho Verdes are sturdier, and generally taste best when chilled.

Vinifera *(Vin-nif′-fer-ah)*: A European or East Asian species of grape vine, the only one of 32 *Vitis* species that gives uniformly good wine — hence the name, which means "wine bearer." Originally native to the region of Transcaucasia on the eastern shores of the Black Sea, varieties of vinifera were transported throughout the ancient world and are now grown in nearly every temperate zone where they are suited.

Vinification: All of the necessary steps by which grapes are made into wine.

Vino *(Vee′-no)*: Italian (and Spanish) for "wine."

Vino Nobile di Montepulciano *(Vee′-no No′-bee-lay dee Mawn-tay-pool-chon′-no)*: Fine Italian red wine produced in the region of TUSCANY, near the town of Montepulciano. The wine was called "noble" not for its qualities but for its original clientele, yet its quality is generally superior: produced from a blend of Sangiovese, Canaiolo, Malvasia and Trebbiano grapes, the wine is full-flavored and has a good bouquet. The region adjoins the CHIANTI area, and select Vino Nobile di Montepulcianos are similar to some of the best Chiantis but are much less well-known. Named for the town of Montepulciano, Vino Nobile di Montepulciano should not be confused with the Montepulciano grape grown in the ABRUZZI region, used for the red wine Montepulciano d'Abruzzo.

Vino Santo: Italian for "wine of the saints," a special type of wine produced in many parts of Italy, especially the TUSCANY region. In the fall, selected Trebbiano or Malvasia grapes are placed in airy lofts to dry during the winter, so that they lose a great deal of water by evaporation. In the spring, they are pressed and the must is allowed to ferment very slowly; Vino Santo is often not put into bottle until its fifth year, and later improves with even more aging. The wine is lusciously rich and intensely sweet, but because so much volume is lost by evaporation, it is produced only in very limited quantities and is very rare on the export market.

Vintage: Term having several different meanings. Technically, the vintage is the annual gathering of the grapes during the harvest and the making of wine from those grapes; hence a vintage wine is one from a particular year. During the 19th century, however, producers in the PORT and CHAMPAGNE districts introduced a new meaning of vintage: the selected wines of a particularly good harvest. In these districts, a wine from an especially fine vintage is superior to one not bearing a vintage date — though a ''vintage'' of course takes place each year in every region where wine is made, without any quality distinction. Many California producers prefer to specify a vintage date only for especially good wines.

In French, the vintage is called *vendange;* in German it is *Weinlese. Cosecha* refers to a vintage-dated wine in Spanish, *Colheita* in Portuguese.

Viognier *(Vee-awn-yay')*: White grape variety grown in the RHÔNE River valley, France, used in blends for the red wines of CÔTE ROTIE and on its own for the rare white wines of CONDRIEU.

Viré *(Veer-ray')*: Little village in the MÂCON region, Burgundy, famous for its good white wines made from the Chardonnay grape, entitled to the appellation ''Mâcon-Viré.''

330

Viticulture: The science and art of grape-growing, as distinguished from *viniculture,* the science of wine-making.

Vollrads, Schloss *(Fall'-rods)***:** Outstanding wine estate in the RHEINGAU district, Germany, located near the village of WINKEL. The estate has some 92 acres of vineyards, mostly planted in Riesling; it is dominated by a massive, picturesque *Schloss* (castle) that was built around 1300, and superior wine has been produced on the property for centuries. Schloss Vollrads now belongs to the Matuschka-Greiffenclau family, one of the oldest wine-making families in the Rheingau; the late Count Richard Matuschka-Greiffenclau was former president of the German Vintners Association.

Like several other German wine estates, Schloss Vollrads identifies the quality of its wines by means of different colored capsules, in addition to the label bearing the Schloss Vollrads coat-of-arms. No wine below the rank of QUALITÄTSWEIN is sold as Schloss Vollrads; the most basic wine bears a green capsule, and special lots are adorned with a gold stripe. (Occasionally, a red label is also used for Qualitätswein.) The *Kabinett* has a blue capsule, with superior wines bearing a gold stripe. The *Spätlese* capsule is pink, and pink with a gold stripe; the *Auslese* is white, and white with a gold stripe. The extremely rare and costly *Beerenauslese* and *Trockenbeerenauslese* both have gold capsules, and the latter is adorned with a special neck label. In any quality grade, however, a wine labeled Schloss Vollrads displays certain noble qualities — great bouquet and fruitiness, and impeccable balance.

Volnay *(Vawl-nay')***:** Famous wine commune in the CÔTE DE BEAUNE, Burgundy. Located on a hilly slope between the communes of POMMARD and MEURSAULT, Volnay is celebrated for its excellent red wines made from Pinot Noir; rather light in color, but having much fruit and elegance, they are among the most charming red Burgundies and

331

have been prized since the 12th century. Volnay has several notable vineyards rated Premier Cru (First Growth); the most highly acclaimed is CAILLERETS, but the Clos des Ducs, Champans, Frémiets, Santenots, Clos des Chênes, Brouillards, Mitans, and Chevrets also have wide repute. The total vineyard area in the commune is about 526 acres; production averages about 91,700 cases annually.

Vosne-Romanée *(Vone Ro'-man-nay)*: One of the most celebrated wine communes of the CÔTE DE NUITS, Burgundy, and possibly the most famous of the entire CÔTE D'OR. There are only 593 acres in the whole commune, yet the incomparable red wine produced in Vosne-Romanée is in great demand. The commune is named for the La ROMANÉE vineyard, the choicest portion of which in 1760 was called ROMANEÉ-CONTI: these two great vineyards are rated Grand Cru (Great Growth), the highest rank for a Burgundy. Three other Vosne-Romanée Grand Crus — RICHEBOURG, La TÂCHE, and ROMANÉE-SAINT-VIVANT — produce similarly fine wines. The vineyards of ÉCHEZEAUX and GRANDS-ÉCHEZEAUX are technically not within the Vosne-Romanée commune but are generally included with Vosne-Romanée wines, and if they are declassified they are sold as Vosne-Romanées. Several excellent Vosne-Romanée vineyards are rated Premier Cru (First Growth): the more famous include MALCONSORTS, Suchots, Les Beaumonts, La Grande Rue, and Clos des Réas. Average production for the entire commune rarely exceeds 62,500 cases annually.

Vougeot *(Voo'-zho)*: Wine town in the CÔTE DE NUITS, Burgundy, celebrated chiefly for one famous vineyard, the CLOS DE VOUGEOT. Wines labeled Vougeot, on the other hand, are not the same as Clos de Vougeots but come from lesser vineyards nearby; these are usually not quite as fine as Clos de Vougeots but can nevertheless be distinctive. Some 4,500 cases of red Vougeot are produced annually; there is also a tiny production of superior white wine.

Vouvray *(Voo'-vray)***:** Fine white wine region in the LOIRE River valley, France, with some 3,000 acres of vineyard east of the city of Tours in the old province of TOURAINE. The charming, scented white Vouvrays are made from the Chenin Blanc (Pineau de la Loire) grape grown in eight communes — Vouvray, Chancay, Rochecorbon, Noizay, Vernou, Parcay-Veslay, Sainte-Radegonde, and Reugny; occasionally their names will appear on a wine label. There are certain outstanding vineyards in these communes that produce superior wines; among the best are: Le Mont, Les Bidaudières, Moncontour, Le Haut Lieu, and Clos du Bourg. Depending on the vintage, Vouvrays can be dry, semi-dry, or sweet *(moelleux);* the sweeter Vouvrays can improve for decades. In addition to still wines, there is an important production of sparkling Vouvray *(Vouvray mousseux),* bottle-fermented by the CHAMPAGNE process, which are among the best sparkling wines produced outside the Champagne region. Total production of all Vouvray often exceeds 500,000 cases annually.

Wachau *(Vok'-kow)***:** Wine district in eastern Austria, situated along the Donau (Danube) River west of Vienna. One of Austria's most famous wine regions, the Wachau is one of the designated Austrian *Weinbaugebiete*

333

(wine-growing regions) that includes the important wine towns of KREMS, Dürnstein, Baumgarten and Mautern. The vineyards are planted extensively in Grüner Veltliner, Riesling and Müller-Thurgau grapes.

Wachenheim *(Vok'-en-heim):* One of the most famous wine towns in the RHEINPFALZ (Palatinate) district, Germany, with 1,433 acres of vineyard. Wachenheim produces both red and white wines, but the fine white Riesling wines are superior and have fetched world-wide acclaim. Wachenheim lies just to the north of FORST and the wines share many of the same noble characteristics. The best vineyards (EINZELLAGEN) include: Gerümpel, Rechbächel, Goldbächel, Böhlig, Altenburg, Schlossberg, Luginsland, Königswingert, and Mandelgarten; the leading producer is Dr. Bürklin-Wolf, who is the sole owner of Rechbächel.

Waldrach *(Vol'-drock):* Little wine village in the RUWER district, Germany, with some 297 acres of vineyard. Waldrach is noted for its especially light and delicate white wines made from Riesling, though they are generally only at their best in hot years. The best vineyards (EINZELLAGEN) are Krone, Hubertusberg, Meisenberg, Ehrenberg, and Jesuitengarten.

Walluf *(Vol'-loof):* Name recently given to two associated wine communities in Germany's RHEINGAU district, Nieder-Walluf and Ober-Walluf, which have now been combined into one municipality. Walluf lies near the Rhine River just below RAUENTHAL, but the wines are generally somewhat heavier and less fine than the Rauenthalers. In fine vintages, however, Walluf can produce some good wines; the vineyards (EINZELLAGEN) include: Berg Bildstock, Langenstück, Walkenberg, Oberberg, and Fitusberg.

Washington State: One of America's newest and most promising wine regions, Washington is the nation's third largest grape-producing state, with over 18,000 acres of vineyard. Grapes were first planted in the Puget Sound area south of Seattle in 1872, but the wines were mediocre and they were only distributed locally. Following repeal, Washington State vintners concentrated their efforts in making dessert wines and not table wines, but this direction was reversed in the late 1960s when it was demonstrated that outstanding table wines could be made from premium grape varieties grown in the state.

From west to east, Washington State experiences several extreme climatic changes. The west coast near Olympia is the wettest region in the continental U.S., and a rain-forest actually exists there. In the center of the state, the Cascade Range rises up to effectively block most of the rainfall, and in the east it is nearly desert. But since 1906 dam projects in the Cascade Range have allowed irrigation to compensate for the lack of rainfall, and the YAKIMA VALLEY in southeastern Washington is now the state's most important wine region, with 83% of the total vineyard area (over 15,000 acres). Many of the vineyards are planted in table grape varieties, but acreage in wine grape varieties is on the increase. The latitude in the Yakima Valley is the same as in the Burgundy region in France, and many of the finer grapes native to France and Germany have been successfully grown there.

Washington has eight commercial wineries, but only two have national distribution of their products: St. Michelle Vintners, headquartered in Seattle and especially celebrated for their fine white wines; and Seneca Foods Corporation, which sells their wines under the "Boordy Vineyards-Yakima Valley" label.

335

Wehlen *(Vay'-len)***:** World-famous wine town on the MOSEL River, Germany, with some 250 acres of vineyard. Wehlen lies between the celebrated villages of GRAACH ZELTINGEN and likewise profits from a southerly exposure; the steep vineyards lie on slate soil, and in great vintages the elegant Riesling wines of Wehlen are prized for their great delicacy. The most famous vineyard (EINZELLAGE) is Sonnenuhr, or "sun dial"; other good Wehlener Einzellagen are Nonnenberg and Klosterberg. It should be noted, however, that Wehlener Münzlay is not an Einzellage but a composite vineyard or GROSSLAGE that includes all of the vineyards of Wehlen, Graach and Zeltingen.

Wein *(Vine)***:** German for "wine."

Weinbauort *(Vine'-bough-awrt)***:** German for "wine-growing community," an officially delimited township and the surrounding vineyards.

Weingut *(Vine'-goot)***:** German for "wine estate," a specific winery and its cellars or vineyards.

Weinkellerei *(Vine'-keller-rye)***:** German for "wine cellar," usually that of the producer and not the consumer.

Weissherbst *(Vice'-hairbst)***:** German for "white autumn"; specifically, a rosé or pink wine made from black grapes. Under the 1971 German Wine Law, a Weissherbst must meet the minimum requirements for QUALITÄTSWEIN, and must be produced only from one grape variety. Weissherbst can be made in most German wine regions, but much of it comes from the BADEN and RHEINPFALZ areas, where wines of this type are popular.

White Riesling: see JOHANNISBERG RIESLING.

Wiltingen *(Vil'-ting-gen)***:** Famous wine village in the SAAR district, Germany, with 771 acres of vineyard planted mostly in Riesling. The largest and most important town in the Saar, Wiltingen is celebrated chiefly for one great vineyard or EINZELLAGE, the SCHARZHOFBERG, but outstanding wines are also made from other Wiltingen Einzellagen: Kupp, Braunfels, Klosterberg, Hölle, Braune Kupp, Gottesfuss, Rosenberg, Schlossberg and Sandberg. However, under the 1971 German Wine Law, Wiltinger Scharzberg is not an Einzellage but a composite vineyard or GROSSLAGE that includes vineyards from the entire Saar district, and in general the wines will be less good than those from Wiltingen itself.

Wine: As defined throughout this dictionary, and by legal definition in most countries, a beverage produced by the partial or complete fermentation of the juice of fresh grapes. Fermented beverages made from cherries, plums, apricots or other fruits are commonly called ''fruit wines'' but are not wines in the true sense of the word.

Wines fit into the following categories: *Table Wines,* or ''still beverage wines,'' red, white, or rosé wines below 15% alcohol, to accompany a meal; *Fortified Wines,* from 15% to 24% alcohol, to which brandy has been added at some point during vinification; and *Sparkling Wines,* to which a secondary fermentation has been added so that the wine becomes sparkling.

Winkel *(Vink'-el)***:** Village and wine commune in the RHEINGAU district, with 687 acres of vineyard. Winkel is famous chiefly for one great wine estate, Schloss Vollrads (see VOLLRADS, SCHLOSS), which tends to overshadow some of the other fine vineyards or EINZELLAGEN that often give excellent wines. These include: Hasensprung (''hare's leap''), Jesuitengarten, Gutenberg, Bienengarten, Dachsberg, and Schlossberg.

Wintrich *(Vin'-trick)*: Wine village of secondary importance on the MOSEL RIVER, Germany, with 704 acres of vineyard. The vineyards are planted primarily in Riesling and produce light, scented wines, although they are generally at their best only in great vintages. The vineyards (EINZELLAGEN) are: Ohligsberg, Sonnenseite, Grosser Herrgott, and Stefanslay.

Winzer *(Vint'-ser)*: German for "vintner" or "wine-grower."

Winzergenossenschaft *(Vint'-ser-ge-nawss'-en-shoft)*: German for "wine-growers' cooperative association." As distinguished from a WINZERVEREIN (see below), a Winzergenossenschaft is usually a wine cooperative on a somewhat larger scale, with facilities for bottling and marketing in addition to wine-making equipment.

Winzerverein *(Vint'-ser-vair-ryne')*: German for "wine-growers' cooperative," an association of growers that have collectively pooled their vineyard holdings and wine-making equipment, so that the wines are sold under one label.

Worms *(Voorms)*: City in the RHEINHESSEN district, Germany, famous for the Gothic Liebfrauenkirche (church of the blessed mother), whose 26-acre vineyard called Liebfrauenstift is said to have inspired the name for LIEBFRAUMILCH. Under the 1971 German Wine Law, the Liebfrauenstift vineyard has become an EINZELLAGE, and the wines are usually better than most Liebfraumilchs — which are regional wines — although they are apt to be less good than some others from further north in the Rheinhessen district.

338

Württemberg *(Voor'-tem-bairg)*: Wine region in western Germany, located along the Neckar River valley around the cities of Stuttgart and Heilbronn. The fifth largest wine region (ANBAUGEBIET) in Germany, Württemberg has over 18,000 acres of vineyard and is one of Germany's most important red wine regions, although the wines are not well-known in the export trade. The region consists of three sub-regions or BEREICHE: *Remstal-Stuttgart,* along the valley of the River Rems in the vicinity of the city of Stuttgart; *Württembergisch Unterland,* in the center; and *Kocher-Jagst-Tauber,* to the north, named for three tributaries of the Neckar. Among the more important wine towns are Stuttgart, Heilbronn, Stetten, Kleinbottwar, Schwaigern, and Weikersheim.

The traditional specialty of Württemberg is SCHILLERWEIN, a pink wine made from red and white grapes pressed together, but many of Württemberg's producers are turning away from Schillerwein and are concentrating on quality red and white wines. The most widespread grape grown in Württemberg is Trollinger, used for red wine and grown nowhere else in Germany; the Spätburgunder (Pinot Noir) is another important red grape variety. Superior white wine is made from Riesling, Silvaner, Traminer and Müller-Thurgau. Most Württemberg wine is consumed locally, but some better examples are now beginning to appear on the export market.

Würzburg *(Voorts'-boorg)*: City in the region of FRANKEN (Franconia), West Germany. Franconia's capital and largest city, Würzburg is famous for its beer as well as its wines; the wines are bottled in the traditional BOCKSBEUTEL flask native to Franconia. There are some 988 acres of vineyard; the better sites are planted in Riesling and Silvaner, and produce vigorous and scented

339

wines. One particularly good Würzburg vineyard (EINZELLAGE), Stein, was so famous that Franconia wines in general are often called "Steinweine" in the export trade, although in Germany this term is legally restricted to wines produced only from the Stein vineyard. Other good Würzburger Einzellagen include: Abtsleite, Innere Leiste, Kirchberg, Stein/Harfe, Pfaffenberg, and Schlossberg.

Y

Yakima Valley: Wine district in southeastern Washington State, located along the lower Yakima River east of the Cascade Range mountains. Principal wine towns in the valley are: Yakima, Richland, Prosser, Wapato, and Grandview. The Yakima Valley has over 15,000 acres of vineyard, but not all are given over to wine grapes; most are Concords that are sold to neighboring states. Nevertheless, the valley lies on the same latitude as do some of Europe's most famous wine districts, and a number of excellent wines have been made from premium varieties grown there.

Yeasts: Single-celled, asexual plant organisms that bring about fermentation in grape juice. Actually, the yeasts themselves do not cause fermentation; an enzyme they secrete, ZYMASE, converts the grape sugar into ethyl alcohol and carbon dioxide by a complex series of biochemical reactions. One particular strain of yeast, *Saccharomyces ellipsoideus,* is the most useful to the wine-maker because it does the most thorough job of converting the grape sugar.

The selection of the proper yeast is of great importance to the wine-maker. In Europe's traditional wine areas, desirable yeast occurs naturally in the region and collects readily on the surface of the grape skins with the waxy "bloom"; in newer wine regions such as California, harmful wild yeasts collect on the grapes and these must be subdued before fermentation proceeds — most effectively, by adding sulfur dioxide (see SULFUR). Desirable yeast strains are imported from Europe, and are inoculated into the must prior to fermentation.

Yonne *(Yawn)*: River and department (administrative region) in northern BURGUNDY, France, in which the famous CHABLIS district is located.

Yquem, Château d' *(Dee-kem')*: World-famous BORDEAUX wine estate, located in the celebrated commune of SAUTERNES. The château of Yquem was built in the 12th century, and since 1785 has belonged to the Lur-Saluces family; today, it is most renowned for its luscious sweet white wines, considered to be the finest of all the great Sauternes in most vintages. Officially it is ranked as a Grand Premier Cru (Great First Growth) and is among the most costly of all Bordeaux wines: even though there are some 250 acres of Sémillon and Sauvignon Blanc wines, average production is only about 6,700 cases annually, and in unsuccessful vintages the entire crop is declassified and not sold under the château label. In years when the finest sweet wines cannot be produced, the estate also makes an interesting dry white wine known as "Château Y" — pronounced *"Ee'-greck."* Although expensive, Château d'Yquem is among the world's very greatest wines.

Yugoslavia: With over 750,000 acres of vineyard, Yugoslavia is the world's tenth largest wine-producing nation. With a heritage of wine-making dating back some 2,000 years,

341

Yugoslavia has an ethnic and religious diversity reflected in the many different wines she produces. Six different regions — Serbia, Croatia, Slovenia, Bosnia-Herzegovina, Macedonia and Montenegro — make up the federal republic of Yugoslavia, and the wines are as varied as the many ethnic groups.

There are essentially three principal wine regions in Yugoslavia. In the north, bordering Italy and Austria, is Slovenia; in the center is the rugged Dalmatian coast, and further inland are the mountainous regions of Serbia, Herzegovina and Macedonia. The climate ranges from alpine in the north to mediterranean in the south, and the wines reflect these climatic differences: in general they are lighter and more aromatic in the north, and sturdier and fuller-flavored in the south.

Much quality wine is produced in Slovenia. Grape varieties indigenous to Italy and Austria grow well there; the town of Ljutomer, east of the city of Ljubljana, is particularly noted for its white wines made from Rizling (Riesling), Traminec (Traminer), and Sipon — the latter variety is grown only in Yugoslavia. The Istrian peninsula south of Trieste is another important Slovenian wine district; its red wines from Cabernet, Merlot and Refosk (Refosco) are particularly well-known, as are its white wines from Pinot Blanc and Muskat (Muscat).

The Dalmatian coast produces an immense variety of red, white and rosé wines, though they are not as widely exported as those of Slovenia. The little islands of Korčula, Hvar and Vis make Grk, Bogdanuša and Plavac, respectively, among the most individual of all Yugoslavian wines. Three Dalmatian specialties are Blatina, a full, soft red wine; Zilavka, a fruity, scented dry white wine, and Opolo, one of the finest rosés in Yugoslavia. As these varieties are native to Yugoslavia, the wines are entitled to a special government *Appellation d'Origine Contrôlée* rating, though this does not correspond to the French system of wine laws.

The native Prokupac grape furnishes most of the ordinary red wines of Serbia and Macedonia, which are best when drunk quite young. Prokupac rosés are often superior to the reds. This grape is now being supplanted by fine French varieties such as Gamay and Cabernet Sauvignon, as is an indigenous white variety, Smederovka, by important new plantings of Sauvignon Blanc.

Yugoslavian wines are well-represented on the U.S. market. Three major wine cooperatives — Slovin in Slovenia, Navip in Serbia, and Hepok in Herzegovina — have united in a joint effort to export wines under their own brand names; the associated Adriatica brand represents virtually all of the country's wine regions.

Z

Zell *(Tsell)***:** Little town on the MOSEL River, Germany, famous for its regional white wine called "Zeller Schwarze Katz" (Black Cat of Zell), sold with a black cat on the label. Because this wine was so well-known, the 1971 German Wine Law authorized Schwarze Katz to be the name of a composite vineyard or GROSSLAGE, and although Zell has several individual vineyards or EINZELLAGEN of its own — Nussberg, Domherrenberg, Kreuzlay, etc. — the Grosslage name is the one most frequently encountered in the trade. Under the wine law, the entire sub-region or BEREICH in which Zell lies is now also called Zell. Despite its great fame, Zeller Schwarze

343

Katz is usually an undistinguished wine and is hardly the best the Mosel region has to offer.

Zeltingen *(Tsel'-ting-gen):* Famous wine town in the MOSEL River, Germany, officially associated with the neighboring village of Rachtig into one municipality, Zeltingen-Rachtig, the largest wine commune in the Mittel-Mosel. Zeltingen-Rachtig has 531 acres of vineyard planted in Riesling; the commune adjoins the equally celebrated village of WEHLEN to the south, and its most famous vineyard or EINZELLAGE is likewise named Sonnenuhr ("sun dial"); other fine Zeltingen Einzellagen are Himmelreich, Schlossberg and Deutschherrenberg. However, Zeltingen also produces a much larger quantity of less distinguished regional wine, and a "Zeltinger" without a vineyard name may be assumed to be a commercial blend; the best Zeltingers are estate-bottled (ERZEUGER-ABFÜLLUNG) from one of the leading Einzellagen.

Zinfandel: Fine red wine grape grown extensively in California, where almost 30,000 acres have been planted. It is of the species VINIFERA and consequently was imported from Europe at some time during the 19th century, though experts disagree over its original location and present-day counterpart; the latest theory is that Zinfandel came from Italy and is related to the Primitivo from the region of APULIA. Zinfandel berries are deep purple when ripe, and when the grape is planted in cool coastal districts the wines are full-bodied and fruity, with a characteristic "bramble" or "berry" flavor. Zinfandel is grown in nearly every wine-producing country in California — most extensively in the warm Central Valley — but the greatest success with this grape seems to be in the North Coast Countries, where some producers have made outstanding Zinfandels that rank with America's best wines.

Zwicker *(Tsvik'-er)*: In the region of ALSACE, France, a wine blended from several different grape varieties. It was recently declared that the term Zwicker shall be superseded by ''Edelzwicker,'' or ''noble Zwicker,'' which must be a blend of better Alsace grapes or *cépage nobles:* Riesling, Gewürztraminer, Tokay d'Alsace, and Muscat.

Zymase: Enzyme produced by yeast, which causes fermentation and converts grape sugar to ethyl alcohol and carbon dioxide. The fermentative properties of zymase were first demonstrated in 1896 by the German chemist Eduard Büchner (1860-1917); zymase is now believed to consist of several related enzymes that collectively act as catalytic agents for the fermentation process.

Appendix

Guides to Wine Service

How Much Wine to Buy

For dinner occasions, a good yardstick is 1 bottle of table wine for each 4 guests (about 6 oz. for each). Champagnes and sparkling wines call for about the same, 1 bottle for each 4 guests. For dry sherry or other aperitif wine, figure 1 bottle for 8 guests (3 oz. servings). An after-dinner wine like port or cream sherry also requires 1 bottle for 8 guests.

When to Open the Wine

Red table wine: Uncork and allow to stand at least an hour before serving. Wine is a living body. When the bottle is opened, the wine absorbs oxygen from the air. Oxidation activates the development of the bouquet and aroma. An hour or so of "breathing" gives depth and smoothness to the wine.

White table wine; Rose wine: Uncork just before serving. These wines have a delicate fruity fragrance which lose their freshness when exposed to air for too long a time.

Wine Serving Temperatures

Red table wines *About 62°F., but not above 70°.* This is the range of "cool room temperature" at which most people prefer red wine. Some red wines that are young, fruity and crisp — the beaujolais is a typical example — may be enjoyed more if a little cooler.

White table wines, Rose wines, Champagnes, Sparkling wines *42° to 48°F., (about 2 hours in the refrigerator — sweeter types somewhat longer).* Do not over-refrigerate. The refreshing, fruity qualities of these wines are brought out best when the wine is served cold.

346

Dessert wines, aperitif wines *White types* are generally preferred cold, *about 42° to 48°F.* *Red types* are often preferred at cool room temperatures, *about 62°F., but not above 70°.*

If There Is Sediment In the Wine

Sometimes, a natural wine sediment may be deposited in a bottle of an older wine as a result of aging. The sediment consists of natural wine solids; it is harmless and does *not* affect the quality of the wine. Sediment is more likely to occur in an old red table wine than in any other wine.

How to serve a wine with sediment deposit in the bottle:

1. An hour or two before the wine is to be served, uncork the bottle and allow it to stand upright so that the sediment settles to the bottom. Avoid shaking the bottle, and pour gently for guests so that only clear wine is served. Or . . .

2. Decant the wine. Again, uncork the bottle, remove the foil from the neck and allow the bottle to stand upright for an hour or two until the sediment fully settles to the bottom. Now, transfer the wine slowly in one firm motion from the original bottle to another container. Stop the wine the moment the sediment begins to come over to the other container.

Serving the Wine

There are certain formal wine customs:

1. The host pours a little wine into his own glass first. This allows him to taste the wine, to assure that it is sound.

2. Guests are served clockwise, left to right, ladies first, then the men, and, finally, the host pours into his own glass.

3. Pour to fill no more than half the glass. The air space above the wine gathers the aroma and bouquet of the wine so necessary for its full enjoyment.

Wine and Food Pairings

One indisputable standard for the choice of the wine to serve with dinner is simply the wine that pleases the buyer.

Traditional pairings are **red wines with red meats . . . white wines with white meats.** But there is nothing wrong with having a white wine with hamburgers, or a red wine with fish. A great many people do.

Nevertheless, certain wines by their nature go better with certain foods than others, and it is helpful for the host and hostess to know combinations of wines and foods that, over the years, have proven most enjoyable to most people.

First, a rule: the richer the food the richer the wine. Even within traditional pairings, some may prefer a dryer wine, or a wine with the slightest touch of sweetness. Bear in mind that for various dishes the sauces used or the stuffing, rather than the meat itself, should be the determining factor in selecting a wine.

Here is a general guide to wine-food combinations:

Wine-Food Selector

Cocktail Snacks, Smoked Salmon, Canapes — dry sherry, dry madeira, full-bodied dry white wines.

Appetizers, pates — light red or dry full-bodied white wines; **raw oysters:** light dry white wines; **clams:** bone dry or medium dry white wines; **shrimp:** light dry to medium white wines.

Soups, Thick — dry sherry, dry marsala, dry madeira.

Salads — no wine.

Fish, Seafood Dishes — dry to medium dry white wines, rose wines, light red wines; **highly flavored fish dishes:** rose and medium-bodied red wines.

Chicken, Turkey, white meat — dry to medium dry full-bodied white wines, rose wines, light red wines; **dark meat:** full-bodied dry white wines, medium red and rose wines.

Duck, Goose — medium-bodied red wines.

Pork — medium dry white wines, light red and rose wines.

Lamb — medium-bodied red wines.

Veal — full-bodied dry white wines, medium-bodied red and rose wines.

Baked Ham — medium dry white wines.

Game — full-bodied red wines; **if not too rich:** medium-bodied red wines and rose wines.

Beefsteak, Roast Beef, Barbecued Meat — medium-bodied red wines.

Strongly Seasoned Hearty Dishes — full-bodied red wines.

Cheese — full-bodied red wines; lighter flavored cheeses: dry white wines.

Outdoor Cold Buffet — rose wines.

349

Fruits and Sweet Desserts — cream sherry, port and other sweet dessert wines, sweet table wines, extra dry and dry labeled champagnes and sparkling wines.

Wine-Cheese Affinities

Wine is a perfect flavormate to cheese. Earthy and tangy cheeses demand hearty red wines. Fresh sourish cheeses are well suited to dry light white wine. The greater the fat content (often stated on the cheese label) the better the cheese will go with subtle wines. Many of the best combinations of wine and cheese are closely related by regions of origin.

Following is a sampling of some of the popular cheeses and wines which they match.

BLUE CHEESES
Stilton, blue Cheshire, Danish Blue
Robust, full-bodied red wines of some weight
Roquefort, Gorgonzola, Dolcelatte, Bleu de Bresse
Less weighty red wines but still robust and fruity

HARD, MATURED CHEESES
Cheddar, Lancashire, Gloucester
Weighty and robust red wines.
Emmental, Gruyere, Swiss, Appenzell, Yarlsberg, Tilsiter, hard cheeses made from goat's and ewe's milk
More delicate and fruity red wines.

SOFT AND SEMI-SOFT FAT FULL CHEESES
Brie, Camembert, Carre de l'Est, Pont-l'Eveque, Bel Paese, Gouda, Munster.
Fine red wines or full-bodied bone dry or dry white wines

FRESH CREAM CHEESES
American cream cheese, Crema Dania, Boursault
Medium dry white wine or light red wine. Cream cheeses with salty taste require more robust wines

FLAVORED CHEESES
Smoked, semi-hard cheeses, cheeses covered with nuts, dried black grape skins, spiced cheeses such as Boulette D'Avesnes, anise-flavored Munster, buttermilk cheese
Red wines, fairly robust

Holding A Wine Tasting

Wine tasting parties are a growing pastime . . . on the testimony of thousands of Americans. They are easy to give. Here are some guidelines:

How many people to invite? A half dozen or so. **How many wines?** Unless you are a professional, do not taste more than a dozen wines at a time. Big tastings are tiring and confusing. Six wines are ideal.

What you will need: A uniform set of glasses: clear, to see the wine, stemmed, tulip-shaped and of 6 oz. capacity or larger to enjoy the bouquet of the wine. Provide one glass for each person. Have ice buckets to chill the white and rose wines and champagnes and sparkling wines, if you serve them. A pitcher or two of water for participants to drink between wines and to rinse their glasses between tastings. Containers for the tasters to dispose of rinse water or wine they discard. Also paper napkins, pencils and scorecards for the tasters to record their judgments of the wines. **Food?** For the tasting session, water biscuits, little cubes of bread. No cheese.

Which wines to compare? A tasting compares wines against each other, and so must have a purpose. Some suggestions: wines of the same color from different districts of the same general area; wines of the same color from entirely different areas; wines of the same color from different grape varieties; wines of the same grape variety from different wineries within a general price range. Other combinations may be used.

Cover the bottles: The tasting should be blind, with all labels covered and familiar bottle shapes disguised so that the taster will not be influenced by his knowledge of the brand name. Assign an identifying number to each bottle.

351

Order of tasting: If you are comparing separate groups of red and white wines, taste the white wines first. Begin with the youngest wine and proceed to the oldest. When tasting white wines, move from the driest to the sweetest. When tasting reds, move from the lightest to the heaviest.

How to taste the wine: Pour 1 oz. or so of the wine into the glass of each taster. The taster holds the glass by the stem, lifts it to examine the color and clarity of the wine. The glass is put back on the table and swirled to release the bouquet. It is lifted to the nose to inhale the aroma. The taster then takes a sip and swishes the wine inside the mouth to get the full flavor. The wine is not swallowed, but spat into the receptacles provided.

Between wine samples: Tasters may drink water, or eat a water biscuit or a small cube of bread to return their taste to neutral. Some like to nibble on a mild cheese on the theory that it will set off the wine to best advantage. Actually, the cheese tends to flatter the wine by neutralizing the astringent tannin.

Record judgment of the wine: Immediately after tasting the wine, write down your impressions of the wine's appearance, aroma and taste. Many tasters assign each wine a numerical value for its overall quality. Others assign a series of ratings for different aspects of the wine.

Comparing notes: When judgments of all the wines have finally been made, everyone compares notes. The wrappings come off the labels, and the host supplies information on the price of each of the wines.

For professional wine tasters, the judgments they make are the basis of buying decisions involving substantial sums of money. The non-professional wine taster carries no such responsibilities. It's a labor of fun for all to learn more about wines.

Storing Wine at Home

Wine is a living thing. It is affected by temperature, light, vibrations, air. The longer wine is kept, the more important it is to observe these few basic rules to preserve the quality of the wine and, in many instances, to assure the conditions for its continued development in the bottle.

1. Cool, even temperature. *50° to 60°F. is ideal — 70° is considered the highest safe temperature for long-term storage.* The temperature should be fairly even with no sudden changes or extremes. The storage area should be relatively dry. Avoid storage near a furnace, hot water heater, steam pipes or radiators. Wall temperatures tend to change sharply; do not store wine against an outside wall.

2. Avoid sunlight. Wine intended for aging should be kept away from direct exposure to daylight. The sun and other sources of ultraviolet rays have a deteriorating effect on the flavor of wine. Wine to be consumed within a year or two are not likely to be affected by any light except direct sunlight.

3. Vibration is harmful. Do not store near washers, dryers, refrigerators or similar equipment. Do not keep wines where they are likely to be jostled, as in a closet where brooms or vacuum cleaners are kept.

4. Store corked wines on their sides. Air is an enemy of wine. Corked wines should rest on their sides, if stored for a long period, so that the corks stay moist and airtight. If you leave corked bottles of wine in their case, turn the case on its side. Bottles with screw caps and sparkling wines with plastic closures should be stored upright, so that the wine does not touch the closure.

Questions People Ask About Wines:

Why are red wines generally enjoyed best at room temperatures and white wines chilled? Due to the tannin in red wines, the bouquet and flavor are enhanced at room temperatures. White wines contain no tannin, and have a higher acidity than red wines. Chilling white wines brings out the fruity flavor of the wines, makes the acidity less pronounced and the wines more enjoyable and refreshing. Light red wines, such as beaujolais, have little or no tannin, but relatively higher acidity, and may be enjoyed slightly chilled.

Can wine that is served chilled be safely stored in the refrigerator? Yes, but some feel it is best to use the wine within one or two weeks to avoid slight impairment of flavor. Once the wine is chilled, however, it should not be stored again at room temperature.

How long can opened bottles of wine be kept? Bottles of red table wines, if promptly recorked, may be kept in a cool place for several days to a week. Rose or white table wines, if promptly recorked, may be kept up to 10 days to two weeks in a refrigerator. Champagne and sparkling wine must be consumed when opened, since it is very difficult to recork these bottles in a manner that will retain their sparkle. Wines of more than 14% alcohol — sherry, dessert wines — will keep perfectly well after opening and partial consumption.

The Professional Wine Reference
Is Published By
Beverage Media, Ltd.
251 Park Avenue South
New York, New York 10010
(212) 677-3300

Readers are invited to address any questions, comments or inquiries about this book to the Wine Publications Editor.